1.00

Collins Illustrated Guide to

ALL CHINA

Charis Chan

COLLINS
8 Grafton Street, London W1
1989

William Collins Sons & Co. Ltd
London • Glasgow • Sydney • Auckland
Toronto • Johannesburg

Whilst every care is taken in compiling the text, neither the Publisher nor
the Authors or their respective agents shall be responsible for any loss or
damage occasioned by any error or misleading information contained therein
or any omission therefrom.

British Library Cataloguing in Publication Data

Collins illustrated guide to all China.
1. China — Visitors' guides
915.1′0458

ISBN 0-00-215239-8

First published 1988
Reprinted 1989
© The Guidebook Company Ltd 1989, 1988

Series Editors: May Holdsworth and Sallie Coolidge
Contributing Editor: Michael Atkins
Picture Editor: Carolyn Watts

Additional text contributions by David Dodwell and Martin Williams

Cover photograph by Basil Pao

Photography by Airphoto International (238); Magnus Bartlett (17, 52−3, 56, 98, 124,
146−7, 177, 185, 208); Anthony Cassidy (7 except bottom right, 24, 29, 57, 76−7,
135); Chan Yuen Kai, China Photo Library (193 top left/bottom right); China Guides
Series (7 bottom right, 44, 93 top right, 193 top right); China Photo Library (89,
142−3, 204, 224); Bob Davis, Stockhouse (128); Katherine Forestier (106−7);
William Giddings (69); Han Wei, China Photo Library (113); Lam Lai Hing, China
Photo Library (229); Pat Lam (84−5); Joan Law (92 top left/top right/bottom, 213,
234−5); Leong Ka Tai (5); Luo Zhong Ming (36); James Montgomery (11, 14, 32−3,
41, 110, 111, 138, 180); Tom Nebbia (8, 193 bottom left, 196); Wang Gang Feng
(220−1); Herman Wong (150, 192); Z.D. Xu, China Photo Library (154−5); Jacky
Yip, China Photo Library (48, 49, 60, 65, 92 middle right, 93 top left and bottom
three, 96, 120−1, 151, 162−3, 170−1, 175, 188); Zhong Ling (166)

Design by Joan Law Design & Photography

Printed in Hong Kong

Acknowledgements

The author acknowledges with much gratitude the advice, research material and contributions of the following people: T.Z. Chang, Paddy Booz, David Dodwell, Tony and Irmgard Lawrence, Judy Bonavia, Martin Williams, Jonathan Mirsky, Professor Frank King of Hong Kong University, Alethea and Ato Rinpoche, P.T. Lu and Barry Girling. Many other people have helped with the organization of this book: Edward Chan, Daisy Chan, Agnes Chang, Lina Chow, Ah Siu, Wendy Ng and Nurizar Cokelek.

Contents

Special Topics

Maps

*Colourful wood-block
prints for peace and
good fortune*

Introduction: Tours and Expeditions

This guide to travel in China has been designed to give up-to-date information on the most attractive destinations in China today. It is not comprehensive, and so does not include every city and expedition that can be covered on a China tour. Included are the places most worthwhile to visit as well as a selection of exotic and adventurous expeditions that can be enjoyed either as part of a tour or be undertaken independently. The layout of the book has been designed to reflect the way in which many people arrange their travel programmes for China: an itinerary which includes a selection of cities or an extended journey to one or more special regions. My hope is that people choosing their first tour to China, or setting out alone for their second or third tour, will find this book an inspiration to informed and enjoyable travelling — and when the trip is over, perhaps the photographs will conjure up memories of the variety and beauty of China's peoples and landscapes.

Tours

The organized China tour, with its ready solution to the problems of time, language and money, is a blessing for first-time travellers. A well-organized tour with a Chinese-speaking escort is highly recommended even to those who would arrange their own itinerary elsewhere in the world. People who have lived and worked in China also like the problem-free nature of a tour, since they are all too well aware of what can go wrong in some of China's more far-flung regions.

As the Chinese open more and more destinations to international tour operators, independent travellers are finding their options both extended and restricted. There are more places to visit, but there are also more people travelling. The economic reforms of the last few years have meant that ordinary Chinese people now have more money to go sightseeing, and this has strained to the limits China's inadequate transport systems. Often the independent traveller has to fight and cajole his or her way onto a plane or train, while hotels in most major cities are full to bursting during the popular tourist seasons of spring and autumn. This means that independent travellers who have not booked in advance may have to sleep on floors or journey out to dormitory hostels far from the centre of town. Unless you have connections in China (which could mean anything from an official contact to a friend in a foreign embassy), getting things done while 'on the road' is so time-consuming that basic organization can spoil the holiday. Your status and connections in China may be the only deciding factor in the allocation of flights, seats and rooms; for 'first come, first served' is definitely not a Chinese motto. However, by taking an organized tour, your connection becomes the tour operator and China International Travel Service (CITS) — which means that the effort is taken out of travelling.

If, for reasons of time and convenience, you choose a tour, it is worth remembering that you can select either a specialist tour (anything from bicycling to botany) or a series of general tours with a good mixture of contrasting destinations. If you have a scientific or educational interest in China, the Chinese embassy in your capital can often advise you of cost-price tours arranged for specialist or academic groups. However, a general tour meets most people's requirements and gives an excellent introduction to the history, culture and people of China.

Once you have decided on a general tour, do not hesitate to ask your tour operator for more details of your schedule within any given city or region — especially if you are keen to visit a particular place. Tour operators, if notified in advance, can let CITS know of any special requests and probably come back to you with an answer. However, visits to advertised venues are not always possible, even on arrival, and CITS has the exasperating habit of changing schedules at the last minute, when there is little that the tour operator's representative can do — except argue. CITS also has the habit of taking tour groups to as many Friendship Stores as possible in order to lighten their visitors' purses. The intelligent traveller will ask for an alternative to the umpteenth visit to a Friendship Store.

If you do decide to make your own way for a day or half a day while on tour, it is possible to arrange hired or public transport, to use your own maps and the advice of a sympathetic guide. But be warned: CITS guides are like good shepherds. They like to keep their flock together for their own peace of mind. Thus you must be tactful when asking for personal amendments to the schedule and also take into account the feelings and needs of your fellow travellers — do not make arrangements that will mean they have to wait a long time for you to catch up. If you want to do something special, simply keep a low profile. On a group visit to a commune in Inner Mongolia, I managed to duck out of a factory visit by telling the head of the commune that I love riding. He gave me a horse for the day and let me go off unescorted. There were no problems except that he hadn't told me the technique for riding on a wooden saddle (the technique is not to sit astride, but to ride with one leg forward and one leg back, alternating the legs for comfort). The next day I was so bruised I could hardly walk — much to the delight of my fellow journalists, who had been so bored at the factory that they had longed to set out on horses, too.

In order to look at the choice of China tours and possible variations, the city destinations in this book have been divided into three categories: Cultural Capitals, Cities Traditional and Modern, and Cities in a Landscape. There should not be any rules for choosing destinations, but I would suggest at least one from each category, so that you can see the range and contrast of Chinese cities. Look at the regional map on pages 20–1 to get an idea of the choice of northern and southern destinations. That way you can plan to experience a variety of climates, architecture and food.

Expeditions

This section has been devised for those choosing a regional tour in China, as well as for those wanting to make their own travel arrangements. Indeed, the word 'expedition' should not discourage the comfort-loving traveller who may think that choosing an adventurous itinerary in China necessitates hardship. In the last five years many regions of China that were either closed to foreigners or solely the domain of Chinese-speaking backpackers have been opened up by enterprising travel agents. These agents, in co-operation with the Chinese government, have helped to develop facilities where previously there were none, and they have also urged that more historical and archaeological sites be included on tourist itineraries — sites which once were known only to scholars.

An organized itinerary for adventure travel does not mean that the adventure is lost. Often it can mean that the tourist has more access to little-known places, which would be difficult to visit independently. Perhaps this is best illustrated by the tours to the Yangzi River. The independent traveller has the fun of booking a berth on a regular passenger steamer and travelling downstream in the company of a boat full of Chinese people on their daily business or even on holiday themselves. The tourist who chooses to go on a luxury cruise loses this day-to-day contact with ordinary people, but does get the chance to make side trips and stop at small towns which the steamer just glides past. As a generalization, one could say that the organized expedition is for those with less time but few financial restrictions, while the independent journey is for those with plenty of time but less cash.

If you decide to forego the organized tour in favour of a do-it-yourself journey, then take Baden-Powell's maxim to heart: *Be prepared!* A China tour that is not well thought out can entail a series of very expensive, bureaucratic nightmares. If possible, go to the visa section of your Chinese embassy and talk to the staff there about your plans. Their advice and knowledge can come in useful. The officials of your national Chinese Friendship Society (in Britain it is called the 'Society of Anglo-Chinese Understanding') can be helpful because they are often people who have travelled extensively in China and have organized tour itineraries for other people. Check up on vaccination requirements, especially if you plan to visit some of the poorer border regions, and make sure you have altitude sickness tablets if you are visiting Tibet. Unless you are planning to scale a Himalayan peak, you will not need specialist equipment for mountain walking. The best thing you can take to China is a pair of well-worn, stout walking shoes; most other daily necessities for budget travelling (except tents and sleeping bags) can easily be bought in Chinese department stores.

The list of dos and don'ts for independent travel in China will vary according to your age, health, and willingness to pick up some of the Chinese language. Make sure that you buy a phrase book before you go to China, since most people encounter language difficulties when going beyond the major cities. When sightseeing, you can always join up with a CITS-organized day tour in major cities like Xi'an, where getting to the sights beyond the city is not always easy or cheap. Going by bus is fun but time-consuming. Meeting up with someone and sharing a taxi for the day can often be the best solution. In fact, it is good to share meals too, since Chinese food is always better when there are a few people eating together.

Above all, China travellers who go it alone should be models of patience, tolerance and forbearance in adversity. The Chinese have never admired someone who loses his temper easily. There is a Chinese saying that you should be able to 'hold a boat in your stomach', the English equivalent of which is 'turn the other cheek'! Common problems on China expeditions range from no hot water to no bed for the night. I have seen a grown man go pink in the face because he couldn't get a cold beer half-way up a mountain that had no electricity and where all supplies had to be carried up on the backs of porters. If warm beer is the kind of problem that could make you lose your cool, then avoid China, since travel in China has been known to test the patience of sages.

There are many off-the-beaten-track destinations in China waiting to be explored, and I trust that the expeditions detailed in this book offer fun and insight to adventurous travellers. The list is by no means comprehensive, but it does cover the most interesting — as well as some of the most popular — destinations in the border regions and in a few of the most scenic provinces.

Finally, Hong Kong has been included as an extra destination — even though it will not be returned to Chinese sovereignty until 1997. Its function as a 'Gateway to China' makes it the most popular and the most logical of stopping-over places in which to begin or end a tour to China itself. No companion to China travel would be complete without some reference to its unique blend of Chinese and Western experience.

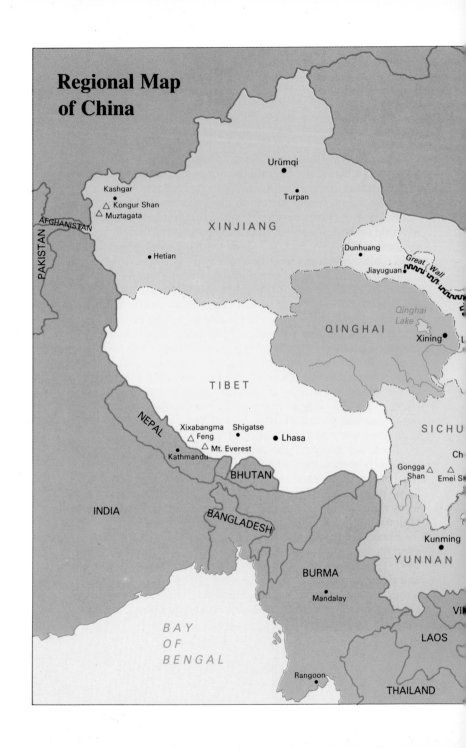

**Regional Map
of China**

Urümqi

Kashgar
• Kongur Shan
△ Muztagata

XINJIANG

AFGHANISTAN

PAKISTAN

Turpan

Dunhuang

Jiayuguan •

Great Wall

• Hetian

Qinghai
Lake

QINGHAI

Xining •

TIBET

NEPAL

Xixabangma
△ Feng

Shigatse
•

• Lhasa

SICHU

△ Mt. Everest

Kathmandu •

Ch

BHUTAN

Gongga △
Shan

△
Emei S

INDIA

BANGLADESH

Kunming
•

YUNNAN

BURMA

Mandalay
•

VI

BAY
OF
BENGAL

LAOS

Rangoon·

THAILAND

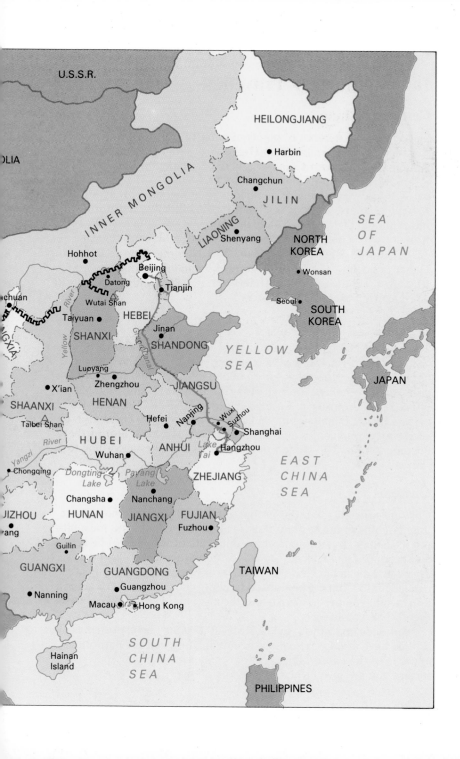

Information for Travellers

Getting to China

Since 1985, the number of points of entry to China has increased considerably. The Karakoram Highway — linking Pakistan and Xinjiang in northwest China — and the Kathmandu-Lhasa Highway — linking Nepal and Tibet — are now travelled by the patient and hardy. Once-weekly flights come into Kunming from Rangoon and Bangkok. Boats can be taken from Japan and Hong Kong. International flights arrive daily in Beijing and Shanghai. The Hong Kong-based airline, Dragonair, has regular flights on Boeing 737−200s to Xiamen, Guilin, Hangzhou,Nanjing, Tianjin, Kunming, Dalian, Fuzhou, Xi'an, Chengdu, Haikou and Shantou. And, of course, for the inveterate train-lover,the Trans-Siberian Railway leaves once a week from Moscow.

Visas

Tourists travelling as part of a group enter China on a group visa — a single document listing all members of the group. The visa is obtained by the tour operator on behalf of his clients. Individual visas can be obtained through Hong Kong travel agents, the Visa Office of the Ministry of Foreign Affairs of the PRC in Hong Kong, or, at Chinese embassies in your respective country. These visas give access to all open cities and regions so there is no need for further documentation. The fee for an individual visa varies according to its source.

Customs

Customs officials treat tour groups gently and you need not expect long holdups in the customs hall. On entering China, you must fill out a customs declaration form, a duplicate of which *must* be kept and produced again when you leave. You are asked to list items such as cameras, watches, jewellery, radios and recorders that you are bringing into China. These listed items are not to be sold or given away while you are in China, and the customs officer may ask to see them when you leave.

Antiques up to the value of RMB 10,000 may be exported as long as they have a red wax seal on them indicating that the authorities approve of the exportation. Customs may ask to see the special receipt you are given when buying an antique.

Money

Renminbi and Currency Certificates Chinese currency is called
renminbi (meaning 'people's currency') and is abbreviated to RMB.
The standard unit is *yuan* (referred to as *kuai* in everyday speech).
The yuan or kuai is divided into ten *jiao* (referred to as *mao*) and 100
fen. Ten fen make one mao and ten mao make one kuai. Yuan
(kuai) and jiao (mao) are available in note forms and fen as small
nickel coins. Since the introduction of foreign exchange certificates
in May 1980, tourists have not been given RMB by banks handling
exchange transactions. Instead they are issued with equivalents
called Foreign Exchange Certificates (FECs). These certificates can
be used anywhere, although their official use is for payment in
hotels, Friendship Stores and for taxis and airline tickets. This has
led to a large black market exchange between RMB and FECs.

    Foreign Currency There is no limit to the amount of foreign
currency you can bring into China. You should keep all your
exchange memos because the bank may demand to see them when
you come to reconvert your currency certificates on leaving China.

    All major freely negotiable currencies can be exchanged for
currency certificates at branches of the Bank of China, in hotels and
stores. The rates of exchange fluctuate with the international money
market.

    Cheques and Credit Cards All the major European, American
and Japanese travellers cheques are accepted. Major international
credit cards are now also quite freely accepted in shops and hotels of
major cities. It is possible to cash American Express travellers
cheques in 52 cities.

    Tipping While tipping is officially not required, it is beginning to
be expected in major cities.

Health

CITS asks those who are unfit because of 'mental illness, contagious
or serious chronic disease, disability, pregnancy, senility or physical
handicap' not to take a China tour. Experience has shown this to be
sound advice. A tour that is exhausting but stimulating for the fit
becomes a gruelling experience for those who are not.

    If you do become ill in China, you will be taken to the local
hospital and given the best treatment available (not always of a
standard that Westerners are used to) and you will be put in a
private room if possible. Costs — particularly of medicines — are
high, so it is important to invest in some form of health insurance
before visiting China.

There are no mandatory vaccination requirements, but gammaglobulin, up-to-date polio and tetanus shots, and B-encephalitis for those travelling between April and October are recommended. Anti-malaria precaution is advisable for those visiting southwest China. Anyone coming from a cholera-infected area should have an inoculation.

Climate and Clothing

Within the ten million square kilometres (four million square miles) of China's vast territory it is hardly surprising to find immense variations in climate. Even generalizations about relatively small areas are difficult because of the effects of altitude and other local conditions. Before deciding on the best season to take a tour, it is worth checking carefully on the weather of each city on the itinerary. Of course, if you choose the most attractive season to visit a city, you also choose the time when tourist spots and hotels are most crowded.

As a basic guide, winters in the north are harsh: Beijing's average minimum temperature between December and March is only −5°C (23°F), and its maximum is around 0°C (32°F). If you go further north towards Harbin, or west into Inner Mongolia, it is much colder. By contrast, summer in the north can be uncomfortably hot and sticky. Temperatures in Beijing may soar to over 38°C (100°F), while the average minimum between June and September is 25°C (75°F). The city has a rainy season in July and August. Spring and autumn are undoubtedly the best times for touring in the north, when you can expect less rain, clear skies and comfortable temperatures — the average maximum spring and autumn day time temperature in Beijing is 21°C (70°F), but nights are chilly.

Moving south, the Yangzi Valley area (which includes Shanghai) has semi-tropical conditions. Summers are long, hot and sticky, with notoriously unpleasant conditions at Wuhan, Chongqing and Nanjing — cities which the Chinese have, with good reason, called the three furnaces. Winters are short and cold, with temperatures dipping below freezing, while spring and autumn are the most attractive seasons with cool nights and daytime highs of around 24°C (the mid-70s°F). Humidity remains high throughout the year — the average rainfall in Shanghai is 114 centimetres (45 inches).

The sub-tropical south (Guangzhou is on the Tropic of Cancer) has a hot and humid six-month period from April to September, with days of heavy rain (Guangzhou's average rainfall is 65 inches), but has a very pleasant dry, sunny autumn, with daytime temperatures around 24°C (mid-70s). Spring can be cloudy and wet, while the short winter from January to March produces some surprisingly chilly days.

Apart from mid-summer, when virtually everywhere open to foreign tourists is hot, most tour itineraries lead the tourist through several different weather zones. But people who decide to travel with several complete changes of wardrobe may find themselves with crippling excess baggage charges — the Chinese tend to be strict about their 20-kilogram (44-lb) baggage allowance. A more practical policy would be to plan on wearing layers that can be discarded or added to as the weather dictates.

The Chinese themselves are informal about dress, and will not expect tourists to dress formally for any occasion — even a banquet. So take casual, practical clothes, and strong, comfortable shoes — you are bound to be doing a lot of walking. Men need nothing smarter than a sports jacket and women can feel properly dressed wearing slacks on any occasion. Although the Chinese are becoming a little more adventurous with their own clothes, they are still offended by anything too flamboyant, and particularly by exposure of too much flesh. But in rapidly changing China even attitudes towards dress are relaxing. Nevertheless, women should leave their scanty clothes at home.

Winter in the far northwest and in Tibet demands very heavy clothing — thermal underwear, thick coats, sweaters, lined boots, gloves, and some form of headgear as protection against the biting wind. Hotel and tour buses are usually well heated, while museums, communes and even some theatres and restaurants are not.

For summer anywhere in China keep clothes as light as possible — many of the places you visit will not be air-conditioned. You may be sightseeing during the heat of the day, so take plenty of protection against the sun, particularly if you are planning to visit Tibet or Xinjiang, where sunglasses are a must. A light raincoat is a wise addition to your luggage at any time.

You need bring only a few changes of clothing since hotel laundry everywhere is fast, cheap and efficient. Dry cleaning is possible, although it may be wiser to wait until you are home to get your most treasured clothes cleaned.

What to Pack

Food, Drink and Tobacco The days when tourists who wanted Western liquor had to bring it with them are happily over. An ever-increasing number of shops and Friendship Stores sell imported wines and spirits at prices which compare favourably with those in the West. Imported cigarettes are also sold, again at very reasonable prices. But if you want to play safe and bring along your own brands, a loosely enforced customs regulation allows you to import duty-free 400 cigarettes and two bottles of liquor.

Coffee is now much more easily available than it was when China first opened its doors to tourists — breakfast coffee in many hotels has become quite drinkable. But if you like it at all times of the day, bring some instant coffee (and powdered milk and sugar) and take advantage of the thermoses of hot water in your room and on the trains. Tea drinkers who prefer Indian rather than Chinese tea should also bring along their own. Many hotel shops sell Chinese peanuts, biscuits, chocolates and sweets.

Film Many tourists bitterly regret not bringing more film with them. Film is available in China — Kodak claims over 100 outlets — but the right type is not always available at the right time. You are, in fact, allowed to import up to six dozen rolls and 3,000 feet of movie film, so why not bring enough to make sure you do not run out half-way through China?

Medicine and Toiletries Bring any prescription medicines you know you will need, and a supply of medicines for your general health. Some of these drugs are available in China, but it is safer (and you will avoid losing time shopping around) if you plan to be self-sufficient.

Apart from some imported cosmetics, most Western-produced toothpastes, shampoos, shaving creams and so on are not available, although there are of course Chinese brands of these items. Sanitary towels and tampons are not widely available in China and travellers should bring their own supply.

Electrical Appliances Voltage may vary from region to region, but it is mostly 220−240V. There is no consistency in the size and shape of plugs, so men should bring normal razors and blades with them. Hotels and Friendship Stores sometimes have adapters, but if you really cannot live without an electrical appliance, it would be best to bring a selection of adapters with you.

Reading Material Until the end of the 1970s, almost the only reading material available to a tourist comprised copies of *China Reconstructs*, a magazine published in a great many languages which puts China's positive socialist face forward, and the press releases of the New China News Agency. Today, visitors to China can purchase copies of international magazines in the larger hotels, as well as regional and international newspapers brought in from Hong Kong. Foreign books are also displayed for sale in hotel lobbies, but look out for China's own English-language daily newspaper, *China Daily*, and the many new English-language paperbacks published in China.

CITS

Although an ever-increasing number of foreigners travel around China independently or use the services of other agencies, many still rely on the ubiquitous CITS (China International Travel Service), which can look after every aspect of the tour. They plan the itinerary, allocate hotels, make travel arrangements, devise daily sightseeing programmes, arrange meals, provide guide-interpreters and much more besides.

Even though CITS is now in a position to offer the foreign tourist a wider choice in matters of hotel accommodation, transport and overall tour itineraries, the mind still reels at the unenviable task that faces CITS whose job it is to manipulate China's limited hotel and transport facilities to accommodate all its foreign visitors. Understandably, once CITS personnel have laid their plans, they are unlikely to want to alter them at the request of tourists, or even tour operators. China's tourist facilities simply cannot operate with a greater degree of flexibility at the moment.

CITS determines in advance the shape of a tour (the order in which places will be visited and the number of days spent in each), but these details are usually not confirmed to the foreign visitors until they arrive in China. Tourists and tour operators are also kept in the dark on other aspects of their tour — until arriving in a city, no one knows for sure where their group will stay or what they will be doing. Perhaps this way of going about things is entirely alien to the experienced Western traveller, but it is one which, at present, has to be accepted in China.

Guides CITS is generous with its guiding services. From the moment a group steps into China, a CITS guide-interpreter will usually meet them and stick by their side through to the final departure lounge. This national guide is joined by at least one local guide in each city the group visits. Standards of guiding vary considerably. Your guides may be knowledgeable and fluent in English. They may, on the other hand, have done little travelling within China, have scant knowledge of the area where they are guiding, and have had little chance to practise their English. But more important, they are almost universally helpful, tireless in their attempts to answer questions, and make good travelling companions.

Daily Programmes Like all enthusiastic hosts, CITS expects its guests to keep up a cracking pace. A day that may start at dawn with a visit to a market could lead on to a morning's sightseeing, an afternoon visit to a school and a shopping session, and not wind up until ten in the evening after a visit to the local opera. Much is expected of the guest's stamina. You may find yourself climbing the

392 steps of Dr Sun Yat-sen's Mausoleum in Nanjing in mid-summer temperatures, travelling in an unheated jeep along a frozen riverbed in the depths of the Mongolian winter, or sitting on hard benches in an airless stadium watching a four-hour acrobatic show.

To get the most out of your China programme you must be prepared sometimes to forego a lengthy break for a shower or a pre-dinner martini. But CITS guides are far from being severe taskmasters. If it all gets too much, they are quite willing to let you rest all day in your hotel, or skip an expedition to wander off on your own.

Transportation

The CITS hosts look after all travel arrangements for their foreign guests. They select the date, time and type of transport, make reservations, see to the necessary security clearances, and ensure that luggage gets from the hotel on to the appropriate train or plane. It is only left for the tourists to pay their own excess baggage charges.

Most foreign tourists travel the long distances between China's major cities by air, and the shorter inter-city distances by train.

Air Travel CAAC (Civil Aviation Administration of China), which once had the monopoly on domestic flights (now a number of semi-independent domestic airlines are appearing), has greatly expanded its services over the past few years. But there is still an element of adventure in flying within China. Flights may be cancelled if bad weather is forecast, reserved seats may mysteriously be filled by others, and sometimes aircraft simply do not turn up. CAAC flies an interesting array of aircraft on internal flights.

You will experience few of the extras associated with commercial airlines in the West. Inflight service has a distinctive CAAC quality to it. Demurely dressed air hostesses serve light refreshments together with gifts of key-rings, fans, vases, or perhaps a butterfly papercut. During longer flights planes may make a special stopover to allow crew and passengers to have a more substantial meal at an airport restaurant. Airports, apart from the new international-style one at Beijing, tend to be spartan places with a minimum of services.

Trains Most foreign tourists enjoy the long-distance train trips, however reluctant they may be at first to embark on their journey. 'Soft Class' — the class reserved for foreigners and high ranking officials (although other classes are available too) — combines charm with comfort and efficiency. Clean, white embroidered seat covers, an endless supply of hot water and green tea, regular mopping of the floors, effective heating in winter, and dining cars which can produce adequate Chinese meals (beer, and sometimes Chinese wine, are available) — all add up to ideal conditions for sitting back and watching China's diverse countryside speed by. Overnight passengers are comfortably housed in velvet-curtained, four-bunked compartments, with a potted plant in each. Each car has washing and toilet facilities that are an improvement on many of their Western counterparts. Another plus for Chinese trains, not always mirrored in the West, is their punctuality — to be on time in China it is still safest to travel by train.

Tour Buses CITS has a range of buses for sightseeing. Foreign groups are usually put in luxury 40-seater Hino buses imported from

Japan. These are equipped with air-conditioning, heating that works, and an effective public address system. Smaller groups may be allocated 16-seater Toyota buses which, although adequate, are designed for Japanese-sized passengers. Occasionally, tourists may find themselves touring in older, unsprung Chinese-made buses.

Taxis For moving around town on your own, taxis provide an easy answer. They are cheap by international standards, and drivers are usually happy to wait while you shop, sightsee and have a meal in a local restaurant. Fares are worked out on a time and distance formula, and in some cities meters are becoming the norm.

Taxis generally do not cruise the streets looking for fares. Fleets of taxis — either imported Toyotas or more distinctive, if old-fashioned, Shanghai-produced vehicles — serve the major hotels in all the most frequented open cities. In these cities there will probably be a special desk in your hotel lobby that arranges taxis. Restaurants, clubs and tourist stores should also be able to call one for you. Whichever city you are in, your CITS escort should be able to arrange a hired car and driver if you want to make a special excursion.

Public Transport Only the most enterprising short-stay visitors would attempt to find their way around on public transport. No doubt there are many efficient bus and trolleybus services in China's cities, but it is difficult to come to grips with the system right away, especially if you do not speak Chinese. Route maps are in Chinese and, since the fare is based on distance travelled, you should also be able to say in Chinese where you are going. You may also have to muster considerable strength to push yourself both on and off the bus.

Communications

China is developing its international communications systems, so it is possible to make long-distance telephone calls or send cables. Most major hotels also have access to telex facilities. Airmail letters and cards do reach their destinations, although they may take some time. If you are thinking about sending any large purchases home, bear in mind that while shipping costs are average, crating charges are high, and the crate may not arrive for many months. Small boxes sent by seamail are often the best solution.

Early Archaeological Treasures

Most visitors to China enjoy tours of archaeological sites and museums, but they are often frustrated by the lack of display signs in major foreign languages. The obvious solution is to make sure that you have your guide or interpreter close at hand. However, if you are part of a large group tour, it is sometimes difficult both to hear what is being said and to see what is actually on display. This introduction to early Chinese treasures is designed to help you find your own way around an exhibition or museum, to go at your own pace and to identify what is on display.

China's first known works of art were pottery vessels and carved jade discs, pendants and sceptres, dating from the Neolithic Period (c. 7000–1500 BC). The pots were made for everyday use and for ritual purposes. The jade pieces were used either as ornaments or in rituals such as burials. The most finely-carved pieces of early Neolithic jade have been found in the eastern coastal region of China — at excavations in Zhejiang Province. Pottery from the Neolithic Period has been found in many sites throughout China: even as far west as present-day Xinjiang Province, long considered outside the orbit of primitive Chinese culture.

The painted pottery of the peoples of the Yellow River plain is best known to foreign visitors because of the famous excavation at Banpo, just outside the city of Xi'an. Banpo is the site of a large riverside village which, from 4000 to 3000 BC, had its own kilns producing distinctive decorated pots. The low-fired red clay pots of Banpo are found throughout the Yellow River region, and are collectively known as 'Yangshao ware'. It is relatively easy to identify Yangshao pottery in a museum, since it is low-fired, unglazed and has rich decorative designs in red, black and occasionally white. Motifs can be bold swirling patterns, faces, fish or bird designs. 'Yangshao ware' is often referred to as Painted Pottery.

In the area around the Shandong Peninsula on China's eastern seaboard, a different kind of pottery was produced in Neolithic times. Known as Black Pottery or 'Longshan ware', the pots have a distinctive black surface which has been polished after firing. Black pottery was wheel-made and, unlike Painted Pottery, has no surface decoration. The potter put all of his skill into creating subtle and elaborate shapes. The ritual vessels are paper-thin and are turned in the most elaborate and impractical forms. Archaeologists believe that the shape of the vessels of the Black Pottery people had an important influence on that of the bronze vessels of the later Shang Dynasty.

During the Shang Dynasty (c.1600−1027 BC), clay pottery was eclipsed by the newly-discovered science of bronze casting. Bronze was more durable than clay and had important military applications. However, the development of bronze was shaped by the potter's skills — the moulds for the cast bronzes were made from clay, and many of the early shapes of Shang bronzes were again derived directly from the refined shapes of 'Longshan ware'. This was particularly true of the high-footed, trumpet-mouthed wine goblets known as *gu*, and the bag-legged, tripod wine heaters (the legs billow out like bags full of water) called *jue*. Both shapes were to die out as the bronze-cast art evolved away from the traditions of the early potters.

The working of bronze was influenced by the skills of the jade carver. The strange animal-mask pattern on Shang bronzes known as *tao tieh* is found as early as 3000 BC, carved on the jade discs of the eastern coastal people. However, the discovery of bronze did not lead to the dying out of jade carving. Because of its translucent hardness, jade continued to be highly prized.

The Shang-Dynasty bronzes are famous for their vigorous shapes and bold designs. The *tao tieh* is the best-known feature of Shang bronzes. In the mask pattern of strong, swirling lines, a pair of savage eyes stare out. Shang bronzes are more like sculptures than decorated vessels. The forms are often the contours of an animal or the mask of a terrified human face. It is not surprising that archaeologists claim these ritual vessels were used at human sacrifices.

With the overthrow of the Shang Dynasty and the triumph of the Zhou in 1027 BC, the function of bronze vessels changed. During the rule of the Shang kings, bronze vessels had a religious function and were important in rituals and sacrifices. Under the Zhou rulers, bronze vessels also became symbols of rank and wealth. Zhou-Dynasty patrons commissioned bronzes of refined shapes with swirling geometric patterns, such as the elegant 'thunder spiral'. Monster and beast shapes disappeared.

There has been much debate on whether the art of bronze casting evolved spontaneously in China or was transmitted from the ancient cultures of the Near East. Chinese bronzes are unique in incorporating lead in the bronze alloy of copper and tin — a fact that argues for the independent evolution of bronze casting in China. The addition of lead to the alloy gives the bronze a grey sheen much prized by connoisseurs.

It is from the bronzes of the Shang and Zhou Dynasties that the earliest developments of the Chinese language have been studied.

The inscriptions on the Shang bronzes describe mainly divination and ritual; on the Zhou bronzes they are of a more political and courtly nature. The bronze vessels are as much historical records as works of art.

Shang and Zhou jade pieces were used to symbolize power. The jade discs and sceptres were the Chinese equivalent of the European royal sceptre and orb. Jade was also important in burial rituals. The jade disc — or *bi* — was buried with rulers in the belief that it would help ease the passage of the soul to the afterlife.

Most of what is preserved from China's early dynasties has been due to these burial customs. Rulers and nobles of ancient China believed that they would need treasures, servants and animals in the afterlife (a tradition which still persists in contemporary Chinese culture, with the burning of paper money, paper houses and possessions for the dead). During the Shang Dynasty, rulers took their wives and servants to the grave with them. In the Zhou Dynasty, figurines of people mainly replaced live examples for these rites. The result was that, by the fourth century BC, the use of tomb figurines was widespread enough for Confucius to declare that the person who initiated the idea of going to the grave with figurines did not deserve to have descendants. In the 1960s, Communist textbooks interpreted the comment to mean that Confucius was recommending the older tradition of human sacrifices. But it is clear from the context — and from other chapters — that Confucius had no interest in the possibility of the afterlife and disliked the tradition of tomb figurines as a reminder of earlier practices.

In the third century BC, Qin Shi Huangdi, China's first emperor, had himself buried with a complete, larger-than-life model army. These warriors and horses, currently being excavated just outside Xi'an, are China's most famous archaeological treasure. The Han-Dynasty historian, Sima Qian, wrote that Qin Shi Huangdi was also buried with fabulous treasures and members of his household. However, the tomb of the emperor has not yet been excavated, and despite being looted in the early years of the Han Dynasty, it is widely believed to contain several undisturbed chambers. Archaeologists are making exploratory digs around the site of the tomb, but they are concerned about the preservation of the contents and the possibility of booby traps — described by Sima Qian as being set up all around the imperial burial chamber.

The Han Dynasty, which succeeded the short-lived Qin Dynasty in 206 BC, also left a legacy of tomb treasures. However, the Han emperors did not make such elaborate tomb preparations as did the megalomaniac Qin Shi Huangdi. No living household members are believed to have been placed in Han tombs. In the early period of the Han Dynasty, known as the Western Han, many precious objects were buried in the tombs of rulers and nobles. By the time of the Eastern Han (25−220 AD), this practice was officially prohibited, and — with some exceptions — bronze vessels were replaced by glazed earthenware or lacquerware, and people and valuable possessions by representational clay figurines.

Jade burial suits are perhaps the most spectacular objects from early Han tombs. Jade was thought to have magical qualities, and the jade burial suit was believed to prevent decay. Bodies of high nobles were encased in jade suits and their orifices sealed with jade discs. One of the finest examples comes from the second-century BC tomb of Princess Dou Wan in Hebei Province. Also from that tomb is one of the finest small pieces of early Han sculpture yet excavated: a gilt-bronze oil lamp in the shape of a kneeling maid-servant. Its purity of form and the individuality of facial expression make the work a rare treasure amongst tomb figurines.

Han-Dynasty tomb figurines are of great interest in providing information about daily life at that time. Models of farms, houses, city gates, animals and utensils as well as models of favourite servants were enclosed in tombs . The painted bricks of Han tombs also tell much of daily life. They can depict anything from court ladies at leisure, nobles out hunting with their bows and arrows, to kitchen workers preparing a feast. Fragments of woven silk and lacquerware have also been found in many Han tombs. By the time of the Han Dynasty, lacquerware had completely replaced bronze vessels as household items, and thus many of the excavated Han tombs have revealed a wealth of red-and-black patterned lacquer boxes and utensils. One of the best exhibitions of Han tomb artefacts is in the Hunan Provincial Museum at Changsha. The museum has the complete collection of the Mawangdui excavation of a first-century BC (Western Han) noblewoman's tomb.

If the later period of the Han Dynasty can be remembered by one object, it is surely the Flying Horse unearthed in Gansu Province, now on display in Lanzhou's museum. The small bronze sculpture has a lightness and fluidity of form far removed from the monumental grandeur of the earlier Zhou and Shang bronzes. Its spirited beauty brings to life the values and interests of a society which, without such works of art, may seem remote and alien.

Pandora's Box: The Chinese Economy
David Dodwell

Any attempt to analyse China's economy is like delving into
Pandora's Box. It can confound even the seasoned economist, let
alone the humble traveller. As one economist, based in Beijing for
the last couple of years, recently remarked: 'How do you expect me
to understand the way this economy operates? There are bureaucrats
here who have been running the economy for the better part of 30
years, and even they can't tell you how it works.'

For a visitor, then, the task of drawing meaningful insights out of
a week or two of dizzying travel between China's main tourist sights
can be a perplexing experience. You are voyaging along one of
China's 'thin red lines' — one of the small but growing number of
well-known tourist routes — and you have a nagging awareness that
what you are seeing is perhaps not typical of the remoter parts of the
country, which are either out of bounds or simply take too much
time to reach. You are travelling at such a pace that you may have
only the most fleeting glimpse of any one city or community —
hardly a sound basis on which to draw conclusions. You have
emerged with a few anecdotes and a fear that they will hardly
provide lessons for a country of more than one billion people and 30
provinces. Yet even the most authoritative economic observers in
Beijing — whether they belong to a diplomatic mission or to the
still-infant World Bank mission — rely on statistical material of a
notoriously uncertain character, and on a similar mixture of
anecdotal experience. Few 'experts' on China could deny that their
claims are based on what, in economic jargon, are termed 'small-
sample generalizations'.

Despite this note of caution, it is nevertheless possible to learn
quite a lot about the country from the window of a tour coach or
railway carriage as you rumble from place to place. Even in hotels,
many of them sanitized to the point of being *in* but not *of* China,
much can be gleaned by reflecting on the problems that constantly
arise — why you have to spend Foreign Exchange Certificates, why
the electricity keeps failing, why service is often so lethargic.

The Hotel and Its Environs
As you will quickly discover on arrival in China, you are not entitled
to use the local currency, but instead have to use a hybrid currency
called *wai hui quan* or Foreign Exchange Certificates ('FECs'). The
system is absurd, leads to all kinds of monetary confusion, and fails
in what it is intended to do: to keep foreign currency out of the

hands of local Chinese. It has spawned local black markets (count the money-changers hovering outside your hotel) and two-tier price systems that in some parts of the country are almost official.

Despite the hopeless confusion that arise from the use of FECs, China's monetary authorities have balked at any suggestion of their abolition. The idiocy of Chinese monetary logic starts with the refusal to allow the local currency — the *renminbi* — to be internationally convertible, while at the same time there is an acute shortage of foreign exchange in the country, which means that it has to be rigorously rationed. Your tourist dollars go into the vaults of the Bank of China, and it takes hell or high water to get them out again.

The hotel you are staying in is one of a number of enterprises in the economy that need to spend foreign exchange — not only on cans of Coke and imported Japanese beer, but on bathroom fittings that work, colour televisions, or the Japanese taxis and mini-buses that wait at the door. Since it cannot earn foreign exchange directly, it has to earn an 'entitlement' to foreign exchange by generating FECs. You, the tourist, are the only significant source of FECs. If there are not enough tourists, or they spend too little, the hotel will soon be facing some insoluble financial problems. It goes without saying that any local Chinese who wants to stay at the hotel is either going to have to discover a source of FECs (some do, by means of foreign relatives), or will be allowed to stay because the hotel is making its foreign exchange ends meet. The system creates irritating examples of discrimination: as when a hotel dining-room is divided into two, with foreign goods available only in the area patronized by FEC-wielding foreigners, or when a taxi driver refuses to give a ride to a local person because he has not achieved his daily quota of FEC income.

One arcane variation of the FEC theme arises in the Pearl River Delta area in the hinterland of Hong Kong. This area has been so heavily influenced by Hong Kong (there are an estimated 12,000 factories in the area, employing about 1.5 million Chinese workers, which manufacture exclusively for Hong Kong companies) that the Hong Kong dollar has become an alternative currency. Banking officials in Hong Kong estimate that 20 per cent of the territory's notes in issue are now circulating inside China, most of them in the Pearl River area. As a result, anyone travelling only to this area really does not need any cash except Hong Kong dollars. Bills will be denominated in Hong Kong currency, menus priced in it, and change will also be paid in Hong Kong dollars. One ironical result of this is that money-changers outside Guangdong hotels — in contrast to their less urbane counterparts elsewhere in the country — are supinely indifferent to offers of FECs.

The reluctance of Chinese hoteliers to accept credit cards (formally declared to be due to problems of credit card fraud) in reality is also closely linked to the need to garner FECs. Any system that puts a layer of bureaucracy between the hotel and its jealously guarded foreign exchange has scant sympathy. It is likely to be some time before these circumstances change.

International phone calls can be difficult to arrange in many cities. In part this is because the digital exchanges and PABXs at the local exchange and in the hotel have to be imported from abroad — again with strictly rationed foreign exchange — and in part because all international calls have to be switched through Beijing or Shanghai. Trunk routes into these cities are often heavily congested (some Shenzhen companies employ staff to do nothing but continuously dial for trunk lines), and sometimes it can take many hours to reach the international exchange itself.

Electricity failures in hotels are infrequent nowadays, but this does not mean that shortages are any less acute nationwide. Most authorities make special arrangements for tourist hotels to have guaranteed power supplies — though the hotel will normally pay a high price for this privilege. Once a standard quota of power is used up, additional power will cost the hotel two or three times the normal electricity tariff. Export companies, or continuous process plants such as aluminium smelters or petrochemical plants, have similar privileges, but most Chinese companies struggle along with electricity for about four or five days a week. Many have diesel generators to deal with brown-outs. Most cities will be 'zoned' so that power is cut, area by area, on a rota basis. Inevitably this rota also applies to domestic users, power being unavailable regularly on certain days of the week, and often between certain hours every day. Even the country itself is 'zoned'. In the torrid summer months, communities south of the Yangzi River are allowed air-conditioning. In winter, you have to live north of the Yangzi to be entitled to heating. This means that life can be unbearably stuffy on the north bank of the Yangzi in summer, while it is rather miserable on the river's south bank in winter.

Yet it is not the difficulties of the climate that are the primary cause of the generally lethargic service so often recalled by tourists to China. Few emerge without some recollection of waitresses indifferent to complaints about the lack of iced water, the filthy crockery, the CAAC office counters closed for seemingly interminable lunch-breaks, or officials' yawning unconcern over the problems caused by cancellation of a flight.

The underlying cause here is what the Chinese call the 'iron rice bowl' — fixed salaries and jobs for life. I wonder how many non-

Chinese would put themselves out, work overtime or anti-social hours, if at the end of the day they took home exactly the same pay as the lazy-bones sitting next to them. With no incentive to provide improved service, to be innovative in one's work, and no punishment for doing nothing, it is perhaps a wonder that any work is done at all. Very few Chinese workers have any say about the job they get after they leave school. This means that graduates in computing science may sometimes find themselves allocated to the local iron foundry rather than an electronics factory. Once allocated, there are very few ways of changing one's job or finding out about alternatives — and this despite the extravagant claims made by the newly created 'talent centres'. Promotion can bring added responsibility, but the material reward is negligible.

This is one of the reasons why many of the goods you will see in hotel shops or Friendship Stores are badly finished. Neither the worker, nor the factory boss he works for, will be paid more (or generate more profits for the company) if they turn out high-quality products. Nor will they be paid less if there is no market for the goods they manufacture. For example, 70 million watches were made in China in 1986, most of them in factories in Shanghai, Tianjin and Datong. A year later, 35 million of them were still in stock but production continued unabated. Out of about 40 million bicycles that will be made in China this year, only 30 million will ever be bought. Like so many other products, the rest will find their way on to the rubbish heap. The idiocy of this policy has recently begun to occur to officials in Beijing, but the road to remedying it appears to be a long one.

Little progress is likely to be made until the fog that surrounds most factory managers is made to lift. Many Chinese factories are in effect little more than processing ventures. Items are delivered to the factory gate, a particular process is carried out on the items in return for a fee, and they are taken away. Delivery and despatch have little to do with the factory, but depend on a ministry to which the factory answers. The fee is fixed by the ministry. Whether there is a ready market for the items thus processed, and whether the factory is being paid a price that bears any relation to the market price of the item, is irrelevant. There is no way of finding new sources of supply if the raw materials are useless (as they often are), and there is no marketing expertise employed to get the best price possible for the end product. As the head of 'Number One Automobile Works' in Changchun — China's biggest car manufacturer — recently remarked, 'We could not even buy an ice cream without approval from a ministry in Beijing.' It does not take a World Bank economist

to conclude that shoddy products are the inevitable result of such a manufacturing process. Again, moves are afoot to tackle these idiocies, but ministry officials in Beijing have a lot to lose from the massive devolution of power that would result. Not surprisingly, progress is slow.

On the Move
It will not take long for you to discover the shortcomings of China's infrastructure — whether you are travelling by train, road or by ferry. But why is it so bad ? First of all, any protracted civil war — which is essentially what China emerged from in 1949 — wreaks havoc with a country's transport system, and rebuilding it in a country the size of China would need cash beyond even the richest country's capabilities.

The Chinese government regards the rail system as the most reliable system — but primarily as a freight, rather than a passenger, network. This is most obvious in China's northeast, where critically important reserves of iron and coal caused the development of a latticework of railway lines. Since it is merely passengers who grumble about matters such as the speed at which a train travels, low priority has been given to the electrification of railway lines and the introduction of diesel trains or double-tracking. Diesel and electric engines may be more fuel-efficient, but in a country where steam coal resources are lying around in almost infinite quantities, and where electricity is in chronically short supply, it is small wonder that China remains one of the few countries in the world still manufacturing steam engines. Passenger journeys will be slow because the pulling power of most steam trains is modest, and because on most lines you will be playing dodgems on a single line with the freight trains, and you can never be sure who is getting the priority (although you hope someone is). North-south travel is also complicated by the fact that there are only two crossings over the Yangzi within 2,000 miles of the coast — one in Nanjing, and the other in Wuhan.

China's trains may not be too fast, but they *are* marvellously reliable. Unhappily, the same cannot be said about China's domestic airline system, about which most visitors have horror stories. Before 1978, when the opening-up policy gave a powerful impetus to tourism as a source of foreign exchange, the airline system was the prerogative of only the highest party officials. The civil infrastructure was therefore sparse in the extreme. As the system has burgeoned over the past decade, so have the country's military airstrips been used *ad hoc* — the only disadvantage being that invariably they are located miles from anywhere. Very few of even the new airports have radar-controlled take-off and landing equipment, so most landings are done by sight. Needless to say, it requires only a modest reduction of visibility for sight-landing to become hazardous — hence the endemic plague of cancellations or long delays.

Maintenance of aircraft is also a major headache because China's fleet is a mixture of domestically made and second-hand imported aircraft. With Boeings, Mcdonnell Douglases, Tristars and Ilyushins in operation on different routes, keeping enough spares in the right place at the right time presents tremendous problems. Many of the aircraft are now so ancient that spare parts are quickly consumed. Shortages of anything can keep large numbers of aircraft on the ground at any one time.

China's road system remains rudimentary, despite huge sums of money being allocated, province by province, for improvement. This resulted in part from Mao Zedong's deliberate policy of making communities self-sufficient, i.e. politically isolated, and hence less likely to generate political protests that could spread across the country. Post-Mao leaders have realized the folly of trying to force self-sufficiency on municipalities, but rebuilding an atrophied road system takes time and money. From the window of a tour bus, the spectacle of traffic jams — and near-miss accidents — makes it very clear that as yet, roads are not primarily intended for motorized passenger transport. They are being built for other priorities, such as conveying short-haul freight between distribution centres, and getting farm and industrial vehicles from place to place. Bicycles also have a higher priority than cars, since in the foreseeable future they will remain the main means of individual transport.

China's river systems — particularly the Yangzi River and the Pearl River — are critically important parts of the infrastructure, both for passengers and for freight. If you travel up the Grand Canal from Suzhou, it is quickly noticeable how much industry backs straight on to the canal bank. Behind Suzhou's pretty face is one of the country's economic powerhouses, with the region embracing Suzhou, Wuxi and Changzhou — called *Suwuchang* by the Chinese — using the Grand Canal network to supply Yangzi River ports such as Zhenjiang and Zhangjiagang, and thus making these some of China's most important inland ports. Until recently, most of the freight barges were state-owned, but recent reforms have put them back into private hands, with a number of quite large independent shipping companies now operating along the Yangzi — for example 'Mingsheng' in Chongqing and 'Data' in Nantong.

In the Countryside
Most visits will involve a sortie of some kind into the countryside,
where the miracles of China's agricultural reform — called the
'responsibility system' — no doubt will be pointed out to you. Of the
two critical elements in China's farm economy, only one will be
apparent: rice. This is the object of back-breaking attention across
the length and breadth of the country at almost all times of the year.
The second — pig-rearing — goes on almost unnoticed by the
average visitor, although provinces such as Sichuan slaughter more
than 300 million pigs every year.

The political priority given to these farm products remains almost
as strong today as it was during the Cultural Revolution, though
many farmers would much prefer to cultivate other more profitable
crops. Under the 'responsibility system', farmers have been freed to
grow and sell their own sideline crops, but only after basic national
needs for grain and pork have been met. The reforms have produced
massive increases in agricultural output in recent years, and have
made many farming communities around big cities such as Shanghai,
Beijing or Canton rich beyond their wildest revolutionary dreams.

But improvements seem to be slowing to a trickle. It is becoming
clear that farmers, who are still not allowed to own land, are
reluctant to invest in its enhancement. Beijing's dogmatic
commitment to meeting basic food needs in terms of grain and pork,
rather than, for example, aquatic products, is leading once again to a
situation in which land which would be better used for cash crops is
being used exclusively for basic staples. The commitment to rice, a
notoriously labour-intensive crop, has also inhibited the
mechanization of the farming sector. This is why you will see people
actually pulling ploughs through the fields, while the mini-tractors
are used simply for shopping expeditions to nearby towns.

As farmers have become wealthier, their first instinct appears to
have been to invest in their own homes. The dilapidated wattle-and-
daub houses so common along roadsides only a few years ago are
rapidly being replaced by brick-built homes. It is a reflection of just
how much of their paltry earnings can be saved that even the most
modest houses can cost 20 years' average annual income. Most of
these houses are built with locally supplied materials of uncertain
quality, but the effect of this boom nationwide has been to create
massive shortages of construction materials. Most freight trains or
barges, if they are not carrying coal or steel, are carrying sand,
cement or timber for construction. Another consequence has been
labour migration on a tremendous scale — evident from the dozens

of rattan-covered shelters and shanty huts alongside most building sites and outside many townships. 'Boom' areas like the Pearl River Delta have an estimated two million migrant construction workers living in such encampments, most of them from poor inland provinces such as Guangxi, Anhui or Henan.

Postscript
All of this hectic economic activity is transforming China at a pace that impresses some and alarms others. After half a century of impoverishing civil war, the country's current Communist leadership would perhaps more than anything else want to demonstrate its superiority by bringing prosperity to its long-suffering population. To that extent, the story the government wants to tell you as you travel across the country is an economic story.

Not for nothing does Deng Xiaoping talk of black cats being just as good as white cats, as long as they kill the mice. Unhappily, neither the black nor the white cats set loose around the country have been specially successful at catching mice. Industrial development has yet to bring a conspicuous improvement in living standards. The poor planning and slipshod character of much development is doing damage to an already hard-pressed environment, and it is difficult to be confident that all the damage is reversible. Perhaps as you travel through China's countryside, you will find reason for optimism, but at present you may have to search a long way.

Lighting candles and incense during a Buddhist ceremony

Shopping in China

The first thing to say about shopping anywhere in China is that it does not have to be at all expensive. There are many modest items that can give great pleasure, such as cotton T-shirts, vests and *neiku*, which are 'inner trousers' worn in winter for extra warmth. They come in a bright array of colours, shocking pink and electric blue being popular, and make excellent, inexpensive jogging suits and sports clothes. I also have a fondness for the deep indigo-dyed cloth of Guizhou, with its patterns of dragonflies, peonies and frogs, and for ceramic rice bowls, medicine jars and casserole dishes made for the country homes of Guangdong Province.

The choice of textiles and clothing in China is astonishing. However, the best often goes to the export market and is more easily sought out in the large emporiums run by the Chinese in Hong Kong. Silks, cottons and cashmere in China's Friendship Stores are often chosen for their appeal to the overseas shopper. But that should not stop the adventurous buyer from shopping in local Chinese department stores. My most recent find was made at a local shop in Beijing's Wangfujing — the capital's rather simpler version of Fifth Avenue. I found here a pair of turquoise, embroidered cotton pyjamas for an astonishingly low price. I bought a pair and walked away. An hour later, I decided to walk back and buy a few more for friends. The entire mountain of pyjamas had melted away, snapped up by canny Beijing residents with a keen eye for a bargain. So be warned — if you see something you like, do not hesitate. There are hundreds behind you all looking for something special.

Silks are one of China's special attractions. Even the most stuffy men have been known to buy silk shirts. Tailoring is easily available if you are in one place for more than a week, but tailors in Hong Kong are even faster — and usually better at interpreting a foreign style. Heavy brocade silks, displayed in swathes of glittering gold, crimson and emerald, are popular with overseas Chinese visitors. My favourites are the bold checks and stripes of Shantung silk, which is of a suitable weight for jackets and trousers. Silk scarves are now better designed than in the early 1980s, and Shanghai has an excellent selection in its local department stores.

For those who enjoy tea and trying out new varieties, a visit to the southern provinces of China affords a chance to taste some of the finest teas available. On my visit to Fujian, I sat drinking with a group of senior Communist Party members who had ensured an excellent supply of *Oolong* tea. Hangzhou is renowned for its *Longjing* green tea, as is Yunnan for its *Pu Er*. The best accompaniment to a fine caddy of tea is a Yixing teapot. Yixing, in Jiangsu Province, has a centuries-old tradition of making unglazed teaware. The unglazed teapots are remarkable for their stylish simplicity of form. Look out for the pumpkin-shaped versions which have a dragon's head on the lid. When the teapot is tilted for pouring, the dragon will stick out his tongue.

China's precious stones can be enjoyed in the form of jewellery or in carved ornaments made from larger pieces of stone. There are excellent precious stone-carving factories in many Chinese cities, where lapidaries with water drills can spend years carving just one work in jade, coral or rose quartz. Some of the carvings are of strange landscapes, others of Daoist Immortals, with the texture or markings of the stone cleverly worked into special features. Chinese jewellery can be either extremely unattractive or stunning to the Western eye. Chinese river pearls are very pretty and cost less than cultured pearls. Many shops offer ropes of coral beads, amethysts, pearls and other precious stones.

Embroidery remains one of the most popular purchases for overseas visitors. It is not hard to see why. Few Western countries maintain a tradition of hand-embroidered goods because of the high labour costs, so Chinese embroidery is increasingly sought-after. The shopper can spend a fortune on the double-sided embroidery which is a feature of Suzhou. The embroiderer works both sides to equal perfection and can often cleverly create a front-and-back effect. More everyday items which can also make excellent gifts are hand-embroidered tablecloths, napkins, guest towels and pinafores.

Many travellers to China like to return home with a painting or a piece of porcelain. A word of warning, however — there are few bargains to be found in the antique shops of China. It is more likely that what you are looking for can be found on Hong Kong's Hollywood Road. The Chinese customs officers will confiscate anything bought without an official red seal, and the government antique shops rarely offer anything over a hundred years old for sale. At the moment, many fine pieces of very early Chinese pottery are available in Hong Kong, smuggled into the territory from illegal digs in China. Hong Kong is also the best place to acquire an old Chinese painting. Beijing's antiques district — Liulichang — has become very expensive since its redevelopment, even though it has never had anything of great antiquity or rarity. Liulichang can be enjoyed for its good choice of copies from paintings, traditional art supplies, fans, rubbings of stone carvings and second-hand books.

展銷部

傳統顧繡

潮州市金山繡品社

服飾品
戲服益品
彩戲寶龍袍
麻裙帳台繡片
喜幛連花各樣
各挂屏潮繡
傳統工藝微意額
歡迎雅意

地址：北門
中山路卓府埕

Minority handicrafts are becoming widely available in big city stores as well as in the shops of the minority regions. You don't have to go to Yunnan's Stone Forest to buy a Sani cross-stitch satchel, since they can now be found in arts and crafts shops in Beijing. However, it is still true that the best of the minority handicrafts are available in their places of origin. Particular favourites are Tibetan rugs, Mongolian saddle rugs (for their hard wooden saddles), jewellery and clothes from Yunnan, and boots, embroidered caps and daggers from Xinjiang.

It is not only the minorities who have their specialities. The provinces and individual cities are often famous for one particular craft or art. In Fujian, it is lacquerware; Shantou has a tradition of painted porcelain and fine linen sheets with lace-crocheted edging; Shanghai has a wonderful choice of carved wooden chopsticks inlaid with silver filigree; and Sichuan is famous for its bamboo and rattan goods. The list is endless. Ultimately, however, shopping in China is all about finding your own particular treasure.

Eating Out in China

The truism that 'you get what you pay for' generally holds for most restaurants in China. But that is not the whole story. There is a tendency for China tour visitors to be taken to hotel restaurants and the special 'Foreigners Only' sections of city restaurants, where they are feasted on banquets designed to please foreign tastes — or what the Chinese believe are foreign tastes. These banquets can be very expensive as well as uninspiring, since they are prepared to a formula. If you are determined to enjoy the best and widest variety of Chinese cuisine, then you must be prepared for a little adventure and a lot of surprises. It is the off-the-beaten-track meals which often reveal the originality of Chinese cooking at its best — and its least expensive.

The years of the Cultural Revolution did much to damage the tradition of Chinese cuisine. The art of cooking was deemed as bourgeois and decadent as other arts; old master chefs were thrown out of their jobs, and good restaurants were closed down to be replaced by workers' canteens staffed by untrained and unmotivated chefs. Since farms and factories were also in turmoil, there was little incentive to produce good and varied food. China is now recovering from that decade of culinary philistinism.

Nonetheless, the impact of the Cultural Revolution has meant that few restaurants in China reach the universally high standards achieved by chefs in Hong Kong. There are of course notable exceptions.

The re-emergence of family-run restaurants has done much to restore a sense of competition and hence quality. Most tourists in China still eat in specially designated areas of hotel dining-rooms every day. Here the food can be average to good, depending on the area and the season, and there is now a more conscientious attempt to include a sample of local dishes on the menu. Yet hotel dining-rooms are not the best introduction to the regional variety of Chinese food. It is much better to ask your guide or a local contact to recommend a couple of local restaurants. Ask for their names to be written down in Chinese, along with instructions for the taxi driver. You can also ask that person to write out a good selection of local dishes, also in Chinese characters, to give to the waiter when you arrive. Alternatively, you can take an exploratory walk and look for a local restaurant that is busy — always a good sign — indicate that you want to sit down, then order by looking over the shoulders of other diners and choosing something that looks good. There are, of course, ways to do this which avoid a Marx Brothers free-for-all. Most Chinese will not mind if you act with discreet good humour. Indeed, there is often someone who wants to practise his English by helping you. You may even end up with a conversational companion as well as a meal.

Small family-run restaurants offer the best value for money, even if the surroundings can be rather basic. You may find yourself perched on a stool under a canvas awning as half the town passes by, but you may also be tasting a family recipe developed over centuries! Do not be too hasty in judging restaurants by the outward appearance. However, if it is really dirty and unpleasant, do not go in; hygiene is as important as authenticity.

In the past few years, the prices in most famous restaurants have escalated sharply as a result of inflation and the new-found prosperity of local Chinese which is keeping restaurants full. The excellent Sichuan restaurant in Beijing's Xidan district, Sichuan Fandian (see page 255), housed in the former residence of the early 20th-century warlord Yuan Shikai, was once famous only for its spicy food. Now it is famous for its pricey menu too. Nonetheless, the food is still good and the surroundings of traditional courtyards and one-storeyed buildings make it enduringly popular with Beijing's foreign residents and visitors.

Chinese people usually choose their delicacies for their nutritional value. Chinese medicine has a holistic approach to healing, and when a person is ill a Chinese doctor will not only prescribe medicine, but also advise what foods should be eaten or avoided. Foods are given the designations of 'hot' or 'cold', not according to their literal state but as an indication of their effect on the body. Snake and dog meat are traditionally eaten in the winter months because they 'warm' the body. Many foods which Westerners regard as tasteless are delicacies to the Chinese due to their 'strengthening' qualities. Sea slugs and shark's fin are often included in a Chinese banquet simply because they are 'good for you'. Foreigners usually do not know or are simply unexcited by this approach, but recognition of its background will make you more sympathetic to Chinese culinary idiosyncracies.

In a country so large and with so many climatic variations, there are bound to be regional varieties of cuisine. In the seventh century, the Grand Canal was built so that the varied agricultural produce of the south might be brought to the tables of the court in the north. The northern regions of China are generally arid, with long, bitterly cold winters. Food in the north used to be severely limited in the winter season. Thus, the northern schools of cooking have plainer and more limited menus than their southern counterparts. The cuisine of Guangdong Province is the most famous throughout China, as well as in the West, becaue of its variety of ingredients and imaginative techniques of cooking. This is not surprising, since the province also has a benevolent climate and an extensive coastline with a long tradition of deep-sea fishing.

A Chinese banquet

As a general rule, rice is served more regularly with food in the south than in the north of China. In the north, wheat noodles and steamed bread are the staples. In the northeastern provinces of Manchuria, there is a tradition of eating steamed sorghum bread, known as *wotou'r*. The breads of China are nothing like the breads of Europe or America, but they should be tried because usually they are delicious. The traditional northern steamed bread bun is called a *mantou* and is often served with a Chinese breakfast of rice porridge (*zhou*) and soybean milk (*doujiang*). As a treat, try a steamed bun filled with red bean paste (*hongdoubao*). In Shanghai, bread buns are popular, even though the region is in the rice-growing belt. A Shanghainese meal is often served with a *huajuan*, which is a twisted length of steamed bread. These breads are wonderful for mopping up a delicious sauce which remains on the dish. The Cantonese are not so keen on the simple breakfast served in the north, and instead serve an astonishing variety of steamed, fried and baked breakfast snacks, known as *dim sum*. These can be stuffed with sweet or savoury fillings as varied as lotus seed paste or barbecued pork and shrimps. The traditional Chinese breakfast is perhaps the first meal on which you should try your new-found sense of culinary adventure — that is, if you can just once renounce the coffee, toast and eggs served at most first-class hotels.

When eating out in China, it is best to have an open mind and modest expectations. If you have eaten out extensively in Hong Kong or Taiwan, then most restaurants in China will disappoint you. But that does not mean that there will not be moments when, after a hard day's travelling, the simplest bowl of clear soup simmered with a few fresh vegetables does not seem like the best meal you have ever eaten. Personally, I cherish the memory of a cold winter's day in Beijing, when I spent five hours out on a frozen lake learning to skate. The ensuing plain meal of pork dumplings steamed on a bed of fragrant pine needles (*jiaozi*) seemed like a banquet.

Cultural Capitals
Xi'an

It is said of the famous English translator of Chinese literature, Arthur Waley, that he never wished to visit modern China, so as to keep intact his vision of ancient China — a vision he had built up carefully through his knowledge of classical texts. It is also said that, in his mind's eye, he could take a walk through the Tang Dynasty capital of Chang'an — the city known today as Xi'an — and be familiar with all the city districts, their businesses and specialities. In modern Xi'an, the provincial capital of Shaanxi Province, it takes a major feat of the imagination to believe that this dusty, unassuming city was the site of 11 Chinese dynastic capitals, spanning over 1,000 years. But in fact the loess plains around Xi'an and the River Wei, which flows close to Xi'an and empties into the Yellow River, lie at the heart of Chinese civilization and are a continual source of new archaeological discoveries, the most famous of these being the extraordinary terracotta army of the first emperor of China. It is these discoveries which have made — and will continue to make — Xi'an one of the most popular tourist cities in China today.

Early History

A site near present-day Xi'an was the early capital of the Zhou Dynasty (1027–221 BC), the great period of bronze culture. However, archaeologists have unearthed even earlier settlements dating back to Neolithic times, as well as the bones of an early *homo erectus*, said to have originated about 800,000 BC at sites near the modern city. Enthusiasts of early archaeology can visit an excavated Neolithic village at **Banpo**, 11 kilometres (seven miles) to the east of the city, which is remarkable for its Painted Pottery (see page 34). More recent archaeological digs have uncovered Zhou sites, the most exciting being that of a Western Zhou (1027–771 BC) burial chamber at **Zhangjiapo**. The chamber yielded two bronze chariots and the remains of six horses, which can now be seen at a small museum west of the city at the village of Doumen.

Many Zhou artefacts have been taken to the **Shaanxi Provincial Museum** in Xi'an itself, which should be visited for its fine archaeological exhibits, ranging from Zhou bronzes to Tang coloured porcelain. The museum is famous for its 'Forest of Steles'. The steles are inscribed stone tablets, some of which date back to the Tang Dynasty, providing a wealth of historical detail for the nonspecialist visitor as well as the scholar. The Forest of Steles can easily be enjoyed with a well-informed guide and by taking a careful look at the carved illustrations on the steles — the maps and portraits, for example. A rubbing made directly from one of the steles can be expensive. However, the museum shop also sells rubbings made from copies of the steles, which are cheaper. The museum is a good starting place for planning visits to distant archaeological sites, since examples from major excavations at Zhou, Qin, Han and Tang sites are all displayed here.

The feudal ruler of the state of Qin, who in 221 BC conquered his rival kings and unified China, is known as Qin Shi Huangdi, the first emperor. During his rule as first emperor, he undertook military campaigns to the far corners of the known world, a vast public works programme involving forced labour, the persecution of Confucian scholars, and the burning of books. Jia Yi, a Han-Dynasty statesman born in 201 BC, five years after the fall of the Qin Dynasty, wrote a famous discourse on the reasons for the rapid overthrow of the Qin. In it he concluded that the mighty Qin fell 'because it failed to rule with humanity and righteousness, and to realize that the power to attack and the power to retain what one has thereby, are not the same' — a very Confucian judgement on Qin despotism. The estimated 8,000 terracotta soldiers and the horses and chariots which lay buried for 2,000 years, guarding the tomb of the first emperor, are a testament to his power and megalomania.

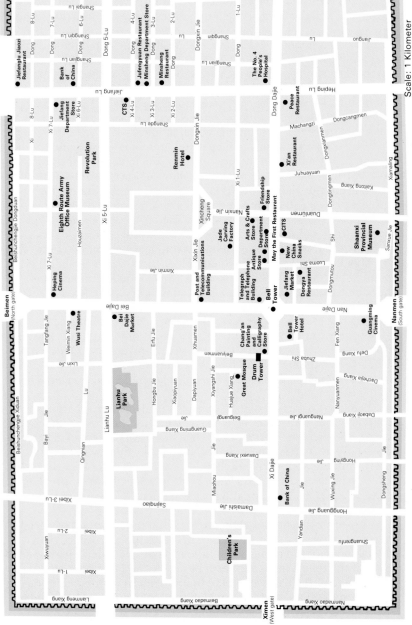

The Walled City of Xi'an

Scale: 1 Kilometer

The **Terracotta Army** was discovered in 1974, when peasants digging a well during a drought uncovered some clay warriors. The excavation site is in Lintong County, a few miles distant from the actual burial mound of the emperor. Visitors can climb the mound, but the burial chambers have not yet been opened for fear of damage to the delicate treasures which are thought to lie within. History tells of the tomb being sealed with traps of poisoned arrows to deter violation. However, the tomb was looted during the Han Dynasty, and one wonders how much is left inside. Archaeological work is taking place at the surrounding burial mounds.

The Terracotta Army, which is still undergoing excavation, can be viewed at the site of the original dig, which has now been roofed over. Special parties are sometimes allowed down into the area of the dig and can walk through the earth corridors separating the groups of larger-than-life-sized warriors. A selection of them has been put on display at the adjacent museum, and you can see how each warrior has different facial features, how the hairstyles and details of uniform vary according to rank, and the contrast between the standing and kneeling soldiers. The figures were originally painted but the colours have leached away. Wooden implements have also rotted, but the original metal weapons have survived. The arrow heads do indeed have poisoned lead tips! Chariots of bronze with figures cast in bronze have also been unearthed here.

For those interested in other Qin excavations, a trip to **Xianyang** is recommended, in order to see the site of the original Qin capital. Unearthed building materials of the Qin period, as well as a model of the first emperor's palace, are on display in the museum attached to the excavations.

The Qin Dynasty lasted 12 years. At its demise, rival armies contended for control of the country, with Liu Bang emerging as the victor. He styled himself Gaozu (High Ancestor) and named his dynasty Han. The name of Han is now synonymous with China itself, Chinese people calling themselves *Han ren* (the Han people). During the first part of the Han reign, known as the Western Han (206 BC–AD 8), the capital was near modern Xi'an and known as Chang'an.

The best collection of Han artefacts is in the Shaanxi Provincial Museum. However, visits to the **Han Tombs** are enjoyable, even though none of the imperial mausoleums have yet been excavated. Nine of the tombs lie to the north of the city and two are to the south. One of the excavated Han tombs open to visitors lies to the northwest of Xi'an, close to the Han tomb of Emperor Wudi and to the Tang-Dynasty tomb at Qianling. This tomb was that of a young

general, Huo Qubing, and it was built for him on the orders of
Emperor Wudi as a mark of imperial favour, since he was killed at
the age of 24 in one of the campaigns against the western tribes.
(These campaigns were crucial to the opening up of the Silk Road
across Central Asia, from China to the Mediterranean.) The young
general's tomb has wonderful stone sculptures of horses, a tiger, a
boar, an elephant and an ox, as well as two strange human figures
which could be depictions of Central Asian gods or demons. The
tomb has a small museum on site.

To the northwest of Xi'an is the site, as yet unexcavated, of the
most famous of the **Tang Tombs**: that of the first Tang emperor,
Taizong. However, some satellite tombs have been worked on, and
the site — known in Chinese as **Zhaoling** — has a small museum,
with a fine collection of funerary artefacts. The six stone horses,
which are the most famous sculptures of the imperial tomb, are no
longer at the site. Four are at the Shaanxi Provincial Museum, and
the other two are in the Museum of the University of Philadelphia.

The other main burial site of the Tang imperial family is to the
west of the city, and known as **Qianling**. It is the resting-place of the
famous Empress Wu, who in the late seventh century temporarily
usurped the Tang-Dynasty throne in favour of her own family. The
main tomb of the empress and that of Emperor Gaozang have never
been excavated, but of great interest is the excavated tomb of the
Princess Yongtai, granddaughter of the Empress Wu, who is said to
have been murdered on her grandmother's orders.

The tomb contains fine murals showing Tang women in costumes
heavily influenced by Central Asian dress. The composition of the
murals is light and graceful, with draperies drawn in flowing lines
and with figures depicted both in full face and in three-quarter
profile. In the tomb are also paintings of soldiers, grooms with
horses, the Tiger of the West and the Dragon of the East. The tomb
of the princess's brother, Prince Yide, also a victim of his grandmother's political ambition, is open and has fine paintings showing
court attendants and a hunting scene. The nearby tomb of the Crown
Prince Zhanghuai, forced to commit suicide by his mother, the
Empress Wu, has a fine mural depicting a polo match. These tombs
all show the influence of Central Asia at the court, at a time when
the Silk Road was flourishing under the protection of Chinese
military outposts.

Close to the excavation of the first emperor's Terracotta Army
are the **Huaqing Hotsprings**, originally a Tang-Dynasty pleasure
resort and now still used for bathing. The present buildings are late
Qing, and the resort is set against an attractive mountain which is

home to several Buddhist and Daoist temples. The resort became famous in recent times as the place where Generalissimo Chiang Kai-shek was captured in his pyjamas by a rebellious young general intent on forcing Chiang into an alliance with the Communists against the Japanese. This episode, known as the Xi'an Incident, occurred in 1936 and ended with Chiang's eventual release, his reneging on the promised truce with the Communists, and the execution of the young general as a traitor.

Buddhist Temples

In the Tang Dynasty, Chang'an was not only a city of vast wealth but also a major religious centre, with Buddhist pilgrims from Central Asia and India arriving to teach and live in the capital. During this period, the monk Xuanzang went to India to bring back the Buddhist scriptures for translation. Scholars from Japan and Korea also came to Chang'an to study Buddhism, and much of the temple architecture that survives in Japan today was directly inspired by the buildings of the Tang era.

Sadly, little remains of Tang-Dynasty architecture in modern Xi'an, or elsewhere in China, because of a major religious persecution undertaken by the Tang Emperor Wuzong in the mid-eighth century. However, many fine Buddhist sites do remain, the most famous of which are the **Big Goose Pagoda** and the **Little Goose Pagoda** in the city centre, both of which formed part of large religious establishments which now no longer exist. The seven-storey Big Goose Pagoda was built in 652 at the request of the pilgrim monk, Xuanzang. It is adjacent to the **Dacien Temple**, of which only a portion remains after the destructions of the reign of Emperor Wuzong. The Little Goose Pagoda was built in 707 and has only 13 storeys — the top two storeys having been lost after earthquake damage. Both pagodas are fine examples of Tang masonry, displaying bold, simple lines on a square plan. You can climb to the top of both pagodas through the interior staircases, with the Little Goose Pagoda offering a particularly fine view over the city to the north.

Beyond Xi'an, in the surrounding countryside, are the remains of many Tang temples which have been rebuilt in later dynasties. Although they have been in a poor state of repair for many years, many of them are being restored, some with the help of funds from Japanese Buddhist foundations. The **Xingjiao Temple**, 22 kilometres (14 miles) southeast of Xi'an, is still a religious centre and has three pagodas, a white jade Buddha and several Ming-Dynasty Buddhas.

The **Daxingshan Temple** is a 1950s reconstruction of a famous Sui and Tang temple. It lies in Xinfeng Park, south of Little Goose Pagoda.

One of my own favourites is the **Xiangji Temple**, 19 kilometres (12 miles) to the south of Xi'an and set in pretty countryside. It has kept its fine eighth-century, 11-storey pagoda, and is the home of the Pure Land Sect of Buddhism — a sect which has a large following in modern Japan, but in China is nothing more than a part of religious history. Japanese donations have allowed for extensive restoration work, and a shop which sells rubbings has a superb one taken from a Tang carved illustration of the temple.

If time allows, there are other temples to be explored around Xi'an, with the help of a guide, a map and a hired taxi. Some 56 kilometres (35 miles) to the southwest of the city is **Caotang Temple**, and the **Huayan Temple** is 19 kilometres (12 miles) to the south of Xi'an. This list is not comprehensive. Indeed, as time passes, more temples will be restored and opened to the public.

City Sights

The city of Xi'an as it is laid out today dates from the Ming Dynasty, and is much smaller in size than it was in Tang times. The three Ming sites worthy of visiting are all easily accessible and within close walking-distance of each other: the **Bell Tower**, the **Drum Tower** and the **Great Mosque**. The bell in question was used to signal the dawn when the city gates opened, and the drum the dusk when they closed. The Bell Tower now dominates a busy traffic intersection and houses a small antique shop. The Drum Tower, just a short walk to the west of the Bell Tower, is also open daily and overlooks the main Moslem quarter of the city. Just around the corner from the Drum Tower is the Great Mosque, a fine place for a quiet walk, with its cool fountain and pretty Ming pavilion — the Chinese counterpart to the Arab minaret. The mosque is a repository of many Chinese Islamic artefacts and possesses a Qing-Dynasty map of the Islamic world. The large prayer hall is always busy with visitors and worshippers; it contains a name board given by the Ming Emperor Yongle. The Ming city walls and gates have been renovated, and you can stroll along the reconstructed ramparts.

There are three Daoist temples open in Xi'an. The **Temple of the Eight Immortals** is now restored as a Daoist centre, and Daoist monks with their long hair (it is Buddhist monks who shave their heads) are once more in residence. The **Eastern Peak Temple** is now part of a school in the northwest corner of the East Gate district, and the **Temple of the Town God** has its buildings used for a school and a shop warehouse.

Xi'an has much else to offer, especially for shopping and entertainment. Many visitors enjoy buying local embroidery brought to the city by the peasants from the surrounding countryside. For children, there are wonderful tiger padded shoes, pillows and hats, padded trousers with knee patches of embroidered frogs, and pinafores embroidered with scorpions and spiders to keep evil away from the wearer. Local opera troupes offer excellent value — hotels and guides can supply details of venues and programmes. The local film studios are considered the most progressive and interesting in China; the film *Yellow Earth* — which was made in the Shaanxi countryside — has won international acclaim. The local restaurants are known to lay on splendid banquets, and the local rice wine can be much recommended: milky-white and innocuous-looking, it packs a good punch.

Luoyang

The ancient city of Luoyang, which lies just to the north of the Yellow River in Henan Province, has a distinguished history as a dynastic capital second only to Xi'an. The Zhou Dynasty established its capital on the present site of Luoyang in 1027 BC, and over the next 2,000 years the city served as the capital of nine dynasties.

Luoyang is best known for the Buddhist carvings of the **Longmen Caves**, which lie just to the south of the city. The caves were worked from the fifth century, when the Northern Wei established their capital at Luoyang, until the ninth century, when persecution of the Buddhist faith led to the closure of monasteries and the end of the patronage of Buddhist arts. However, the area around Luoyang is also famous for its rich heritage of archaeological treasures. Major art works, from Neolithic times until China's early dynasties, have been unearthed in the region and put on display in the **Luoyang Museum**.

The modern landscape of Luoyang is heavily marked by industrialization, but the city's gardens are renowned for their peonies, grown in the region since peony cultivation began under imperial patronage in the Sui and Tang Dynasties. The best place to view the peonies, especially when they bloom in early summer, is in the city's **Huangcheng Park**. The park is also notable for its lantern festival, held at the New Year (lantern-making is a traditional craft in Luoyang), and the two Han tombs which have been excavated beneath the park gardens. The tombs are open to the public and have fine wall paintings.

The famous **East is Red Tractor Factory** is in Luoyang. The bright red tractors were an important symbol of China's reconstruction in the 1960s and the factory, with its model facilities for workers, was then considered worthy of foreign tour groups. In the present climate of economic reform, it is no longer an inevitable part of tour itineraries.

Outings from Luoyang

Thirteen kilometres (eight miles) to the south of Luoyang, on the banks of the River Yi, lie the Longmen Caves. The craftsmen actually used the cliffs of the River Yi to create their monumental cave sculptures. There are in all 1,352 caves, over 40 pagodas, and some 97,000 statues: a daunting challenge to any visitor!

Carving of the caves began in the Northern Wei Dynasty, when the Emperor Xiaowen moved his capital to Luoyang in 494. The Wei emperors were devout Buddhists, and they manifested their devotion in the form of these cave workings. The caves are scattered in various locations, but there are six which are the most frequently visited: the **Binyang, Lianhua** and **Guyang** caves of the Northern Wei Dynasty, and the three Tang-Dynasty caves of **Qianxi, Fengxian** and the **Ten Thousand Buddhas**.

Many of these caves have been badly damaged by earthquakes, water erosion and looters (both Chinese and foreign), but most of what remains is outstandingly beautiful. The sculptures from the Northern Wei Dynasty are highly textured and dynamic in form. The Northern Wei sculptors are famous for their flying *apsaras* (Buddhist angels) who float through flower- and cloud-filled skies, trailing fluttering ribbons. In the Sui-Dynasty carvings, there is a more static feel to the sculptures, whose huge faces and fore-shortened limbs create a deliberately imposing effect. In contrast, the Tang sculptures (particularly those in the Fengxian cave) have great freedom of form and a liveliness of feature. The sculptures seem to be independent of the rock face from which they are carved, and the torsos twist and move in dance-like postures.

Just over ten kilometres (six miles) to the east of Luoyang lies the **White Horse Temple**. This is considered to be one of the earliest Buddhist foundations in China, dating from the Eastern Han Dynasty of the first century, when the capital was at Luoyang. The surviving temple structures all date from the Ming Dynasty, but many of the buildings have the original Han bricks. The temple is a centre for Chan — better known by its Japanese name, Zen — learning.

A half-day drive southeast from the Longmen Caves, the **Songyue Temple Pagoda** looms on Mount Song. As the earliest surviving brick pagoda in China, it has obvious value as an architectural rarity. It was built around 520, in Indian style, and rises 40 metres (130 feet) in 12 storeys. It was once part of a thriving monastery founded in the Northern Wei Dynasty.

Eighty kilometres (50 miles) southeast of Luoyang lies the **Gaocheng Observatory**. Built in the Yuan Dynasty, it is one of a series established throughout China. It is an imposing brick structure, looking like a blunt-ended pyramid. The Yuan-Dynasty imperial astronomer, Guo Shoujing, worked here and in 1280 calculated the length of the year to be 365.2425 days — some 300 years before the same calculation was made in the West.

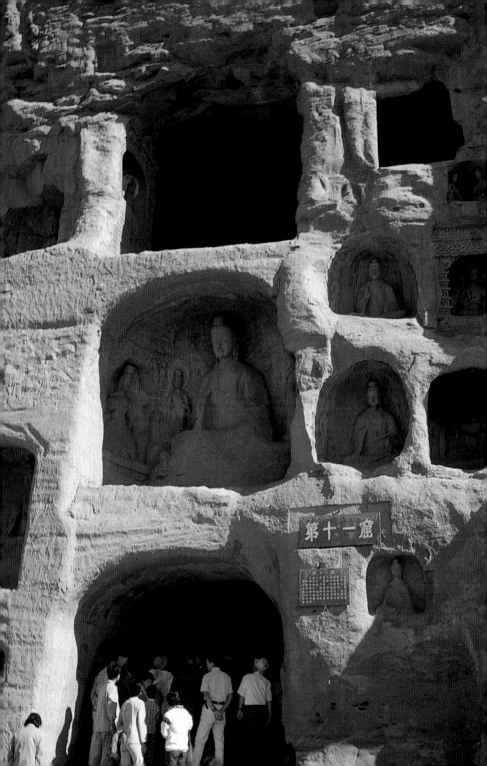

第十一窟

Kaifeng

Kaifeng was the capital of the Northern Song Dynasty (960–1127). Like Xi'an under the Tang emperors, it was the centre of power and learning in a glorious period of Chinese civilization. The city had previously served as the capital of six dynasties before the Song, but today, sadly, little of that imperial heritage has survived. The city has suffered from several disasters, one of which was a sacking in 1127 when the Jin Tartars moved into north China from Central Asia, causing the Song court to flee southwards; another was the deliberate flooding of the city in 1644 by Ming loyalists, desperate to push back the Manchu troops threatening the city. Kaifeng also suffered from periodic floods when the Yellow River overflowed its banks, so it is perhaps not surprising that the city has never developed into a major metropolis in recent centuries.

The original city walls still remain, however, revealing that the Song city was laid out in three concentric circles. The city architects of the later Ming Dynasty built their cities on a rectangular plan.

Visitors to Kaifeng must include a stop at the **Youguo Temple Pagoda**, also known as the Iron Pagoda, which lies in the northeastern part of the city. The exterior of the pagoda is inlaid with iron-coloured glazed bricks. Its eaves, pillars, and lintels are made from bricks glazed to resemble wood. The pagoda was built in 1044 on the site of an earlier wooden pagoda which had been struck by lightning. The pagoda has an elegant octagonal shape and rises in 13 storeys. Its base was badly damaged in a flood in 1841, but its fabric has survived very well. The bricks have been carved in a very naturalistic style, with motifs of Buddhist immortals, musicians, flowers, plants and animals. Close to the pagoda stands a small pavilion which covers a Song Dynasty bronze statue of a minor deity. It is considered to be one of the finest surviving masterpieces of Song bronze casting.

The **Xiangguo Monastery**, close to the city centre, was founded in the sixth century but came into its own as a major centre of Buddhist learning only in the Northern Song Dynasty. The monastery was completely destroyed in the flooding of the city in 1644, and the present buildings date from the Qing Dynasty. One of the temple halls is octagonal, with a small six-sided pavilion rising from the centre of the roof — a curiosity, since temple halls are usually rectangular.

Within the old city walls, **Yuwangtai** — sometimes known as the Old Music Terrace — can also be visited. It is set in landscaped gardens and is named after the legendary Emperor Yu, who tamed the floods — an appropriate tribute from a city bedevilled by flood-waters. More recently, the temple was popular with poets of the T'ang Dynasty who came here to compose and carouse.

Northwest of the city, but close to the old walls, is the **Dragon Pavilion**. Set on a series of rising terraces overlooking lakes and gardens, this was the site of a Song Dynasty imperial palace and also a Ming Dynasty palace originally built by the King of Zhou. Like much of Kaifeng, the whole site was flooded in 1644, and all earlier buildings were lost. The park was redeveloped in the Qing Dynasty, when it assumed the name of Dragon Pavilion. Prior to the Qing, it had been known simply as Coal Hill. The name of Dragon Pavilion is believed to be derived from the magnificent cube of carved stone which stands inside the pavilion. The four sides of the stone are carved with curling dragons.

Nanjing

In its present form, Nanjing is a Ming-Dynasty creation — like Beijing. It was the capital of the first Ming ruler, Emperor Hongwu, who called the city Yingtianfu. On becoming emperor in 1368, he commissioned a magnificent palace and massive city walls, inter-sected by 13 gates and enclosing a 130-square-kilometre (50-square-mile) city. When Hongwu's son usurped the throne to become Emperor Yongle, he moved the capital north to Beijing. Yongle set about eclipsing his father's capital with an even grander design for his chosen city. With the move of the capital to Beijing in 1420, Nanjing received its present name — the Southern Capital.

Unfortunately it has suffered more damage from war and rebellion than Beijing. Even though it is still the proud possessor of Drum and Bell Towers, it has lost sections of the original walls and some of the gates. The Ming palace was destroyed in the 19th century. Nanjing no longer has the air of a proud imperial city, but rather the peaceful atmosphere of a provincial capital overseeing its fertile and wealthy hinterland. Jiangsu Province, of which Nanjing is the capital, is China's most prosperous region and famous for its silk industry.

The location of the city is strikingly attractive, swept on its northern flank by the Yangzi River and surrounded by mountains. The river and mountains have made the city of strategic importance throughout history. It has been the capital of eight dynasties, and the setting of many bloody battles. The Rape of Nanjing must be the worst example of these bloodbaths in recent times. In 1937, the Japanese occupied the city in the wake of the fleeing Kuomintang

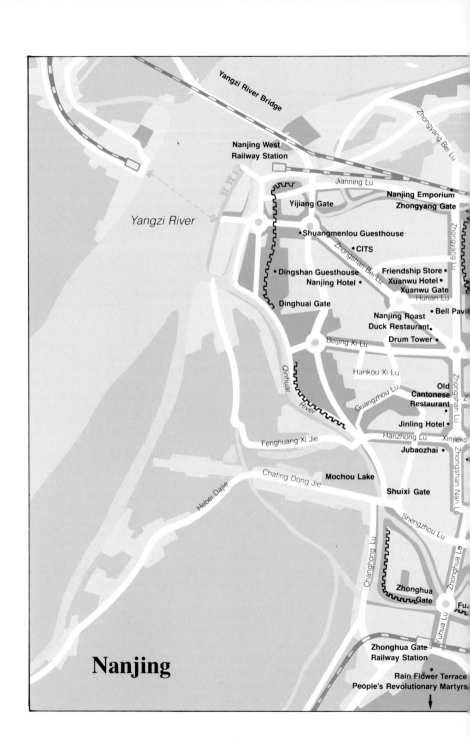

Yangzi River Bridge

Zhongyang Bei Lu

Nanjing West
Railway Station

Jianning Lu

Nanjing Emporium
Zhongyang Gate

Yijiang Gate

Yangzi River

Zhongyang Lu

Shuangmenlou Guesthouse

Zhongshan Bei Lu

CITS

Dingshan Guesthouse
Nanjing Hotel

Friendship Store
Xuanwu Hotel
Xuanwu Gate

Hunan Lu

Dinghuai Gate

Nanjing Roast
Duck Restaurant

Bell Pavil

Beijing Xi Lu

Drum Tower

Qinhuai River

Hankou Xi Lu

Zhongshan Lu

Guangzhou Lu

Old
Cantonese
Restaurant

Fenghuang Xi Jie

Hanzhong Lu

Xinjieko

Jinling Hotel

Zhongshan Nan Lu

Jubaozhai

Chating Dong Jie

Mochou Lake

Hebei Dajie

Shuixi Gate

Shengzhou Lu

Changhong Lu

Zhonghua
Gate

Fu.

Nanjing

Yunhua Lu

Zhonghua Gate
Railway Station

Rain Flower Terrace
People's Revolutionary Martyrs

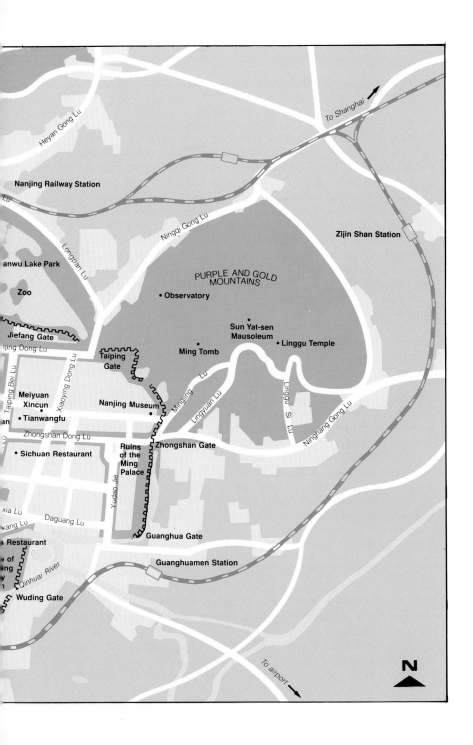

(Nationalist) army, which had made the city its temporary capital after the Japanese conquest of northern China. The occupation was followed by the brutal massacre of 400,000 civilians.

In the 19th century, Nanjing had already experienced tumult. In 1853, Nanjing was proclaimed the Capital of the Celestial Kingdom of Heavenly Peace, even while the Qing emperor was still holding court in Beijing. This proclamation was the result of an uprising led by a young scholar named Hong Xiuquan who believed himself to be the younger brother of Jesus Christ. Soon, the uprising turned into a tidal wave, which at times came very close to toppling the Qing Dynasty. Known as the Taiping Rebellion, its form of messianic Christian despotism — which allowed women an unprecedented amount of freedom — controlled southern China, until the self-interest of the West combined with the outrage of the Qing rulers to ensure the Celestial Kingdom's destruction in 1864. During the campaign, Emperor Hongwu's palace was destroyed and his tomb looted.

Only two decades earlier, Nanjing had been the site of another tragedy — at least for the Chinese: the signing of the 1842 treaty with the English which was to end the first Opium War and lead to the opening up of China to trade with the West (on unequal terms). The Treaty of Nanjing in 1842 therefore marks a turning point in Chinese history. Scholars may argue about the extent of Western economic penetration of China, but what is undisputed is the humiliation felt in China about the Qing government's inability to defend the nation from Western navies and opium traders.

Yet if the city has suffered in history, it has also seen days of splendour and fame as a centre of culture and Buddhist scholarship, particularly during the Tang Dynasty. It was then that Nanjing was the home of the poets Li Bai (Li Po) and Bai Juyi (Po Chu-i), whose works are considered among the finest in Chinese literature.

City Sights

The **Nanjing Museum** houses an excellent collection representing over 30 centuries of Chinese history. Here you can see a jade burial suit, dating from the Han Dynasty, which was believed to prevent physical decay. Small rectangles of jade were wired together to cover the body from head to foot, and a jade disc was then inserted into the corpse's mouth. Archaeologists discovered that the suit, alas, did not have the desired effect. The 400,000 exhibits of the museum have been arranged chronologically, so visitors with little time can select the dynastic period in which they are most interested.

The **Museum of the Taiping Heavenly Kingdom** is fascinating for two reasons: its exhibits give a detailed picture of the strange kingdom set up by Hong Xiuquan, the 19th-century scholar who believed he could set up the Kingdom of Heaven on earth, and it has a fine Ming-Dynasty garden which has survived the political vicissitudes of the city.

The old city walls, more extensive than anything that remains in Beijing today, are worth exploring — perhaps as part of an evening stroll. In the 17th century, these walls were the longest in the world and today, even in a state of decay, they are still a magnificent sight. The **Zhonghua Gate** and the **Heping Gate**, built with a mortar mixture of rice-gruel, paste and lime, are the only two to have survived from the Ming Dynasty, and they vividly illustrate the insecure nature of those times — when the possibility of insurrection meant that hundreds of thousands of ordinary Chinese were made to undergo forced labour.

Within walking distance of each other, in the city centre, are the Ming **Bell Tower** and **Drum Tower**. The bell was used, as usual elsewhere, to sound the dawn, and the drum was rolled when the city gates were closed at dusk. Nearby is the Ming **Examination Hall**, where the aspiring scholars of the region would gather in the hope of securing work in the imperial bureaucracy. Now, however, it is a ruin, with only the stone tower and bridge of the original structure remaining.

On Mochou Road is a **Confucius Temple**, which houses archaeological exhibits in a set of Qing-Dynasty halls. The **Cock Crow Temple** also has halls from the Qing Dynasty, but is most famous for its Ming statues. The **Sanzang Pagoda** is a modern construction, but legend has it that it contains the remains of the famous Tang monk, Xuanzang, who went on a pilgrimage to India to bring the Buddhist scriptures to China. The **Sheli Stupa** is also modern, built in 1911, and is dedicated to a monk who lived and worked on the site printing Buddhist tracts. (These sights are usually excluded from tour itineraries, so include them on an evening walk and ask your local guide for a street map and/or directions.)

Beyond the city walls to the east, set in the Purple and Gold Mountains, lies the **Mingxiaoling**, the tomb of the first emperor of the Ming Dynasty. The tomb was looted during the Taiping Rebellion, and today most visitors come to see the pastoral site of the old tomb and its quiet Spirit Avenue, lined with stone warriors, scholars and beasts.

Modern Nanjing

A great achievement of Nanjing is its bridge over the Yangzi River, which was built despite the withdrawal of the Russian engineers who designed it. The **Yangzi Bridge**, with its road and rail platforms, is six-and-a-half kilometres (four miles) long, and was completed in 1968. The bridge is a symbol of national pride and is important in Chinese communications. Before its construction, all north-south traffic through China had to make the crossing by ferry.

In the city centre, at 30 Meiyuanxincun, travellers interested in Chinese Communist history can visit the house where the late premier, Zhou Enlai, lived and worked when negotiating with the Kuomintang after the defeat of the Japanese.

Another popular place to visit, particularly for Chinese tourists, is the **People's Revolutionary Martyrs' Memorial**. It stands on the original site of the Rainbow Terrace, a place of Buddhist pilgrimage. It is said to have won its name after the eloquent preaching of a Liang-Dynasty monk so moved the Buddha that he sent down a shower of flowers which turned to pebbles. These pretty agate pebbles are collected, polished and sold as souvenirs. The area's pebbles are at their most beautiful when they glisten in water — whether wet with rain or in a small bowl, displayed along with New Year narcissi or goldfish.

Outings from Nanjing

East of the city are the **Purple and Gold Mountains**, which are home to some of the most famous sights of Nanjing. An example of these is the **Observatory**, built on the summit of one of the peaks. It houses a fine collection of astronomical instruments, including a Ming copy of a Han-Dynasty earthquake detector. Also in the collection is a bronze armillary sphere, designed by the Yuan-Dynasty astronomer, Guo Shoujing, in 1275.

The most visited sight in the Purple and Gold Mountains is the **Sun Zhongshan Mausoleum**. Sun Zhongshan, better known by the Cantonese spelling of his name, Sun Yat-sen, is considered the father of the Chinese Republican Revolution. He rose to prominence in the early years of this century as an activist in the anti-imperial movement. After the 1911 Revolution, when the Qing Dynasty was overthrown, Dr Sun came back home — after a narrow escape in London, when he was nearly kidnapped by Chinese secret service agents — and became the first president of the new republic. He did not have the support or personality to stop military leaders from taking power into their own hands, and he died a disappointed man in Beijing in 1925. You reach the mausoleum, which has a roof of brilliant, sky-blue tiles, after a spectacular climb up nearly 400 wide granite steps.

Also in the mountains is the **Linggu Monastery**, which is worth visiting to see the Ming **Beamless Hall**. This hall is made of bricks without any supporting pillars. It was constructed over a mound of earth and subsequently excavated on completion of the building, thereby leaving the hall standing in pillarless splendour.

The wooded **Qixia Mountain** lies 25 kilometres (16 miles) east of Nanjing, and is home to one of the oldest surviving monasteries in southern China. The present buildings of **Qixia Monastery** all date from this century, but there is a famous library with many ancient Buddhist scriptures. Within the monastic grounds there is an octagonal stone stupa, carved with images from the life of Buddha, which dates back to 601. A short walk from this stupa is a rock face carved with Buddha images. It is known as **Thousand Buddha Cliff** (a name used at many sites throughout China), and has carvings dating from the early seventh century.

One hour by car, to the northeast of the city, there are stone carvings from the fourth and fifth centuries. This was a period of political chaos in China, when a series of short-lived dynasties ruled different regions of the country, and the carvings reflect this. They are scattered over the fields at 31 different sites, and all are remains of aristocratic and imperial tombs of the period. They are known collectively as the **Southern Dynasties' Stone Carvings**.

Beijing

Beijing lies just south of the rim of the Central Asian steppes and is separated from the Gobi Desert by a green chain of mountains, over which the Great Wall runs. The Great Wall was built and rebuilt by a succession of Chinese emperors to keep out the marauding hordes of nomads who from time to time swept into China — in much the same way as the wind from the Gobi still sweeps in seasonal sand storms which suffocate the city. The rocks beneath the city yield bitter water, which is barely drinkable, and only the presence of a few sweet springs made the growth of an imperial capital possible.

Modern Beijing lies in fact on the site of countless human settlements which date back half a million years. Visitors can see the site, outside the city at **Zhoukoudian**, where *Homo erectus Pekinensis*, better known as Peking Man, was discovered in 1929. The name Beijing — or Northern Capital — is by Chinese standards a modern term. It dates back to the 15th century, when the Ming Emperor Yongle planned and built the city in its present form. One

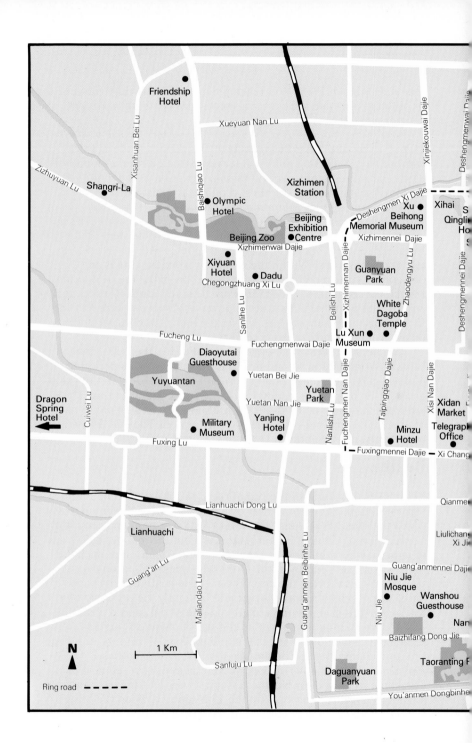

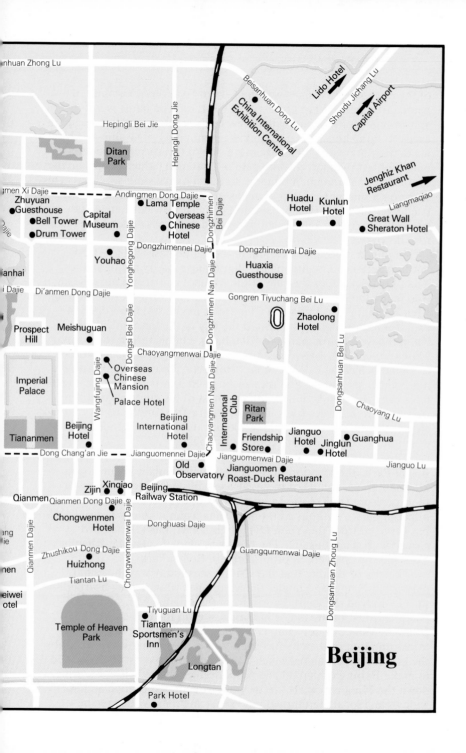

Beijing

of the city's earlier names was the City of Swallows (Yanjing), a name given in the Liao Dynasty (947—1126). The name is still appropriate, for in a land where few birds are seen in cities except in cages, Beijing boasts a large summer community of swallows, which make their homes in the capacious eaves of the ancient wooden buildings. At twilight, the city gate of Qianmen, which stands on the south side of Tiananmen Square, is circled by roosting swallows. This scene on a summer evening remains much the same as it must have been over the centuries, except that the gate now lies lonely and obsolete, no longer buttressed by the old city walls which have been torn down over the years.

Beijing first became a capital in the Jin Dynasty (1115—1234), but it experienced its first phase of grandiose city planning in the Yuan Dynasty under the rule of the Mongol emperor Kublai Khan, who made the city his winter capital in the late 13th century. Kublai Khan's Beijing was known in Chinese as Dadu, but the Venetian explorer Marco Polo, who visited the city at the time of Kublai Khan, knew it by the name of Khanbaliq. On his return to Europe, Marco Polo wrote a vivid account of his travels across Central Asia to China, which he called Cathay. However, his contemporaries did not believe his stories, and they nicknamed him *Il Milione*, saying his tales were thousands of lies. In fact, most of his descriptions of Cathay were accurate (despite some interesting omissions — chopsticks, for example), and his book can be recommended for an eyewitness account of 13th-century Khanbaliq.

Little of it remains in today's Beijing, except for the layout of **Beihai Park**, the creation of the water-loving Kublai Khan whose kinsmen, the Moghuls of India, also established water palaces for their pleasure (unlike the Ming creators of the Forbidden City, an imperial palace without a hint of flowing water). One treasure which has survived from the Yuan Dynasty is a vast, black jade bowl carved with sea monsters. The bowl was made for Kublai Khan in 1265 and is displayed, appropriately, in Beihai Park.

The city of Beijing that the visitors sees today was the grand concept of Emperor Yongle, the Ming ruler who, having usurped the throne, moved the capital north from the original Ming choice of Nanjing. Most of the major historical sites in the city date either from the Ming or later Qing Dynasties. The major modern transformation of the city has been 'achieved' (if that is the word) by the present government, which on coming to power in 1949 decided to make Beijing its capital and to modernize the old city by tearing down the Ming city walls, destroying the commemorative arches (to widows and local dignitaries), and replacing them with wide new roads and concrete housing blocks. The intimate network of *hutongs* — or lanes — was largely redeveloped, thus taking away the distinct pattern of neighbourhoods which had given the city such human proportions. A few of the old *hutong* districts remain north and south of the Forbidden City, but the city centre is dominated by the imposing Stalinesque buildings put up around Tiananmen Square in the 1950s.

The Cultural Revolution, from 1966 to 1976, also caused the destruction of many of Beijing's historic and religious treasures in the name of revolutionary purity. During the anti-intellectual purges of the Cultural Revolution, there were many cases of famous scholars being killed or committing suicide. Perhaps the most infamous was the death by drowning of the writer, Lao She, in the moat of the Forbidden City. Of all the writers of the 20th century, it is Lao She who writes with the most authentic voice about Beijing, its people, neighbourhoods and low life, especially before 1949.

The leadership of the present Chinese government is trying to make good the ravages of the Cultural Revolution with restoration work and rebuilding. The problem is that the skilled craftsmen, whose forefathers built and maintained the imperial city over generations, are a dying breed, and today's craftsmen often lack the necessary skills and knowledge of materials to save buildings, frescoes and carvings. Some restored murals have crude colouring and lines worthy of chocolate-box design. Even so, there is still enough to see in the city, and beyond, to keep an enthusiastic sightseer busy for a long time.

Most of us, however, have only a limited time in Beijing, so the list of places below is selective. The best way to enjoy the city is not to bury your head in the guidebook as you move around, but to keep your eyes open for details and ask as many questions as possible.

City Sights

The **Forbidden City** (Imperial Palace) was the home of emperors from its creation by Emperor Yongle in 1420 until the last Qing Emperor, Henry Puyi, left it in 1924. The vast pageant of halls, white marble terraces and deep red walls is now used to display many exhibitions ranging from court costumes to the imperial collection of clocks and, in the dry autumn months, rare paintings. (Much of the imperial art collection was taken to Taiwan in 1949.) The entire complex of the Forbidden City covers 74 hectares (183 acres), designed to overawe the visitor while reinforcing the majesty of the Son of Heaven — the name by which every Chinese emperor

Peking opera

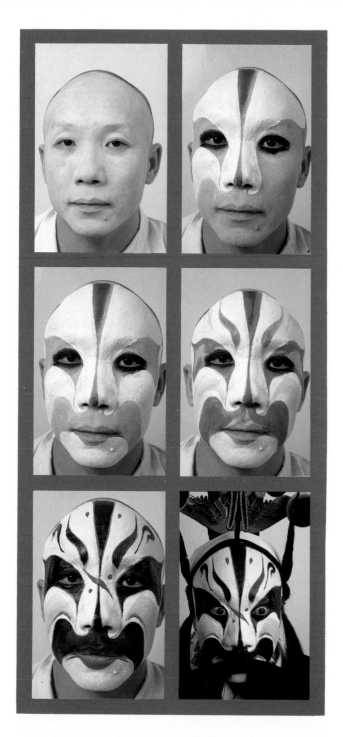

The stages of make-up for an actor

Chinese Opera

Peking Opera has its origins in southern China, but was adopted by the Qing court in the 19th century and thus came to be known as Jing Ju, meaning 'capital opera'. It is best known for its percussive style of music and the use of wooden clappers (rather like oblong castanets), which are used to mark the time of the actors' movements. There are only four tempos which set the mood of the scene: the slow tempo is used for scenes of reflection or when the actor is thinking out loud; the medium tempo is used during narrative; a fast tempo is used for moods of gaiety or excitement; and a free tempo is used for interludes between the action. Actors either sing in a falsetto style or in natural voice. The warrior characters have special techniques for singing, pushing their voice through the lower front part of their cheeks in order to create a deep, gruff effect. Chinese audiences love to applaud a particularly fine solo, which requires great voice control and range.

Chinese opera is different from its Western counterpart in many ways, but no difference is as striking as the painted faces seen on the Chinese stage. Ancient Greek dramas were performed behind masks for dramatic effect, but the Chinese opera demands that many of its characters have their faces painted in elaborate patterns to denote personality. This colour and pattern effect worked in the past because the audiences could tell the good and bad characters apart, through their familiarity with the art. The illiterate and poor learnt their history and legends through opera performances. Modern audiences have had less contact with traditional opera. They have to read the programme notes to know, for example, that red faces belong to heroes and white faces denote treachery.

Not all painted faces are elaborate and multicoloured. Some roles demand a layer of rouge over the face with white contours around the eyes and thick black eyebrows (the eyes are emphasized by the actor sticking his or her skin with sellotape to make the eyes sweep up at the corners). As a rough guide, the young female and male 'good characters' have unpatterned, rouged faces, while the warriors have elaborate face markings. Clown characters are easy to distinguish with their white blob of face paint in the centre of their faces. Maidservants and page boys usually have little makeup and two little jaunty topknots of hair. The faces of the gods are painted a brilliant gold, and the animal spirits have face markings made to resemble the animal in question.

There are few props on the stage of a Chinese opera, and the actors mime an action in order to tell the audience what is happening. Watch carefully and you may see a character 'row' across the stage by bending his body as if balancing on a boat and sculling from the stern with one oar. A character who is about to ride a horse takes his tasselled whip and makes a mounting movement. A man who is leaving a room takes an elaborate step while pulling at the hem of his robe (all traditional Chinese houses have raised steps in their doorways). Great emotion is expressed by the shaking of the hands in the sleeves of the tunic. Shy love is shown by the woman turning her head behind her hand. These and other tiny gestures by the actors give important information to the audience, gestures which can be read after only a little experience of Chinese opera.

The stories of traditional operas usually have complex plots full of twists and turns. Plot rather than character development is the way in which suspense is injected into the drama. This is because there is no character development as we know it in the West; the painted faces of the characters are given at the beginning of the play and there is no change of either character or make-up in the course of the action. Bad characters are vanquished, not transformed. It is understandable that the plays most popular with foreign visitors are the acrobatic martial operas, which need little explanation. Yet even the martial spectacles are more exciting for having their plots unravelled. A particular favourite is *San Cha Kou* or 'Where Three Roads Meet'. This tale is of mistaken identity and a fight in the dark between two heroes and an innkeeper. The three actors mime a fight as if they were in the pitch dark. It is so captivating that you forget the actors can really see each other as they move across the stage. Their eyes never meet, and at one point one of the actors moves his sword into the air as if trying to catch the moonlight on its blade. It is thrilling stuff, so much so that it inspired the English playwright Peter Shaeffer to write *Black Comedy* after he saw a performance in the late 1950s.

Regional Chinese opera can be just as exciting and colourful as its metropolitan cousin. In Sichuan and Shaanxi operas you will often find the role of a comic dame sung by a man. In the Yue Ju style of opera of the Zhejiang region, all the parts are played by women and the music is softer, with more strings, wind instruments, and less percussion than northern opera. The classical Kun Qu style, which originated from Suzhou, is still popular with older audiences in present-day China. There is a Kun Qu troupe based in Beijing which performs quite regularly in the capital. They have one lively story in their repertoire concerning a wastrel husband who, as a young man, sold his wife. His punishment is to be taken into her service, on her secret instructions, and then to run errands while she pretends that she does not know who he is. He is filled with shame and heats her wine with trembling hands, dreading that she will recognise him. The story has a fine comic climax, in which the man is persuaded to marry an unknown bride, who turns out to be — yes — his wife, who has of course forgiven him. Chinese audiences delight in these tales of misfortune, forgiveness and reconciliation.

was known. The palace requires a visit of at least half a day, and it can be daunting in the heat of summer, the time at which the emperor and his court retreated to their cooler lakeside palaces.

The palace is at its most beautiful after a light winter snowfall. To see the golden roofs at their most brilliant at any time of year, try to get a view of the palace from an upper floor on the west wing of the **Beijing Hotel** at dawn.

Another important sight is the **Temple of Heaven**. This is actually a wonderful sequence of temples and altars set in a park as part of Emperor Yongle's grand design. Heaven — or *tian* — was considered the source of harmony and spiritual authority by Chinese philosophers, and so it came to symbolize the source of imperial power. The Temple of Heaven was the site of imperial sacrifices at the winter solstice to keep order and harmony on earth. The architecture reflects that sense of order: the northern wall of the complex is curved in a half-circle to symbolize heaven, and the southern wall is built as a square to symbolize earth. The blue tiles of the roofs echo the colour of the sky, whereas most imperial buildings have yellow tiles (the imperial colour). The main buildings and altars are also built in tiers of three to create nine dimensions of surface. Nine is the mystical number in Chinese tradition, and it also symbolizes heaven. In addition, the emperor made his sacrifices at the **Altars of the Sun, Moon and Earth**. These sites have been transformed into public parks and can be found in the east, west and north of the city, respectively.

The original water park of Kublai Khan is now **Beihai Park**. It boasts a Tibetan-style white dagoba — built in 1651 to honour the Dalai Lama's visit — which dominates the small hill at the centre of the lake. The lake is actually only half of a larger one. The southern half lies hidden behind the high red walls of **Zhongnanhai**, once also part of the imperial park and now the residential complex of senior Communist Party leaders, including Deng Xiaoping. No foreigner, unless he is a high-ranking dignitary, can visit the lakeside villas and steam-heated tennis courts used by China's privileged few. Ordinary Chinese and foreign tourists must take their pleasures on the north shores of the lake at Beihai, with boating in the summer and skating in the winter. There are guided tours of the lakeside temples and pavilions. Emperor Yongle was the main architect of Beihai, but most of the buildings visited today are Qing-Dynasty additions or restorations. The park's **Fangshan Restaurant** is a popular place to host lunches and dinners. Indeed, its splendid setting and choice of recipes from the imperial palace kitchens make it *the* place to visit.

Directly to the north of the Forbidden City lies **Coal Hill**, also known as Prospect Hill, which offers a fine view over the Imperial Palace to the south and Beihai Park to the west. It played a sad part in Chinese history, since it was here that the last Ming emperor hung himself when his capital was overrun by Manchu troops in 1644.

In the early dynasties, Chinese science — astronomy in particular — was well in advance of the West's. A Chinese astronomer calculated the length of the year 300 years before it was discovered in the West. By the time the Jesuit fathers arrived in China, as missionaries in the Ming Dynasty, much of China's previous scientific knowledge had been lost, due to dynastic change and the resulting destruction and upheaval. In order to impress the Chinese emperors with the superiority of the Christian faith (a faith that had persecuted Galileo for his scientific discoveries), the Jesuit fathers set about casting fine astronomical instruments and challenging the accuracy of the Chinese court astronomers' predictions. This was not a minor challenge, since the emperor — as Son of Heaven — was responsible for the accuracy of the calendar, and thus the harmony of the empire. The Jesuits' astronomical instruments are on display at the **Imperial Observatory**, alongside Ming and Qing pieces, on an open-air platform which was once a section of the city wall. Yet despite their great prestige at the Qing courts of Emperors Kangxi and Qianlong, and their work in the field of science, the Jesuits failed to achieve their objective of converting the imperial household.

Tiananmen Square is a vast 20th-century creation named after the Forbidden City's southernmost gate — the **Gate of Heavenly Peace**. Until the appearance of **Chairman Mao's Mausoleum** (open to the public only at limited times) in 1977, the square gave an uninterrupted view from the city gate of **Qianmen** to the outer walls of the Forbidden City. On the west side of the square sits the Stalinesque **Great Hall of the People**, where party and national congresses are held. On the eastern side are the very worthwhile **Museum of Chinese History** and **Museum of the Chinese Revolution**. Perhaps the most charming quality of this vast square, once used for staging political rallies and the site of the declaration of the People's Republic by Mao Zedong in 1949, is that it is now a gathering place for every out-of-town visitor on a first trip to the capital. Groups and families like to have their photographs taken with the Gate of Heavenly Peace and a dour (and nowadays rare) picture of Chairman Mao in the background. On a windy day, children old and young come into the square to fly kites — another Chinese custom that is now being revived with pleasure.

Many of the city's old temples are also being restored and opened
to the public. Over the last few years, the government has allocated
money for the renovation of these, which since the mid 60s had
functioned as schools, warehouses and dormitories for soldiers.
There are many throughout the city — and they can be found with
the help of a guide, a hired taxi and some good maps/notes. A
favourite of mine is the **White Dagoba Monastery** (Baitasi), whose
white dagoba makes it easy to spot. It lies in the west of the city, in
the Taipingqiao district. It has a very fine collection of Tibetan
thankas (religious paintings), and is a quiet place seldom visited by
tourists. The people put in charge of its maintenance are woefully
ignorant of its history — as is the case at many important historical
and religious sites throughout China — but within their limitations
they are very helpful. However, it is best to take an English-speaking
guide if possible.

It was at this temple that I first heard a flock of pigeons whistling,
literally whistling, through the air. A neighbouring pigeon fancier
had revived yet another old custom — attaching pitch whistles of
differing frequencies to his birds, thereby making them sing in the air
as they flew by.

Beijing Nightlife

As the capital of China, Beijing offers some of the best entertainment in the country, although perhaps not in the Western sense of
nightlife. Most of China's millions rise with the dawn and go to bed
early. The English-language newspaper *China Daily* offers a guide
to what's on in Beijing, and that can mean anything from a
traditional opera to an American film (although the choice of films is
often subject to current political thinking), or a concert by a visiting
international orchestra. If you have a sense of adventure, then a
night at the opera (Chinese style, not the Marx Brothers) is the best
value. Beijing has many fine opera troupes, but of special interest is
the Jingju — or Peking — Opera, and Kun Qu, the older form of
opera, which is popular with more traditional Chinese people. I once
sat one row behind Deng Xiaoping's wife at a Kun Qu Opera
performance and she obviously enjoyed it as much as any ordinary
member of the audience.

If you insist on having a 'night on the town', the new
internationally-operated hotels all have bars, while some have
discotheques and nightclubs with live music and video shows. The
local hotel staff can always tell you what is happening and where,
and they can point out a local café popular with fashionable young

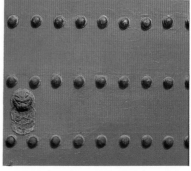

people. Fast-food shops have mushroomed in the capital, but their mock-Western fare is poor. It is far better to try the Chinese fast-food on offer on the streets. There can be no better guide to where to eat dumplings except to follow the crowds. Whichever food stall looks busy will be a good place to try.

Street entertainers have returned to the capital. They are usually poor peasants who take up acrobatics or singing as a respectable form of begging. Still, they do not make a happy sight. In the cold of winter, some stallholders serve late-night hot chocolate under canvas awnings, mainly to cyclists passing by. Also in winter, peasants come into the capital to sell toffee crab-apples on sticks, which are always popular with the children. Generally, however, street life at night in Beijing is fairly low-key, compared to southern cities such as Guangzhou (Canton), Xiamen, and of course Hong Kong.

Outings from Beijing

As President Nixon is supposed to have said on his visit in 1972, 'the **Great Wall** is . . . a great wall.' There is perhaps little one can add, except that helicopter tours are now available and these save considerable time for those whose stay in Beijing is limited to a matter of days. The wall is now open to visitors at two sections: the traditional **Badaling**, where you can see the famous landscape of the wall climbing relentlessly over mountain ridges; and **Mutianyu**, which is a quieter place to visit but a little less spectacular. For the Chinese emperors, the Great Wall was a barrier against the barbaric northern nomads. For the ordinary Chinese of today, it is an immense symbol of the common man's suffering and the resilience of his spirit. The wall as it stands now is mainly a Ming creation.

Thirteen of the Ming emperors believed that their spirits could rest in peace in a quiet valley close to the capital. However, this once silent valley is now overwhelmed by hordes of tourist buses and flanked by a Japanese-financed golf course. Nonetheless, the **Ming Tombs** are extremely beautiful, and they should be visited early in the morning or at dusk in order to beat the crowds and enjoy the serenity of the great Spirit Avenue.

Further away from Beijing, and so less crowded with visitors, are the **Eastern Qing Tombs** of Hebei Province. They are set in a peaceful farm landscape, backed with towering mountains. The carvings on their Spirit Avenues are notably different from their Ming counterparts — the officials in the Qing avenues have pigtails in the Manchu fashion and wear Buddhist rosaries (the Manchus were very interested in this religion). The Ming spirit guardians, in contrast, wear the traditional Chinese topknot and carry Confucian tablets. The two long-lived emperors, Kangxi and Qianlong, are interred here — as is the infamous Empress Dowager who, at the end of the 19th century, took control of the government and was responsible for obstructing the necessary reforms that might have strengthened the Qing Dynasty.

A favourite haunt of the Empress Dowager was the wonderful series of lakeside halls and pavilions of the Qing emperors to the northwest of the city. These are poetically called in Chinese **Yiheyuan** (The Garden for the Cultivation of Harmony). We in the West know it as the **Summer Palace**. Here the Empress Dowager had a private opera-stage in the palace, as she did in the Forbidden City, so as to be able to enjoy whole days of theatrical entertainment. The marble boat moored on the north shore of the garden's Kunming Lake is also a folly associated with the Empress — she had the pleasure boat built with misappropriated funds which should have paid for the modernization of the Chinese navy. The Yiheyuan Summer Palace is a popular place for boating in summer, and is glorious for ice-skating in winter, with its willow-fringed shore and marble bridges. It also has a fine restaurant, Tingliguan, which is popular for banquets.

The summer retreat of the early Ming emperors, and later the Qing emperors, is known as the **Yuanmingyuan** (Garden of Perfection and Brightness) . Foreigners often refer to it as the Old Summer Palace. It lies close to the newer Yiheyuan and is a romantic ruin of marble columns, broken fountains and scattered terraces. The garden was designed by the Jesuits for the Ming emperors. It was looted and blown up by foreign troops in 1860, who were part of an expeditionary force sent by European governments to push the Qing government into greater trade concessions. The troops were under the command of Lord Elgin (self-proclaimed saviour of the Parthenon marbles, now in the British Museum). The Yuanmingyuan is still a lovely place for summer picnics, and local people like to come here for painting, courtship and moon-gazing.

A similar day's outing can be made to the **Fragrant Hills**, particularly in the autumn months when the folds of the small mountains are burnt gold and red with the dying leaves. This certainly provides a serene contrast to sightseeing in Beijing. If you plan ahead, you can visit the **Temple of the Sleeping Buddha** (Wofosi) and the **Temple of the Azure Clouds** (Biyunsi), since they are *en route* to the hills. The Temple of the Azure Clouds is also a lonely place to visit in spring, when the peach and almond trees are in blossom. The Fragrant Hills was an imperial park at the time of the nomad emperors of the Jin and Yuan Dynasties. They made it their own game reserve. Sadly, there is little wildlife left, but a series

of small temples set amidst the trees makes the park a quiet haven for peaceful walking, reading poetry and a breath of fresh air. Of particular interest in the park is the 16th-century garden of the Study of Self Knowledge, with its circular pool enclosed by a walkway.

Close to the entrance to the Fragrant Hills park is the Fragrant Hills Hotel, designed by the American-Chinese architect I.M. Pei. It is a wonderfully simple design, inspired by classical Chinese architecture and interpreted in a modern way, but it has been spoilt by just a few short years of neglect. Under better management, the hotel could be one of the best in China.

Chengde was another summer resort favoured by the Qing emperors. It lies beyond the Great Wall, a five-and-a-half hour train journey from Beijing. It was created by the cultured Emperor Kangxi, who planned a palace with lakes and parks in a sheltered river valley surrounded by mountains. Kangxi's grandson, Emperor Qianlong, who had to outdo his grandfather's accomplishments in everything, including length of reign, doubled the number of landscaped beauty spots and had eight magnificent temples built, each of which was to reflect the different religious practices of the various domains of the Chinese empire. Only seven of these remain, since one was dismantled and taken to Japan during the Second World War. The Putzuozongshengmiao is a copy of the Dalai Lama's Potala Palace in Lhasa. Chengde fell from favour as a summer retreat in 1820, when Emperor Jiaqing was struck dead there by lightning.

Cities Traditional and Modern

Guangzhou

Guangzhou (Canton) is the provincial capital of Guangdong Province, one of China's richest and — in the river plains — most fertile regions. With a sub-tropical climate, an extensive coastline and a mesh of tributaries of the Pearl River, which forms a rich alluvial delta, there is an abundance of seafood in the area. Indeed, the amount of fish, meat, vegetables and fruit available throughout the year makes the offerings of a northern Chinese table look poor by comparison. The northern Chinese are often shocked by what the adventurous Cantonese will include on the menu — pangolin, monkey, cat or even bear's paw. But what sets the region apart is the natural diversity of foodstuffs — and the high percentage of their income that the Cantonese spend on eating.

The Cantonese have always been considered a distinct group in the Chinese world. All regions of China have their different dialects, but few are so difficult to master as Cantonese, with its imploding consonants and a more complex tone system than that used in the northern dialect of Mandarin or Putonghua. The northern dialect has lost these imploding consonants, indicating that Cantonese has changed its form the least in the last 1,000 years. Scholars say that if you read a Tang poem in Cantonese, you will be listening to the closest equivalent to the authentic Chinese language spoken in the eighth and ninth centuries. This may be due to the ring of mountains around the north of the province, which kept Cantonese culture relatively isolated from the upheavals of the north, allowing the province to develop its own identity as well as its own spoken language.

The sea has been part of the same process. With a long coastline facing out into the South China Sea, towards the islands of Southeast Asia and the shipping routes to India and the Middle East, Guangdong Province has a history of being a conduit for new ideas and religions. Arab traders made their way up the Pearl River to the city of Guangzhou as early as the seventh century, leaving behind small communities of Moslems, with their mosques and imams. What they took away from China was much more important than the porcelains and silks in their vessels. The Arabs absorbed Chinese ideas and inventions, most of which ultimately were to have a profound impact on the West.

The Christian Crusades against the Arabs in the 12th century brought Europe into contact with such inventions as gunpowder, the magnetic compass, the stern post-rudder and papermaking, all of which had originated in China, unknown to the Europeans who learnt these new sciences from the Arabs.

By the time the 15th-century Portuguese traders arrived in Guangzhou, guided by compasses which had been invented long before in China, they were to find a wealthy, cosmopolitan city which had centuries of experience of trading with foreigners. Indeed the Portuguese were shocked that they were viewed as just one more contingent of barbarians who were after the silks and porcelains of China (rather as they themselves treated the natives of South America). Christian missionaries from Europe followed these traders. Yet until they had the strength to offer a military challenge to the Chinese empire, these European merchants and missionaries behaved in accordance with Chinese law and customs.

By the early 19th century, Western engineers had perfected their use of gunpowder (a Chinese invention) to the point where European naval vessels could threaten potential trading rivals. By this time, the British had also established an extensive mercantile empire in India. This was the setting for the arrival of Guangzhou on the stage of international history.

In 1839 the British opened fire on Guangzhou after the British Parliament had voted to go to war in order to sustain its lucrative opium trade with China. This trade in Indian-grown opium had developed as an easy means of exchange for Chinese silks and teas. It was, however, considered pernicious by many Chinese government officials, who persuaded the Qing court to put a stop to the trade in 1839. The British responded by adopting Palmerston's 'gunboat diplomacy'. The subsequent Opium War ushered in a new era for Guangzhou, since the war brought a humiliating defeat for the Qing troops whose weapons and tactics were too outdated to deal with the superior firepower and the highly maneouvrable ships of the British navy. The Treaty of Nanjing, which concluded the war in 1842, opened four other Chinese ports to foreign trade and thus broke Guangzhou's monopoly. By the early 20th century, Shanghai had eclipsed Guangzhou as China's major port.

Nonetheless, the late 19th century was a period of prosperity for Guangzhou. It remained a city of great intellectual and political ferment. By the 1890s, an anti-Qing movement was gathering momentum in Guangdong Province, fuelled by the Qing government's inability to curb the activities of foreign traders and missionaries — activities much resented by the Chinese. This resentment erupted in 1900 in the form of the Boxer Rebellion of north China. In the south, the Cantonese Dr Sun Yat-sen and some small groups of activists solicited overseas Chinese support (and funds) for their planned revolution.

In fact, it was in Guangzhou itself that the October 1911 Revolution, which overthrew the Qing Dynasty, was foreshadowed. In April of that year, an uprising led by anti-Qing activists was defeated by imperial troops at the Battle of Canton. Over 100 young revolutionaries died in the fighting. When the October Revolution came, the city quite peacefully went over to the Republican side, and there was little bloodshed.

Guangzhou was badly damaged and suffered a large loss of civilian life during the Japanese occupation of the 1940s. There was much resistance to the occupation, and many Communist-led cells organized sabotage operations in the area. Yet it was only after the 1949 Revolution, when the Communist Party came to power, that political struggle became an everyday reality in Guangzhou. In the 1950s, the anti-landlord movement led to mass executions of regional peasants who were rich enough to have rented out land or to have employed workers. In the 1960s, the Cultural Revolution brought the fighting into the streets, with various Red Guard factions battling with each other over who was the most politically correct or who had the right to interrogate and beat up those suspected of being 'counter-revolutionaries'. During this period, the city was therefore all but closed to foreigners, except in the most controlled circumstances.

Today, however, the city has a busy and prosperous air. It is famous for its parks, with their seasonal flower shows, temples, traditional restaurants and new international hotels. The economic reforms of the last decade have once again opened Guangzhou to the world. However, its principal contact is still that provided through an intermediary — Hong Kong: its businessmen, television channels and inhabitants.

A good proportion of the people of Guangdong Province have relatives in Hong Kong (many of whom swam there during the troubled times of the Cultural Revolution), and those relatives have helped bring new prosperity, particularly to Guangzhou and the small towns of the Pearl River Delta. In the early 1970s, relatives brought consumer goods such as televisions, washing machines and watches with them. But with the recent relaxation of investment laws, overseas Chinese have built houses and opened their own factories, bringing new life to Guangzhou and its surrounding towns. Three Special Economic Zones, **Shenzhen**, **Zhuhai** and **Shantou**, have been opened to foreign trade and investment in Guangdong Province (see also page 109) but the greatest economic success of

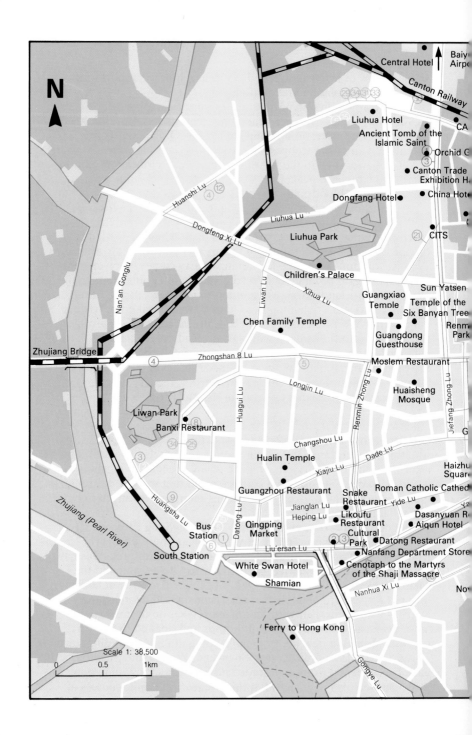

N

Central Hotel

Baiy
Airpo

Canton Railway

㉙㉞㉛㉝

㊴

CA

Liuhua Hotel

Ancient Tomb of the
Islamic Saint

Orchid G

Canton Trade
Exhibition H

Dongfang Hotel

China Hote

Huanshi Lu

⑫

④

Liuhua Lu

㉑

CITS

Dongfeng Xi Lu

Liuhua Park

Children's Palace

Sun Yatsen

Nan'an Gonglu

Liwan Lu

Xihua Lu

Guangxiao
Temple

Temple of the
Six Banyan Tree

Renm
Park

Chen Family Temple

Guangdong
Guesthouse

Zhujiang Bridge

Zhongshan 8 Lu

④

⑤

Moslem Restaurant

Longjin Lu

Renmin Zhong Lu

Huaisheng
Mosque

Jiefang Zhong Lu

G

Liwan Park

Huagui Lu

⑧

Banxi Restaurant

㉞

㉕

Changshou Lu

Hualin Temple

Xiajiu Lu

Dade Lu

Haizhu
Square

③

Guangzhou Restaurant

Snake
Restaurant

Roman Catholic Cathed

Zhujiang (Pearl River)

Huangsha Lu

⑨

Jianglan Lu

Heping Lu

Yide Lu

Likoufu
Restaurant

Dasanyuan R

Aiqun Hotel

Bus
Station

①

Datong Lu

Qingping
Market

②

Cultural
Park

Datong Restaurant

⑥

South Station

Liu'ersan Lu

Nanfang Department Store

White Swan Hotel

Shamian

Cenotaph to the Martyrs
of the Shaji Massacre

Nanhua Xi Lu

No

Ferry to Hong Kong

Gongye Lu

Scale 1: 38,500

0   0.5   1km

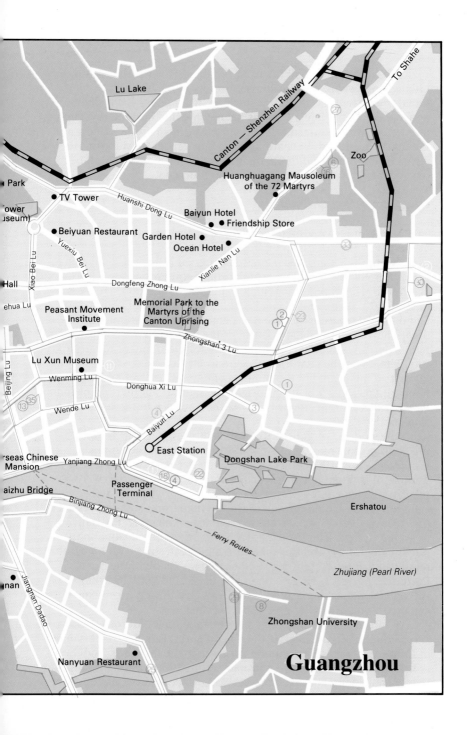

Lu Lake

Canton — Shenzhen Railway

To Shahe

㉗

Zoo

⑥

Huanghuagang Mausoleum
of the 72 Martyrs

Park

● TV Tower

Huanshi Dong Lu

Tower
(useum)

Baiyun Hotel

● ● Friendship Store

● Beiyuan Restaurant

Garden Hotel ●

Yuexiu Bei Lu

Ocean Hotel ●

Xianlie Nan Lu

㉝

Hall

Xiao Bei Lu

Dongfeng Zhong Lu

㉚

ehua Lu

● Peasant Movement
Institute

Memorial Park to the
Martyrs of the
Canton Uprising

② ㉔
①

Zhongshan 3 Lu

Lu Xun Museum
●

⑪

Wenming Lu

Donghua Xi Lu

①

Beiling Lu

⑬ ㉟

Wende Lu

④

Baiyun Lu

③

○ East Station

Dongshan Lake Park

rseas Chinese
Mansion

Yanjiang Zhong Lu

⑱ ④ ㉒

aizhu Bridge

Binjiang Zhong Lu

Passenger
Terminal

Ershatou

Ferry Routes

Zhujiang (Pearl River)

Jiangnan Dadao

nan

⑧

Zhongshan University

● Nanyuan Restaurant

Guangzhou

region has been the small towns of the Pearl River Delta, south of Guangzhou, where new businesses are booming. The city of Guangzhou itself has been transformed: its impoverished, shabby atmosphere of the late 1970s has been converted into the raw energy of a boomtown. Western fashion and music have hit the streets of Guangzhou. Indeed, beneath a paper-thin veneer of Marxism, the city still retains its traditional openness. Guangzhou may well be a city in which future political changes are focused.

City Sights: Traditional

The oldest and least visited temple in Guangzhou is **Guangxiao Temple**. For those with an interest in Zen (Chan in Chinese) Buddhism, the Guangxiao Temple is of great historical significance. It was here in the Tang Dynasty that the Sixth Patriarch of Zen Buddhism, Hui Neng, was initiated into the monkhood. Hui Neng taught that enlightenment can be attained in a flash of illumination, and does not necessarily have to be earned through systematic discipline and study. That doctrine is the core of Zen Buddhism. The temple is also of architectural interest. Despite frequent repairs and rebuilding over the centuries, the Great Hall retains its Song-Dynasty dimensions. In the temple compound you can find an early Song iron pagoda, which was originally built for another temple and moved to its present site in 1235. At the entrance to the temple is a small antique shop.

More popular on tourist itineraries, however, is the **Temple of the Six Banyan Trees**, with its nine-storey pagoda, the Huata. Founded in the fifth century, some time after the Guangxiao Temple, it is nonetheless associated with the Sixth Patriarch. Its present title also dates from the Song Dynasty, when the poet and calligrapher Su Dongpo came south to Guangzhou and, impressed by the trees of the temple, wrote two characters meaning 'Six Banyans' as an inscription. The two characters are engraved on stone in the poet's calligraphy, and this tablet (or stele) can still be seen near the temple entrance. Here is also a Song bronze statue of the Sixth Patriarch, as well as several fine Qing brass Buddhas. The temple is still an active teaching centre, and if you give prior notice, a monk can escort you as well as give you a blessing.

An interesting example of an ancestral temple, few of which have survived in modern China, is the **Chen Family Temple**. Chen (Chan in Cantonese) is a very common surname in the province, and the temple was founded to give a proper setting for ancestor worship and family education. The spirit tablets of the ancestors are no longer in the central hall at the back of the temple, but visitors can enjoy the hall's carvings and ornate decorated tiles.

The arrival of the Arabs in the seventh century also brought a new religious centre to the city. The **Huaisheng Mosque** is one of China's earliest mosques, and is believed to have once stood at the edge of the Pearl River. The river has shifted its course, and the mosque now lies in the city centre, just south of Zhongshan Lu on Guangta Lu. It has a fine, plain, stone minaret, known as the Guangta, indicating the early date of the mosque's foundation — most late mosques having small pavilions in place of the minaret. Visitors can climb the minaret for a view of the city.

For those further interested in the history of the Arabs in China, a little exploration in the north of the city will reveal the **Ancient Tomb of the Islamic Saint**, containing the remains of Mohammed's uncle, who came as a missionary to China.

Finally, still in a traditional mood, there are several old restaurants in the city which offer Cantonese cuisine in a setting of landscaped courtyards with ponds and small galleries. The three most famous are the Panxi, the Beiyuan and the Nanyuan (see also pages 256–7).

City Sights: Modern

In order to gain an impression of how European traders once lived, it is worth visiting **Shamian Island**, a sandbar in the Pearl River. The Chinese authorities gave the Europeans the island in the 19th century as a residential base, along with extraterritorial rights. Once on the island, the Europeans were no longer subject to Chinese law or supervision. Shamian was made an elegant residential area with large mansions, churches, a yacht club and tennis courts. Now the area is shabby and rundown. Nevertheless, it is an interesting place for a leisurely walk. A smart new hotel, the **White Swan**, with a glass atrium lobby, waterfalls, trees and swimming pool, has been built here and makes a convenient place to relax and enjoy a cool drink.

Just west of Haizhu Square on Wende Lu lies the **Roman Catholic Cathedral**, open to worshippers again after serving for many years as a warehouse. It was built in granite by a French architect and was consecrated in 1863.

The **Mausoleum of the 72 Martyrs** was built in 1918 as a memorial to the young revolutionaries who lost their lives in the Battle of Canton (see page 101). Donations for the memorial came from patriotic overseas Chinese as far away as Canada and Chile. The mausoleum is built in a bizarre blend of styles, with a miniature

Statue of Liberty, an Egyptian-style obelisk, and two traditional Chinese guardian lions!

The founding father of the Chinese Republic is commemorated in the **Sun Yat-sen Memorial Hall**, with its brilliant blue tiles. Inside there is a 5,000-seat auditorium used for concerts, operas and other shows.

The city's earliest contribution to Communist revolutionary history is remembered in the **Peasant Movement Institute**, which was once the headquarters of such activists as Mao Zedong, who set up a school to educate young cadres. The Institute is housed in a Ming-Dynasty Confucian temple, and is therefore both historically and architecturally interesting.

Another incident in Communist revolutionary history was the so-called Canton Uprising of 1927. This took place just before the Kuomintang army pushed northwards to unify the country. (The Kuomintang was founded just after the 1911 Revolution. It ruled China, often in name only, until 1949, and now forms the government of Taiwan.) In the early 1920s, the Kuomintang had formed an uneasy alliance with the Communists, who then proceeded to infiltrate Kuomintang ranks. In 1927 the Kuomintang took the opportunity to crush the Canton commune, putting to death about 5,000 people whom they knew to be Communist activists or supporters. This tragedy is remembered in the **Memorial Park to the Martyrs of the Canton Uprising**, where local people now go boating or strolling. In autumn, there is a fine chrysanthemum fair here.

Botanists and amateur gardeners will also enjoy the **South China Botanical Garden**, the finest in China. Founded in 1958, it is administered by the Chinese Academy of Science and is set in 300 hectares (750 acres) — large enough to find a quiet spot, even in hectic Guangzhou.

Finally, the **Municipal Museum** is worth visiting for three main reasons. It is housed in a Ming-Dynasty watchtower. It gives a fine view over the city and a neighbouring football stadium (football is now a major sport in China). And it has a fine collection of historical documents. Well worth looking out for in the museum are the Tang-Dynasty glazed figurines of Arab traders, recognizable from their very un-Chinese hooked noses.

Outings from Guangzhou

Many adventurous travellers explore the countryside of Guangdong Province by bus. This is quite easy to do, since there are good bus services to the towns and villages, now that peasants are allowed to come to the city to sell their wares. The Pearl River Delta towns, such as **Nanhai**, give a good impression of the new prosperity of the region and the mushrooming of mini-factories set up by Hong Kong businessmen.

Trips to the three Special Economic Zones of Shenzhen, Zhuhai and Shantou are interesting if you have a desire to see what economic progress is taking place in China today. Shantou is the furthest from Guangzhou, but is the most attractive. In terms or attracting foreign investments, it has not done very well. Nonetheless, it is a charming town, with a city centre unspoilt by modern buildings. In Shantou you can buy lovely lace-edged cotton sheets and pretty hand-painted porcelain.

One of the most popular trips from Guangzhou is to **Foshan**, 20 kilometres (12 miles) southwest of the city. The town has a famous ceramics industry, and is also well known for its folk arts such as paper-cutting, lantern-making and carving. The town has many fine old temples which, like most Cantonese temples, are brightly decorated with roof figures, colourful murals and carved doors.

Tianjin

The municipality of Tianjin is not a major destination for foreign travellers unless they are in China on business. The city has few of the attractions of China's other major cities, having suffered extensive damage during the catastrophic Tangshan earthquake of 1976. The old treaty port's European-style buildings have survived and are now being renovated, but modern housing blocks of characterless uniformity are the major feature of the city.

Tianjin is only a two-hour rail journey from Beijing. It is an important industrial centre, and is considered by foreign businessmen to be more go-ahead than Shanghai in its efforts to attract foreign capital. Tianjin has had a special opportunity to redevelop its urban infrastructure, due to the extensive rebuilding programme undertaken after the 1976 earthquake. It is strange to contemplate a spaghetti-junction flyover with little moving over it except for occasional trucks, bicycles and mule-drawn carts, but the city is planning for the future, and its road system will be very important as traffic increases on China's highways.

Visitors to Tianjin usually go to one of the city's famous carpet factories. The carpets are woven by hand from painted patterns placed on the weaver's loom. The weaver is responsible for interpreting the pattern and matching the colours of the wool to be used. The carpets are made in a variety of designs and sizes, the most popular still being the classic designs using traditional motifs.

After being woven, the carpets are hand-trimmed with electric scissors to create an embossed effect.

The Tianjin region is famous for its handicrafts, two of which — kites and New Year posters — are famous throughout China. The kites are made in fabric or paper, and are stretched over thin bamboo frames. Designs can range from a basket of peonies to a goldfish. The New Year poster workshops — located outside the city centre, in Hexi district — produce the brightly decorated pictures which the Chinese like to paste up in their homes during the lunar New Year. The posters traditionally feature fat babies, the god of longevity, maidens plucking lotuses (lotus seeds being symbols of fertility), and door gods. After the overthrow of the so-called 'Gang of Four', when Mao's widow — Jiang Qing — and three others were arrested for political crimes, the poster workshops produced jolly pictures of small children sticking knives and spears into caricatures of the famous four. Recently these political themes have disappeared from the posters — perhaps forever.

Tianjin's traditional arts and crafts can be purchased at a newly created **Culture Street** on the banks of the River Hai. The street incorporates the renovated **Linmoniang Temple**, dedicated to the local goddess of fishermen. While exploring Culture Street, try the famous Tianjin steamed dumplings called *goubuli baozi*. The name

Tianjin docks

means, disconcertingly, 'dogs won't touch them'. Yet despite their name, they are delicious.

Businessmen whose itineraries demand extended stays in Tianjin are often taken to the famous orchards of the region to try the apples and pears of late summer. Other such day trips can be made to the lakeland region of **Baiyangdian** to the south, in Hebei Province. Here, tourists make water tours of the lakeside villages, which thrive on fishing, ducks and reed weaving. To the north of the city, within the municipal boundary, is the **Temple of Singular Happiness** (Dulesi), in Jixian district. This Buddhist temple was founded in the seventh century and is famous for the 11-headed Guanyin (Bodhisattva of Mercy) statue. The eastern gate of the temple is the earliest of its kind extant in China.

Shanghai

By Chinese standards, Shanghai is a very modern incarnation. Although its antecedents date back to the Warring States period (475–221 BC), when it was just a small fishing village on a tidal creek at the mouth of the Yangzi River, its present-day position — as the world's third largest and China's largest city, as well as the nation's biggest port and manufacturing base — is a far cry from its genesis. It was that very position at the mouth of the Yangzi, China's main trade artery until well into this century, which made it so attractive to 19th-century merchants from Europe and America. They turned a prosperous regional trading centre into a treaty port, with an international settlement and international importance. Modern Shanghai owes its development, cityscape and pre-eminence to that strange conjunction of Western traders and regional Chinese entrepreneurs who flocked to Shanghai and together made it their home and their fortune.

As a maritime trading city, Shanghai's waterfront was for a long time the focus of business. Known in Chinese as the Waitan, and to the foreigner as the **Bund**, the waterfront thoroughfare (now known as Zhongshan Dong Lu) was, in the '30s, Shanghai's equivalent to Wall Street. That same '30s skyline remains, little changed, though rather more drab, certainly less imposing than it was in its heyday. Yet it is still exciting for the traveller lucky enough to arrive by ship.

Shanghai has remained China's major commercial centre, despite the Communist government's suspicion of its history of decadent prosperity, entrepreneurial spirit and political independence. After 1949, the new leadership was keen to cash in on the city's wealth and business infrastructure. Yet it starved the city of the funds needed

for redevelopment and modernization, while much of the money the city generated was syphoned off to develop the poorer inland regions. The Shanghainese have always resented this, just as they have resented the sufferings caused by excessive political campaigns, many of which were focused and fomented in Shanghai during the Cultural Revolution.

All these problems have left the city poorly serviced, shabby and hopelessly overcrowded. Workers in China are given one day off a week, and that day is staggered — for if everyone had the *same* rest day (or two), there would be no room at all to walk in the already crammed shopping districts of the city. Official fear of further political change, plus the well-known Shanghainese trait of overweaning self-confidence, and outdated manufacturing processes, have ensured that China's major industrial city remains a nightmare for the modern China trader. However, things do look set to change, and the Shanghai Stock Exchange — founded in mid-1986 — is prospering, with no one willing to sell shares and everyone eager to buy new issues.

Indeed, despite the drawbacks for Chinese and foreign business-men, Shanghai still has many compensations — even if few of them are as wild and wicked as in the past. With its mere handful of tradi-tional buildings, the city mainly attracts visitors interested in China's urban landscape. Just as you don't go to New York to see colonial-style village America, you don't go to Shanghai for a glimpse of China's imperial past. What the city does offer is a good view of treaty port identity, modern Chinese life, and perhaps a look at the nation's future — in the new industrial estates, in the emergence of a new generation of young people who, in all but name, have left behind their revolutionary heritage and are getting on with the good things in life.

City Sights: Traditional

Although Shanghai is a modern and industrial city, most Chinese and foreign visitors like to start their sightseeing with a trip to the old Chinese quarter, known as Nanshi. Here the streets are not built on an orderly grid system, as they are in the International Settlement area, but run hugger-mugger in a mesh of lanes and alleyways. This is part of the charm of the place, but it is probably less picturesque for those who live here — the overcrowding means that homework, knitting, chess, preparing the dinner and even family quarrels often take place in the street.

It is also an area famed for its shopping. Unlike the large department stores of the famous **Nanjing Lu**, which sell anything from cameras to canned food, these small shops are speciality ones. Look out for shops with tea, fans, bonsai (miniature trees, known in Chinese as *penjing*) and singing birds. In the old city south of Nanjing Lu, you can add to your list long cotton underwear for less than a dollar, fans with Chinese opera characters, pot plants and patterned silks.

This quarter is popular with locals, too, thanks to its restaurants and the **Huxinting Teahouse**. This is set in the middle of a small lake and is reached by a nine-turn, zigzag bridge. It has arched eaves and is painted red, making it a perfect setting for a leisurely cup of tea and traditional Chinese snacks.

On the other side of the lake is a slightly scruffier establishment, which serves delicious steamed dumplings known as Nanxiang dumplings. Made of minced pork, steamed in a thin pastry skin and dipped in vinegar and slices of ginger, they are so popular that the small restaurant can be identified simply by the sight of steam escaping from its windows and the crowds around its door.

A grander restaurant to visit nearby is the **Lubolang** (Walkway of the Jade Waves). This is my favourite in all of Shanghai because of its steamed and baked Shanghai-style snacks, which include such lyrically named delights as Moth Eyebrow dumpling, a baked crescent of wafer-light pastry filled with shrimps and delicate vegetables. If you can't get a seat in the restaurant — and it's always packed, especially near the windows which overlook the lake — you can buy snacks from the window downstairs to take away.

The **Yu Garden**, adjacent to the Lubolang restaurant, is a good place to walk off that lunch; it has marvellous vistas of pools, pavilions and rock gardens. The garden is attractive but it is often overcrowded with sightseers. It dates back to the 16th century, when a Ming official laid out the landscape to please his father. Only two hectares (five acres) in size, it recreates a wild landscape in miniature, with strange rocks, still pools, running water, meandering paths which offer changing vistas, and small pavilions in which to sit, dream, play chess or watch the moon. The garden also has an interesting history as the headquarters of the 'Society of Little Swords', an offshoot of the Taiping Rebellion in the mid-19th century. In fact, this association saved the garden from the destructions of the Cultural Revolution, since the 'Little Swords' were deemed to be early revolutionaries.

The city has some attractive temples, too. In the old quarter, there is the Daoist **Temple of the Town God**, but it is no longer used and stands merely as an architectural curiosity.

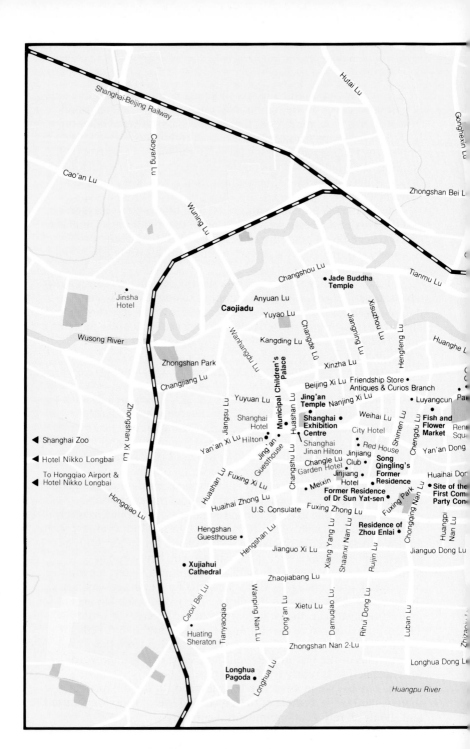

Shanghai-Beijing Railway

Hutai Lu

Gonghexin Lu

Cao'an Lu

Caoyang Lu

Zhongshan Bei Lu

Wuning Lu

Tianmu Lu

Changshou Lu

Jade Buddha
Temple

Xisuzhou Lu

Jinsha
Hotel

Anyuan Lu

Caojiadu

Yuyao Lu

Jiangning Lu

Hengfeng Lu

Huanghe Lu

Wusong River

Kangding Lu

Changde Lu

Xinzha Lu

Zhongshan Park

Wanhangdu Lu

Changjiang Lu

Beijing Xi Lu

Friendship Store •
Antiques & Curios Branch

Yuyuan Lu

**Municipal Children's
Palace**

**Jing'an
Temple**

Nanjing Xi Lu

• Luyangcun Pa

Jiangsu Lu

Shanghai
Hotel

Huashan Lu

Weihai Lu

Shimen Lu

Chengdu Lu

**Fish and
Flower
Market**

Ren
Squ

◀ Shanghai Zoo

**Shanghai
Exhibition
Centre**

City Hotel

◀ Hotel Nikko Longbai

Yan'an Xi Lu

Hilton

Shanghai
Jinan Hilton

• Red House

Yan'an Dong

To Hongqiao Airport &
Hotel Nikko Longbai ◀

Jing'an
Guesthouse

Shanghai
Garden Hotel

Changshu Lu

Changle Lu
• Jinjiang
Club

**Song
Qingling's
Former
Residence**

Zhongshan Xi Lu

Huashan Lu

Fuxing Xi Lu

Jinjiang
Hotel

Huaihai Don

Hongqiao Lu

• Meixin

**Former Residence
of Dr Sun Yat-sen**

Fuxing Park

**Site of the
First Com
Party Con**

Huaihai Zhong Lu

U.S. Consulate

Fuxing Zhong Lu

Chongqing Nan Lu

Huangpi
Nan Lu

Hengshan
Guesthouse •

Hengshan Lu

Xiang Yang Nan Lu

Shaanxi Nan Lu

Rujin Lu

**Residence of
Zhou Enlai** •

Jianguo Dong Lu

Jianguo Xi Lu

**• Xujiahui
Cathedral**

Zhaojiabang Lu

Caoxi Bei Lu

Wanping Nan Lu

Dong an Lu

Xietu Lu

Damuqiao Lu

Rihui Dong Lu

Luban Lu

Tianyaoqiao

Zhongshan Nan 2-Lu

Longhua Dong L

**Huating
Sheraton**

**Longhua
Pagoda** •

Longhua Lu

Huangpu River

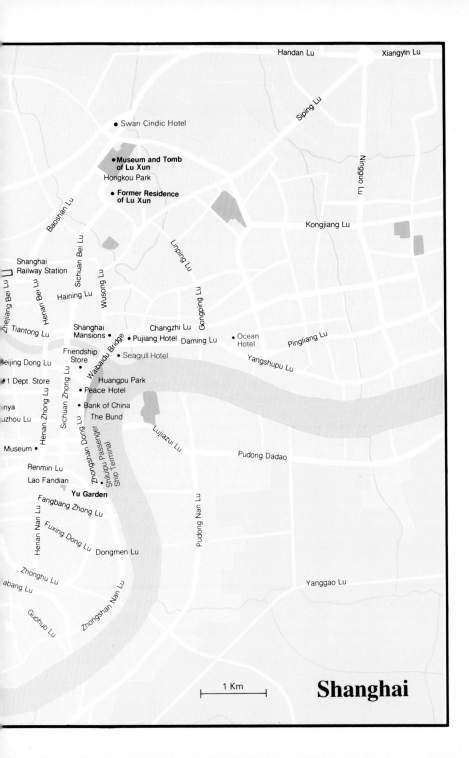

Handan Lu   Xiangyin Lu

Siping Lu

Ningguo Lu

● Swan Cindic Hotel

●Museum and Tomb
of Lu Xun
Hongkou Park

Kongjiang Lu

● Former Residence
of Lu Xun

Baoshan Lu

Linping Lu

Shanghai
Railway Station

Sichuan Bei Lu

Wusong Lu

Gongping Lu

Zhejiang Bei Lu

Henan Bei Lu

Haining Lu

Tiantong Lu

Shanghai
Mansions ●

Changzhi Lu

● Ocean
Hotel

Pingliang Lu

Friendship
Store

● Pujiang Hotel

Daming Lu

Beijing Dong Lu

Sichuan Zhong Lu

Waibaidu Bridge

● Seagull Hotel

Yangshupu Lu

#1 Dept. Store

Huangpu Park

nya

Henan Zhong Lu

● Peace Hotel

uzhou Lu

Zhongshan Zhong Lu

● Bank of China

The Bund

Zhongshan Dong Lu

Shilupu Passenger
Ship Terminal

Lujiazui Lu

Museum ●

Pudong Dadao

Renmin Lu

Lao Fandian

Yu Garden

Pudong Nan Lu

Fangbang Zhong Lu

Henan Nan Lu

Fuxing Dong Lu

Dongmen Lu

Zhonghu Lu

abang Lu

Guohuo Lu

Zhongshan Nan Lu

Yanggao Lu

├─── 1 Km ───┤

Shanghai

In the northwest of the city stands the **Temple of the Jade Buddha** (Yufosi), named after its two exquisite milk-white jade Buddhas, brought from Burma in the 19th century. One of the Buddhas is seated, and the other is recumbent, the latter position symbolizing the Buddha's attainment of enlightenment. Monks live, work and study in this temple, and visitors can observe the religious services and eat at the temple's vegetarian restaurant.

At the western end of the Nanjing Lu is the **Jing'an Temple**, dating back to the last century, when it was popularly known to foreign residents as the Bubbling Well Temple. It has a colourful history, including an abbot of the temple who was famous for his rich wife, seven concubines and White Russian bodyguard.

To the southwest of the city, near a small park, stands the **Longhua Temple**, with its pagoda. The temple site dates from the third century, and the pagoda in its present form dates from the tenth century. The temple buildings are all from the Qing Dynasty, and the temple halls are famous for their flower and small rock gardens. There is an excellent vegetarian restaurant here.

City Sights: Modern

On the face of it, modern Shanghai has little intrinsically Chinese in character — be it traditional or modern Communist. The city is largely a product of European colonialism, and much of the architecture, whether civic or suburban, reflects that heritage. The Bund and the **Xujiahui Cathedral**, formerly the Cathedral of St. Ignatius, are part of the Western legacy. The Cathedral, built by the Jesuits in 1906, is still an active centre of Roman Catholic worship and is in the southwest of the city. The old Hongkong and Shanghai Bank, now the Municipal Party Committee Headquarters, may not be the tallest building on the Bund, but with its broad facade, portico and dome it is still an impressive sight.

The port, the largest in China, is worth visiting just to gain an idea of the amount of traffic which flows through it. Shanghai's wharves stretch for 56 kilometres (35 miles) along the shores of the Huangpu Creek and, unlike the northern ports which ship more than they receive, the bulk of Shanghai's port traffic is incoming.

The **Municipal Children's Palace** is as interesting for its setting as for its child prodigies. The palace is housed in the pre-1949 residence of the wealthy stock-broking family of Kadoorie. The Kadoories left Shanghai for Hong Kong, where today they are of considerable influence in the Hong Kong business community. Their former mansion is now a centre for children of exceptional abilities, who can pursue their studies or activities with special coaching facilities. Visitors can see athletic or musical performances given by the children. For those who cannot resist pandas, even if they are in captivity, **Shanghai Zoo** in the western suburbs is of interest. There are also golden-haired monkeys, which once lived wild in the Yangzi gorges, and rare Yangzi River alligators.

Chinese revolutionary history was made in Shanghai with the founding of the Chinese Communist Party in 1921. The house where the founding members gathered, and the **site of the First National Congress of the Chinese Communist Party**, can be visited at 76 Xingye Lu, just north of Fuxing Park. In the north of the city, you can also find the residence of the writer Lu Xun (1881–1936). He was a pioneer of modern Chinese language and literature. A museum of his life and work can be found in the nearby **Hongkou Park**, where his tomb is placed at the bottom of a bronze statue of the writer.

Shanghai's **Museum of Art and History** houses a particularly fine collection of bronzes and traditional and modern paintings. The museum's setting is rather austere and bleak, particularly in the winter months, but its fine exhibitions justify a good half-day's visit.

Shanghai Nightlife

If you prefer to eat, drink and listen to an old dance-band, rather than sitting up in the evening with a book and a cup of jasmine tea, then Shanghai is the city for you. It has innumerable restaurants featuring cuisines of nearly all of China's culinary regions. The international hotels now offer anything from saunas to discos, and the old hotels of the '30s have their own attractions — such as art deco interiors, shabby but grand dining rooms, and billiard tables. The **Dongfeng Hotel**, once the old Shanghai Club, is the home of the Long Bar, which in its day was the longest bar in the world. The **Peace Hotel** on the Bund features a jazz band whose members' ages, if added up, would figure in the 200s.

On most tour group itineraries is the **Shanghai Acrobatic Theatre**. It is certainly worth obtaining tickets for its virtuoso performances of juggling, tumbling and plate-spinning. The local opera performed in the Shanghai region is known as Yueju. A more melodic relative of the Peking Opera school, it has less percussion and more choruses than the northern style. The CITS office in the Peace Hotel can help you with bookings.

Cities in a Landscape

Wuxi

Wuxi's strange name which means 'without tin', is connected with the city's early origins. The town was founded in the Zhou Dynasty (1027−256 BC) by two princes from the north. After a city was established on a site close to the present-day location of Wuxi and tin reserves was discovered, they called the place Youxi or 'with tin'. When the tin ran out in the Han Dynasty, the city's name was changed to Wuxi, 'without tin'.

Wuxi, which lies in the south of Jiangsu Province, has the Grand Canal running through its centre. The Grand Canal was built in the early years of the seventh century by the Sui Emperor Yangdi, in order to link the north and south of his realm. Visitors can stand on any of the city's many bridges and watch boats pass by, just as they have done for over 1,000 years. Yet despite the city's strategic location on the canal, Wuxi never prospered as did neighbouring Yangzhou. Wuxi remains a quiet, provincial town, despite the rapid development of its industrial infrastructure in recent decades.

The great attraction of Wuxi is Tai Lake, which lies beyond the city. Its expanse of shining water set between soft hills mirrors the sky in all its moods, and fishermen trawl its waters for the fish which play such an important part in the regional cooking of Wuxi. Along the shores are orchards growing the best of sweet oranges, peaches and Chinese plums. The shallow edges of the lake are harvested for their lotus roots, seeds and water chestnuts. The lotus seeds are ground into a sweet paste for buns or simmered in a sugary soup; the water chestnuts are used in savoury dishes to create a crisp, light contrast to the meat. And beyond the orchards are the mulberry fields, where the leaves are picked to feed the countless silkworm larvae whose cocoons will be spun into silk thread for the factories of Jiangsu Province.

City Sights

The **Plum Garden** is a particularly popular place in spring, when thousands of plum trees are in blossom. The best time to eat the plums themselves is in late summer. Another sylvan pleasure is the **Li Garden**, which is modern by neighbouring Suzhou standards. Yet it is well worth seeing, since it contains all the elements of a classical Chinese garden in an idyllic setting.

For many Chinese, however, Wuxi is famous for its *ni ren* or clay dolls, made at the **Huishan Clay Figurine Workshop**. The tradition of making clay figures dates back to the Ming Dynasty. The workshop turns out brightly painted figures in traditional round shapes of dozing monks, fat babies and smiling children holding fish, coins or lotus flowers (the symbols of plenty, prosperity and fertility). In recent years, new shapes have been introduced which reveal the influence of Western cartoons. Look out for a Chinese 'Snow White and the Seven Dwarfs', as well as some very blonde nymphs.

Much of Wuxi's surrounding arable land is patterned with groves of mulberry bushes, so it is hardly surprising to learn that there is a thriving silk industry here. Visitors are often taken to the **Number One Silk Reeling Mill** or the **Number One Silk Weaving Factory**. The **Zhonghua Embroidery Factory** is also open to visitors. (During the Cultural Revolution, the traditionally lyrical names of shops and businesses were considered a 'feudal' relic and all factories were renamed by their size, be it Number One or Two, or by some patriotic label such as Red Flag or East is Red. Sadly, these names have stuck.)

Outings from Wuxi

Tai Lake has 90 islands in all. The visitor can enjoy them and their related sights either by taking one of the shallow-draft ferry boats or by cruising across the lake in a grander dragon boat (in fact, a gaily decorated barge). The lake is a popular rest resort for Chinese holiday-makers from neighbouring cities and for government officials escaping the heat of a Beijing summer, so the shores of the lake are the site of many sanatoriums and government holiday villas. **Turtle Head Island** is the most popular destination for pleasure craft on the lake. Here visitors can walk through bamboo glades and paths lined with flowering shrubs, or climb to get a view of the entire lake from **Deer Peak Hill**. Chinese holiday-makers like to savour the peace of the island by finding a quiet spot on the rocky foreshore to read, chat and enjoy a family picnic.

From Wuxi, a trip on the **Grand Canal** can be arranged through the CITS office. The canal links the northern city of Luoyang, which the Sui Emperor Yangdi chose as his capital, with the southern city of Hangzhou in Zhejiang Province. The canal's construction was completed in an astonishing six years, bringing great suffering to the conscript labourers who excavated the canal and lined it with vast slabs of stone. During the six years, bridges were also constructed across the canal and its embankment was paved to make roads. The canal was of economic, political and military importance, ensuring the emperor a constant supply of food from the river-washed farmlands of the Yangzi basin to the arid lands of the north. The

canal was also important for the speedy despatch of troops to the south. However, the vast public works scheme undertaken by Sui Yangdi undermined the popularity and finances of the dynasty. The result was that in 618, only one year after Yangdi died, the country was swept by a rebellion bringing the Tang Dynasty to power. Today, the canal is less important as a strategic artery, but it does function as a commercial route. Barges ply between canal cities, carrying agricultural produce and bulk goods expensive to freight by the overworked rail system.

Finally, a day trip to the neighbouring city of **Yixing** is highly recommended, both for its teapots and its tea. Yixing is the home of the famous **Purple Sand Pottery Factory**, where you can see traditional clay teapots being made. The dark, reddy-brown and blue teapots are unglazed, their fame resting on a sophisticated simplicity of form. Older versions of Yixing ware can be seen in the city's **Pottery Museum**. Modern craftsmen can turn out teapots shaped as pumpkins with a dragon's head as the lid handle — when the tea is poured the dragon's tongue protrudes! Other designs include small squirrels running across branches carved from the clay sides of the pot, or a handle shaped as a simple twist of bamboo.

Suzhou

Suzhou is notable for its intimacy of scale as a city and its traditions as a centre for refined garden design. If Hangzhou can be described as a city set within a landscape (see page 130), Suzhou is a series of landscapes set within a city. But a casual stroll around Suzhou will not immediately reveal the gardens; they are hidden behind high walls and doors. The gardens were the creations of scholar-artists, who made their own private, landscaped retreats from the cares of the outside world. They are not simply areas for tending and planting. The gardens are artistic conceits designed in harmony with rocks, pools, plants, decorative windows, pebble mosaics, walkways and carefully devised vistas. In addition, they are conceived as settings in which to entertain as well as retire, to observe the changing moods of the seasons as well as the light and shade of the passing day.

Suzhou's fame dates back to the Tang Dynasty, when its beauty and affluence were praised in poetry. Yet its origins can be traced much earlier. It is believed that a settlement was first built on the present city site during the Zhou Dynasty (1027−256 BC), when the marshlands of the region were reclaimed. From these earliest times, Suzhou was known for its canals, which criss-crossed the low-lying land. The canals had steep humpbacked bridges, under which sailed the river craft which carried the city's traffic. During the 13th century, when Marco Polo visited the city, he claimed the city canals had 6,000 stone bridges. Most of those canals have disappeared in the last few decades, as the government has reclaimed more and more land for building, with the result that only 168 of the original thousands of stone bridges are left standing. Nevertheless, Suzhou remains an attractive and graceful city, with its low-eaved, white-washed houses and tree-shaded streets. In the old city quarters, there is even a flavour of traditional village life, now that Deng Xiaoping's economic reforms have allowed families once more to set up their own street stalls, selling anything from steamed dumplings to handmade inkstones.

According to Chinese tradition, Suzhou women are among the fairest of their sisters, and their local dialect is so charming that even a quarrel is attractive to overhear. Suzhou women are also famed for their skills as needlewomen, and Suzhou embroidery is still a prized possession among Chinese women. The Research Institute for Embroidery, set up in 1957, is well worth a visit. Some of the most outstanding examples of embroidery show perfect stitching on both sides of the silk, and the reversed image is made to stunning effect.

City Sights

The great period of garden-making in Suzhou was during the Ming Dynasty (1368−1644), when it was recorded that the city contained over 250 gardens. Today, it is known that over 100 still remain, but only a handful of the more famous ones have been renovated and opened to the public.

One of the smallest and yet most remarkable is known as the **Garden of the Master of the Fishing Nets**. A garden was first built here in the Song Dynasty, but its present form and name date from the Ming Dynasty, when the scholar Song Zongyuan bought the property. A walk through the garden with its bridges and carefully devised views is particularly rewarding. Visitors may recognize the Hall for Eternal Spring, which has been recreated in the Metropolitan Museum of New York.

The larger and more open garden known as the **Garden of the Humble Administrator** is part-park and part a restored Ming garden. In the park section, visitors can stroll by the small lake and enjoy hot snacks served at a lakeside stall. The classical Ming garden has a pool patterned with islands and bridges, one island of which — the Xiangzhou — is said to suggest a moored boat. In the small enclosed Loquat Garden are a series of decorative pebble pictures.

The oldest extant garden in the city is reputed to be the **Pavilion of the Blue Waves**, dating back to the Song Dynasty. The garden was re-landscaped in the Ming Dynasty and then destroyed in the Taiping rebellion of the mid-19th century. It was restored in 1873. The garden has an imposing artificial hill, and an open vista to an adjacent, willow-fringed canal.

Another seductively named garden is the **Lingering Garden**. With stylized landscapes in an ornamental setting, this large 16th-century garden is famous for its classical round doorways known as Moon Gates. These and other geometrically-shaped doorways provide natural frames for viewing the plants, pools and rocks beyond. The garden pool is framed by vast rock formations, which create the impression of mountains. The garden was restored in the early part of this century.

For the connoisseur of rocks, the **Forest of Lions Garden** is a favourite. It was laid out in the Yuan Dynasty (1279−1368) under the supervision of the painter Ni Zan, and is thus one of Suzhou's most highly-regarded gardens. It has a fine collection of rocks, one of which is so large and eroded that it has small caverns and grottoes through which you can actually walk.

The **Garden of Harmony** is a Qing-Dynasty garden which has been modelled on earlier Ming ones. It too has a number of rocks dredged from Tai Lake, which have been arranged as a mountain frame for the pond. It is interesting to note that this, like other classical Chinese gardens, does not have the dynamic, fluid quality of the Japanese garden. In the Chinese version there is a pleasure in the composed harmony of elements and the appreciation of devised contrasts.

East of the city is the quieter **Plough Garden** (Ouyuan), which is recommended if you want to escape the crowds. This is an important consideration, since in the warmer months the crowds in Suzhou's gardens almost obscure the view. The best idea is to visit the gardens just as they open in the morning or — if you want to take special photographs — go to your guide and see if you can arrange a visit before opening time.

As far as temples are concerned, staying in Suzhou would be incomplete without a visit to the **Cold Mountain Monastery**. This monastery has been immortalized in a Tang-Dynasty poem by Zhang Ji, copies of which are painted on fans or carved on inkstones and sold as Suzhou souvenirs. The temple was founded in the fifth century and is adjacent to a small, attractive canal, spanned by a high-arched bridge which is featured in the poem, 'Midnight at Maple Bridge':

> The moon sets, a bird calls and frost is in the air
> The dark maples and fishermen's lamps dance in my own sad dream
> Cold Mountain Monastery stands outside the city walls
> And its midnight bell carries to this a stranger's boat.

The monastery's bell has disappeared and the Ming replacement was taken to Japan and lost. The present bell, cast in 1906, was given as a gift by a Japanese Buddhist delegation.

Opposite the Lingering Garden, you will find the **West Garden Temple**. The gardens of both areas were designed by the same Ming scholar, Xu Shitai, in the Ming Dynasty. The main curiosity is a pond where, reputedly, a 300-year-old turtle lives.

Of the many stone bridges remaining in Suzhou, the most famous lies in the southeast of the city and is known as the **Precious Belt Bridge**. It is over 1,000 years old, built in 816, and it has 53 arches. In its present form, it is a 19th-century restoration of the original. The bridge is so named because an early governor of the city is said to have sold a precious belt in order to raise funds to build it.

Other stone curiosities include the **North Temple Pagoda**, easy to find because of its height. It was built in 1582 and it has recently been renovated so that visitors can climb up to get a good view of the city. In the central district of the city stand the **Twin Pagodas**, which were built in the Song Dynasty. They are all that remain of an earlier Tang temple.

The **Folk Custom Museum** and the **Drama and Opera Museum** are fascinating places to visit for those interested in Chinese culture. The city's old Confucius Temple now houses a **Museum of Stelae** (stelae are inscribed stone tablets). The most interesting of these is a Song-Dynasty constellation chart and a Yuan city map, which shows Suzhou as Marco Polo must have seen it. The best place to buy the city's famous embroidery is the **Research Institute for Embroidery**, which has its own museum showing the development of embroidery stitches and motifs. Suzhou also has a tradition of making intricately carved sandalwood fans, which can be bought at the **Sandalwood Fan Factory**. The fans keep their fragrance for years, and traditionally were dowry gifts. Silk is made in Suzhou, and the **Silk Garment Factory** is a popular place to tour and buy goods.

Outings from Suzhou

To the northwest of the city is **Tiger Hill**. It is a wonderful sight, with its leaning pagoda, waterfalls, spring, rocks and landscaped paths. The hill was built in the Zhou Dynasty (1027−256 BC) as a burial mound for a local ruler, the King of Wu. Legend has it that a tiger guards the tomb — hence the name of the hill.

Finally, 18 kilometres (11 miles) southwest of the city is the **Sky Flat Mountain**, which with its tabletop summit, slopes of maple, woodland, and traditional pavilions makes a scenic half-day outing.

Hangzhou

It is somehow quite appropriate that visitors to Hangzhou, capital of Zhejiang Province, can buy fans which unfold to show a picture map and a guide to the city and its famous West Lake. For although Hangzhou was once an imperial city in the Southern Song Dynasty (1127–1279), the city is better known as a pleasure resort for those with the time and ease to take boat trips across West Lake, fan in hand of course, to see the many lakeside views and pavilions celebrated over the centuries in both song and verse. Marco Polo, who visited Hangzhou in the 13th century, wrote lyrically of the pleasures of the lake and concluded, 'indeed a voyage on this lake offers more refreshment and delectation than any other experience on earth.'

Without West Lake, Hangzhou would have been just another prosperous city thriving on its position as the southern terminus of the Grand Canal, and on its two agricultural industries of tea and silk. But with West Lake, Hangzhou has gained a status not far short of paradise. To quote a well-used saying: 'In heaven there is paradise, on earth Suzhou and Hangzhou'. If Suzhou's loveliness as a city of gardens is almost entirely man-made, Hangzhou has little need of such to enhance its natural beauty. The city skirts the shore of a wide, shallow lake rimmed by green and gentle hills, in which are grown the famous Longjing tea of the region and mulberry leaves for the silkworm larvae.

The modern city is, alas, less prepossessing. It was virtually destroyed during the Taiping rebellion of the mid-19th century, and underwent extensive modernization and industralization in the last decades. Walking around Hangzhou today gives the visitor little idea of the glories of its time as the capital of the Southern Song, a period famous for great cultural achievements. Little remains, too, of its later imperial heritage. It is only when contemplating the lake that one understands why, in the Yuan, Ming and Qing Dynasties, Hangzhou was an imperial resort, and why the two famous long-lived Qing emperors, Kangxi and Qianlong, each made six visits to the city.

Hangzhou has a rich literary heritage. The city and West Lake have been the setting of numerous folk-tales and scholars' stories. In

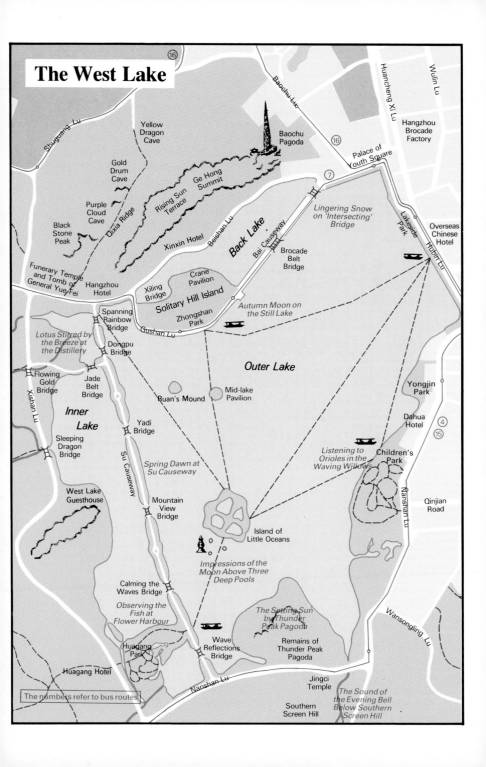

The West Lake

Shuguang Lu

Yellow Dragon Cave

Gold Drum Cave

Purple Cloud Cave

Black Stone Peak

Baochu Lu

Baochu Pagoda

Palace of Youth Square

Hangzhou Brocade Factory

Huancheng Xi Lu

Wulin Lu

Ge Hong Summit

Rising Sun Terrace

Dixia Ridge

Xinxin Hotel

Beishan Lu

Back Lake

Bai Causeway

Lingering Snow on 'Intersecting' Bridge

Lakeside Park

Overseas Chinese Hotel

Hubin Lu

Funerary Temple and Tomb of General Yue Fei

Hangzhou Hotel

Xiling Bridge

Crane Pavilion

Solitary Hill Island

Zhongshan Park

Gushan Lu

Autumn Moon on the Still Lake

Brocade Belt Bridge

Spanning Rainbow Bridge

Lotus Stirred by the Breeze at the Distillery

Dongpu Bridge

Flowing Gold Bridge

Jade Belt Bridge

Xishan Lu

Inner Lake

Sleeping Dragon Bridge

Outer Lake

Ruan's Mound

Mid-lake Pavilion

Yongjin Park

Dahua Hotel

Yadi Bridge

Su Causeway

Spring Dawn at Su Causeway

West Lake Guesthouse

Mountain View Bridge

Listening to Orioles in the Waving Willows

Children's Park

Nanshan Lu

Qinjian Road

Island of Little Oceans

Calming the Waves Bridge

Observing the Fish at Flower Harbour

Impressions of the Moon Above Three Deep Pools

Huagang Park

Wave Reflections Bridge

The Setting Sun by Thunder Peak Pagoda

Remains of Thunder Peak Pagoda

Wansongling Lu

Huagang Hotel

The numbers refer to bus routes

Nanshan Lu

Jingci Temple

Southern Screen Hill

The Sound of the Evening Bell Below Southern Screen Hill

one tale recorded by a Ming collector of folk legends, Feng Menglong, a white snake maiden, aided by her blue fish maidservant, falls in love with a mortal during a rainstorm on West Lake. The story ends tragically when the white snake and blue fish are captured by a Buddhist monk, made to revert to their original animal forms, and then imprisoned under a pagoda. The pagoda is said to have been the Thunder Peak Pagoda, which tumbled down in 1924, having overlooked the lake from its southern shores. Communist reworkings of the tale, however, have a happy ending for the lovers, and the story is still part of the traditional opera repertoire.

This is not the only such tale. In an earlier story, told by a Tang scholar, the Qiantang estuary to the south of West Lake — which once joined it as part of the same tidal basin — was reputed to be the home of a hot-tempered dragon. It is no wonder then that the estuary is famous for its tidal bore, which can reach six metres (20 feet) in height. Such a phenomenon would be easy to associate with mischievous dragons who are known to make their homes in lakes, rivers and clouds.

West Lake's two most renowned literary associations are with the Tang poet, Bai Juyi (Po Chu-yi), and the Song poet, Su Dongpo. They both served as governors of the city, and both were responsible for major earthwork projects designed to safeguard West Lake from flooding. The lake has two major causeways named after the poet-governors who commissioned their building. The causeways now have attractive lakeside walkways, planted with willows and flowering trees.

City Sights

Traditionally **West Lake** has had Ten Prospects — the places where various scenic aspects of the lake can be enjoyed at different times or at different seasons. The Ten Prospects are known to date from at least the Song Dynasty, but their present sites are all Qing designations. With the help of a map of the lake and a guide, the visitor can still see 'Spring Dawn at Su Causeway', 'Observing the Fish at Flower Harbour', 'Listening to the Orioles in the Swaying Wilows', 'Lotuses Ruffled by the Breeze at the Distillery', 'Setting Sun by Thunder Peak Pagoda' (the pagoda has gone), 'Autumn Moon on the Still Lake', 'Impressions of the Moon above Three Deep Pools', 'Lingering Snow on Intersecting Bridge', the 'Sound of the Evening Bell below Southern Screen Hill' (the bell has disappeared, as has the Jingci Monastery in which it hung), and a little way from the lake, 'Twin Peaks Piercing the Clouds'.

The best way to start a visit to the lake is to take a boat to the central **Island of Little Oceans** (from where can be seen 'Impressions of the Moon above Three Deep Pools'). The island is man-made and has been cleverly contrived to create four small lakes within a lake. Here a small pavilion serves refreshments, including the famous West Lake lotus root simmered into a sweet broth. Three stone lanterns close to the island are sometimes lit with candles at night to create the impression of three moons reflected in the water.

The **Su Causeway**, named after the poet Su Dongpo, is an excellent place to stroll and enjoy a view of the lake. Small bridges intersect the causeway, and thus it is sometimes known as Six Bridge Dyke. The causeway is particularly beautiful in spring when the willow, peach, camphor and horsechestnut trees are in bud and blossom. At the northern end of the Su Causeway is a prospect — 'Lotus Ruffled by the Breeze at the Distillery'. It is here that visitors come in summer to see the deep pink lotus blossoms.

Solitary Hill Island, easily found near the Hangzhou Hotel and the largest of the lake's islands, is linked to the shore by the famous **Bai Causeway**, named after the poet Bai Juyi. On the island is the **Xiling Seal Engraving Society**, where visitors can order a carved seal with the help of a guide. The **Zhejiang Museum** and its adjacent botanical garden on the island are also worth exploring. Another of the Ten Prospects can be seen from the southeast corner of the island — 'The Autumn Moon on the Still Lake' . It was here that Emperor Qianlong of the Qing Dynasty had a pavilion built so as to be able to enjoy the prospect.

On the north shore of the lake stands the **Tomb and Temple of Yue Fei**, a popular place to visit for Chinese tourists because of Yue Fei's reputation as a patriot. A Southern Song-Dynasty general, Yue Fei, led several successful campaigns against the Jin nomads, who had conquered north China and caused the Song emperor to flee south before establishing a new capital in exile at Hangzhou. General Yue Fei incurred the jealousy and distrust of the prime minister, Qin Hui, who had the general murdered in 1141. When Yue Fei's reputation was restored, his remains were interred in Hangzhou and the temple was established.

Also on the north shore of the lake is the slender **Baochu Pagoda**, which was first built in the 10th century. The present structure dates from 1933. A small adjacent teahouse offers an attractive view over to the south of the lake, where there are the remains of the seven-storey brick **Thunder Peak Pagoda** of the white snake legend. The pagoda fell down in 1924.

Overlooking the nearby Qiantang estuary is the impressive 13-storeyed, dark red, wood-and-brick structure of the **Pagoda of the Six Harmonies**. It was first built in 970 on the site of an earlier pagoda which had served as a lighthouse. The pagoda's name refers to the six codes of Buddhism — to obtain the harmony of body, speech and thought, and to renounce physical pleasures, personal opinions and wealth. Visitors can ponder on these codes as they climb the pagoda for a view over the river.

There are other reflective spots in Hangzhou. There are several parks, but the best for real gardening enthusiasts is the **Botanical Garden** on the western outskirts of the city. It has a fine medicinal herb section, and is in a peaceful rural setting where, in midsummer, you can see young farm girls strolling in their wide-brimmed hats. North of the Hangzhou Hotel are three caves, which are open to visitors: Purple Cloud Cave, Gold Drum Cave and Yellow Dragon Cave. They are crowded on wet days, when sightseeing below ground becomes an attractive option.

Visitors who are keen to see the traditional skills of tea and silk manufacturing can usually arrange tours to the **Dragon Well Brigade** to learn about the growing and picking of tea, and to the **Silk Printing and Dyeing Complex** or the **Du Jinsheng Silk Weaving Factory** to learn about sericulture. At the silk factories, you can watch silk-reeling and weaving, as well as buy silk itself.

Outings from Hangzhou

If your plans allow an extended stay in Zhejiang Province, there are several short or day outings to be made from Hangzhou. To the west lies the **Lingyin Temple**, notable because of its woodland setting next to the **Peak that Flew There**. The peak is actually a small outcrop famous for its Yuan-Dynasty Buddhist carvings, but earlier carvings in the rock-face date back to the tenth century. The temple buildings have been destroyed several times since its founding in the fourth century; the present ones date from the 1950s. Within walking distance of the temple is the Taoguang Hermitage, offering walks through bamboo glades and, at the top of the path, a fine view over the city. The open-air teahouse next to the Peak that Flew There is an excellent place to sit and drink a cup of pale green Longjing tea and look at the Buddhist carvings.

A half-day outing to the **Mei Family Gulch** in the hills beyond Hangzhou gives a glimpse of a traditional farming community in a scenic setting. The **Mogan Mountains**, just over one hour away from Hangzhou by car, offer a resort-style setting with tennis, swimming and walks in woodland.

Longer outings from Hangzhou offer a chance to see the neighbouring towns of **Shaoxing** and **Ningbo**. Both towns have old and attractive buildings and temples. Shaoxing is famous for its rice wine and as the birthplace of the 20th-century writer Lu Xun. Ningbo is known for its seafaring traditions, tough mercantile inhabitants who enjoy salty foods (which appear to influence their character), and as the birthplace of the Kuomintang leader, Generalissimo Chiang Kai-shek. **Putuoshan**, one of China's Nine Sacred Mountains, is an island off the Zhejiang coast (see pages 233).

Guilin

Guilin is one of China's best-known cities on account of its beautiful landscape of limestone mountains, likened in a Tang poem to jade hairpins. The city has been popular with sightseers for over 1,000 years, and many famous poets and painters have lived and worked here, celebrating its river and mountain scenery.

Once the capital of Guangxi Province (the capital was moved south to Nanning in 1914), Guilin has always been a prosperous commercial centre, profiting from its proximity to the Ling Canal which links the two major river networks of the Pearl and the Yangzi. This canal was built in the second century BC, under the orders of Qin Shi Huangdi, the first emperor of China, who used it to link the middle regions of his empire around the Yangzi with the far south. But central government control of Guangxi was only intermittent, and the province remained a frontier region of the Chinese empire until the time of the Tang Dynasty (618–907). Many Guangxi people are not ethnic Chinese. The most populous minority group of the province are the Zhuang, who make up around 35 per cent of the population. However, the land they occupy covers over 60 per cent of the province, and thus the province has been designated a Zhuang Minority Autonomous Region.

Guilin lies along the west bank of the Li River, and was once a walled city. However, widespread destruction during the Japanese occupation in the Second World War, along with a recent modernization and industrialization programme, have left the city drab and undistinguished amidst its mountains. Visitors continue to flock here — Chinese sightseers made prosperous by the last few years of economic reform, and foreign tourists encouraged by the increased number and quality of the hotels, as well as more flights into the city. When I first visited Guilin (in 1979), tourism was a rough and ready affair, but it was immensely enjoyable because there were no crowds. Now all that has changed, and the city has been inundated by a tourist tidal wave, forcing prices higher and higher and making life less comfortable. So why come to Guilin at all? The answer is simple — the landscape with abrupt mountains amidst verdant river plains still has the ability to refresh and enchant the senses.

City Sights

Unlike those of most other Chinese cities, the city sights of Guilin are of nature's rather than man's making. However, the small mountains which punctuate the river plain have been embellished with delicate pavilions, winding paths and carvings. It is great fun to climb one of these mountains and gaze out over the city and the Li River, where fishermen pole their bamboo rafts through the lazy current while their cormorants dive for fish.

In the city centre, the best-known peak is **Solitary Beauty Peak**, which was once part of a 14th-century palace of the Emperor Hongwu's nephew, Zhou Shouqian. The calligraphy on the peak's rock-face dates from the Tang and Ming Dynasties.

Close to Solitary Beauty Peak is **Fubo Hill**, named after a famous general of the Han Dynasty. Half-way up the hill is a cave where the Bodhisattva of Mercy, Guan Yin, was worshipped. Fubo Hill has many fine stone inscriptions and carvings; those outside the Cave of Guan Yin are attributed to the Qing painter, Li Pingshou.

Another interesting hill, this time with four peaks, is the **Hill of Many Colours**. It offers sweeping views over the Li River and the city to the south. It also has many fine stone carvings, some again from the hand of Li Pingshou. The hill has several Buddhist altars, which were built in the Five Dynasties and Song period.

To the west of the city, near the railway line, is the **Hidden Hill**, which was badly damaged during the Cultural Revolution and is not often shown to tourists for that reason.

The small group of peaks which make up **West Hill** was once famous for its Buddhist statuary. They are all but gone after Red Guards smashed them in the 1960s. However, when the more popular hills in the centre of town are crowded, this and Hidden Hill are good places to wander quietly and enjoy a view over the countryside.

Two hills, which cannot be climbed but are interesting for their resemblance to animals, are **Camel Hill** and **Elephant Trunk Hill**. The latter juts out into the Li River, and at dusk looks extraordinarily like a larger-than-life elephant drinking from the river.

Across the attractive covered Flower Bridge, you can walk to the **Seven Star Hill and Cave**. Underground caves are a natural corollary of Guilin's limestone landscape, since the rock easily erodes in water, forming vast caverns below ground level. The Seven Star Cave contains dripping stalagmites and stalactite pinnacles, all illuminated with coloured lights. Other caves worth visiting are Reed Flute Cave, White Dragon Cave (beneath South Creek Hill), and Returned Pearl Cave (beneath Fubo Hill).

Outings from Guilin

The **Li River Boat Trip** is undoubtedly the highlight of most people's visits to Guilin. It is not too hard to understand why, for even the most well-travelled visitor finds the quiet, pastoral landscapes along the river enchanting. The boat sets out downstream just beyond the city (return journeys upstream are also available), and it later moors for a lunch served with endless bottles of chilled beer and fizzy orange drink. The landscape to either side of the river is of manicured fields shaded by leafy bamboo glades. On the river, you pass the well-known cormorants who fish for their masters. The mountains along the way have fanciful names, which are in the Chinese tradition of making a picture when looking at landscapes — Crown Rock, Conch Hill, Jade Lotus Peak and Snow Lion Peak, are examples.

The boat ride ends at the small market town of **Yangshuo**, which is reputed to have finer scenery than Guilin. On the way back to Guilin by bus, there is usually an opportunity to stop at the village where the **Thousand Year Banyan Tree** grows. Nowadays, it shelters a mini-market of hawkers' stalls. The village lies at the foot of a limestone peak, and small pigs run amidst the dirt paths alongside hens and children. The tree is an astonishing sight, with its massive spread of branches and house-like trunk.

You can visit the **Ling Canal** by going to the small county town of **Xing'an**. Over 2,000 years old, the canal symbolizes the extent of the military power of China's first dynasty, the Qin, which had its capital at Xi'an, over 1,000 kilometres (620 miles) to the north. The canal joins the two major river systems of the Pearl, which flows into the sea south of Guangzhou, and the Yangzi, which joins the ocean just north of Shanghai. The joining of these two river systems was of great strategic and economic importance. The government could transfer grain from the Yangzi basin to the troops in the south of China via an inland water route, while at the same time it could despatch troops to the south to quell the rebellions of the traditionally troublesome minority peoples.

Chinese Calligraphy

Chinese people have a special reverence for the arts of calligraphy
and painting. In traditional China, the scholar class considered the
practice of calligraphy, painting and poetry to be the highest skills
an educated man could acquire. Scholars who took the imperial
examination were often judged by the quality of their handwriting,
and even the best essay, if written in a poor hand, could result in
failure for a candidate. How a man wielded his brush was believed to
indicate his character and qualities. Even today, when most students
use pens rather than brushes to write their university exam papers, a
good hand is still admired.

Calligraphy is an art form in China because of the special nature
of the Chinese language. The variety of form and strokes of the
Chinese character lend themselves to a creative interpretation. The
earliest Chinese characters were cut on the shells of tortoises or the
bones of animals, and later they were inscribed on bronze vessels.
The use of a sharp implement to write the words influenced their
shape and development. The invention of paper during the Han
Dynasty, and the development of writing by brush, led to a greater
expressiveness in the setting down of characters. The earliest style of
writing Chinese characters is known as *Zhuan Shu* (Seal Script), and
was derived from the carving of the characters on a hard surface. The
strokes of the characters are curved and pictorial in style, reflecting
the representational quality of the early characters. To this day,
calligraphers still practise the writing of Seal Script and — as its name
suggests — it is most commonly used in the carving of seals.

During the Qin Dynasty, a regular script was formulated under
the rule of Qin Shi Huangdi. This script is known as *Li Shu* (Official
Script). The strokes of the characters were made more regular and
compact. Later, in the Han Dynasty, the *Kai Shu* (Regular Script)
was developed, giving even greater regularity of form to the
character. In the Regular Script there is a more geometric and
angular shape to the characters. They are written as if placed in the
centre of an imaginary square.

The Han Dynasty also saw the development of another script,
more cursive and free in form, which is called *Cao Shu* (Grass Script).
Grass Script and the later script of *Xing Shu* (Running Script) both
allow the writer a greater freedom of expression. Yet the strong and
irregular strokes of the two scripts do have their conventions — which
prevent the deforming of the characters. The brush may seem to dip
and dash across the surface in a kind of shorthand Chinese, but the
structural elements of the characters are still respected.

These five scripts of Chinese calligraphy — Seal, Official,
Regular, Grass and Running — allow for great variety and

experimentation of style within given, understood conventions. Chinese scholars who spend a lifetime perfecting their brushwork often try to master more than one style, using different scripts for different occasions. It is common to see the Grass and Running Scripts used for writing poetry at the side of paintings, while the more formal styles of Seal, Official and Regular Scripts are used for official inscriptions, letters and the scroll hangings, with their two-line quotations from a poem or homily, which used to hang in most peoples' houses.

Because of the value that Chinese people have traditionally placed on the words of their language, a character written out in good calligraphy was believed to have a good effect. Shops and restaurants in traditional China always paid large amounts of money to have their sign boards and advertisements written out in fine calligraphy, so as to attract business. And even a poor household, where nobody could read and write, would buy auspicious New Year couplets in good calligraphy, expressing fine sentiments to hang on either side of their doors. The poorest peasant would often have the character *man*, meaning 'full', written out on his rice bucket as a good luck charm. Words were believed to possess the power of their meaning, and the writing of words was a revered art.

The appreciation of such an art form is difficult for those who cannot read Chinese, so it is doubly important to find out what you are looking at if you visit an exhibition of calligraphy. If you have a guide nearby, ask for a translation of the characters and an explanation of which style you are viewing. Then it is up to you to look at the balance of space and characters on the page, the ease or the tension, the regularity or irregularity of the script. Look for the way the brush has been used on the paper. Is the manner firm and tense, or fluid and rhythmic? Are the characters written out in bold isolated units or do they run together like a flowing stream? Answers to these questions will give you some idea of the calligrapher's intentions.

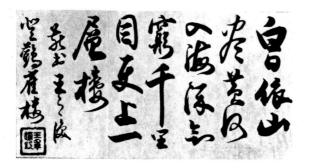

Kunming

Kunming's Lake Dian rests like a blue-glazed dish with a rim of green land circled by distant mountains. The lake's great beauty and Yunnan's gentle climate make Kunming — the capital of the province — appealing even in the winter months when much of the rest of China remains too cold to attract many visitors. But it is the variety of peoples in the region which usually draws travellers to Yunnan. Twenty-four different ethnic minorities live in this southwestern province which borders Burma, Laos, Vietnam and Tibet. Many of these minority peoples have more in common with their Southeast Asian or Tibetan neighbours than with the Chinese. They have their own languages, enjoy distinct customs and rituals, retain many of their religious practices, and wear jewellery of extra-ordinary intricacy above their brightly coloured robes.

For many travellers, Kunming is a staging post for journeys to the towns and villages of the minority peoples, rather than a destination in itself (see pages 195–202). But even if time does not allow a journey far beyond Kunming, there are many opportunities to learn about the minorities and to see their handicrafts in the museums and shops of the city. And the city itself has its own pleasures — wonderful gardens and parks, outings on Lake Dian, local food specialities such as 'Crossing the Bridge Noodles', and many old temples and pavilions.

Yunnan has a different atmosphere to China's northern provinces and, until quite late in its history, was not directly under Chinese control. The earliest inhabitants of the region were the Dian people, the same name that is given to Kunming's lake, and they were known to have lived around Kunming in the first millennium BC. Wonderful bronze implements from their culture have been found in excavations outside the city (these are now on display in the Yunnan Provincial Museum in Kunming itself). During the Tang Dynasty, the Nanzhao Kingdom held sway over Yunnan, later to be replaced by the Dali in the 12th century. In the next century, the Mongol conquerors of China brought Yunnan under the aegis of their Yuan Dynasty. As a means of controlling their new territory, the Mongols brought in Moslems to settle in the area and act as their political agents. Yunnan's Moslem population has grown and thrived to this day. Yet even as late as the Ming and Qing Dynasties, the imperial court saw Yunnan as a distant and unattractive outpost, using it in much the same way as the British used Australia in the 18th century — as a place for dumping unwanted persons.

Nowadays, Yunnan has quite the opposite image in Chinese eyes. Except for the tragic decade of the Cultural Revolution (1966–76), when Yunnan's minority peoples were treated atrociously (like all minorities throughout China), Yunnan is now seen as an exotic and attractive destination, with mild winters and picturesque landscapes. Chinese travellers and anthropologists — as well as Westerners — have now begun to be fascinated by the customs and languages of Yunnan's minorities. Moreover, the province's mountains and valleys are home to over half of China's indigenous trees and flowers, making it an irresistible place to visit for both amateur and professional gardeners and botanists.

Kunming is the ideal place in which to gain a glimpse of Yunnan and its wonderful variety of peoples and landscapes.

City Sights

A good starting place for a visit to Kunming is the **Yunnan Provincial Museum**. It has an excellent section on the minorities, which acts as an introduction to the peoples of Yunnan and their varied lifestyles. You will note that the Dai women, whose villages lie close to the borders of Laos and Burma, wear the sarong that is seen all over Southeast Asia. It is here that you will also see the fine bronzes of the Dian Kingdom, which has been dated back to 1200 BC. These bronzes deserve careful scrutiny, since they show detailed scenes of daily life. The animal bronzes are especially noteworthy.

Close to the zoo in the north of the city is the Buddhist **Yuantong Temple** and its adjacent park. The park is famed for its flowering shrubs and trees: cherry in spring, rhododendrons in summer, chrysanthemums in autumn and camellia or magnolia in winter. The temple itself dates back a thousand years or so, and has been attractively restored.

Just to the northwest of the city, in a woodland setting, lies the **Bamboo Temple**. A legend tells of the temple's foundation in the Tang, when two princes chased a rhinoceros to a spot where monks appeared holding staves of bamboo, which then miraculously turned into groves of bamboo. The temple is noted for its 500 Luohan, or Bodhisattvas, carved in the 19th century.

In the northeast of the city, the **Copper Temple** can be reached after a dramatic climb through pine woods. The attractive temple with its wrought-copper roof stands on a marble terrace and is dedicated to the Daoist deity, Zishi.

Just south of Jinbi Lu are two ancient pagodas dating from the ninth century — **East and West Temple Pagodas**. The former can be visited and is notable for its four golden (copper) roosters on the summit. The latter is visible from the street but cannot be visited at the moment.

Yunnan's large Moslem community dates back to the Yuan Dynasty. Five mosques are open in Kunming, and can be visited if proper attire is worn and cameras are used with discretion. The largest mosque is on Shuncheng Jie, in an Islamic neighbourhood which is also worth exploring for its small shops and *halal* (Moslem) restaurants.

Most travellers to Kunming will want to take one of the numerous ferries which traverse **Dian Lake** at various points. Details of short or longer ferry rides can be obtained from the CITS office. The western shores of the lake rise steeply to and from **Western Hill**, famous for its temples and magnificent views. The **Huating Temple**, Kunming's largest Buddhist monastery, has an imposing garden with an ornamental lake, the enclosing decorative wall of which is intersected by stupas. Higher up the mountain is the **Taihua Temple**, which also has a garden setting of great charm. The back of the temple has a hall dedicated to the Guan Yin, Bodhisattva of Mercy. In her Indian incarnation, she was depicted as a male. However, the Chinese have endowed her with the grace and compassion of a Buddhist Virgin Mary. In this temple she is even portrayed holding a male child.

Beyond the Huating Temple rises the **Sanqing Temple**, a Daoist shrine. There is little left of the original interiors, but a rest at the temple teahouse is recommended before a walk to **Dragon Gate**, where the view of the lake below is unsurpassable.

Daguan Park, on the north shore of the lake, is worth visiting with a Chinese-speaking guide since it houses a cultural treasure in the form of a poem inscribed on a stone. Written by a Qing-Dynasty scholar, it extols the beauty of the scenery of Kunming. The park itself is attractive, with a landscape of lakes and willow-edged causeways.

On the eastern and southern shores of Lake Dian, fields and villages stretch down to the water. A bus or taxi journey to some of the smaller villages and towns will show rural life just beyond the city. A visit to the small town of **Jinning** is recommended for its museum honouring the birthplace of Zheng He, the great Ming-Dynasty eunuch admiral. His expeditions as far as Arabia and Africa rival the later journeys of the Portuguese and Spanish explorers (in the 15th century). The museum shows the extent of his seven great voyages, which he achieved with the aid of the Chinese-invented compass.

Outings from Kunming

Seventeen kilometres (ten miles) northwest of the city lies the
Kunming Botanical Garden. Travellers interested in gardening
should make a point of visiting here. Yunnan is the original home of
many flowering shrubs, such as the rhododendron and camellia,
which people from the West now see as a natural part of their own
landscape. Close to the garden is the colourful Daoist temple known
as **Black Dragon Pool**. As with many dragon legends, the dragons of
this story were destructive, only being mastered by a Daoist scholar
who banished nine of them and tamed the tenth. This one is said to
live in the pool.

The most popular one- or two-day outing from Kunming is the
Stone Forest, 126 kilometres (79 miles) southeast of the city. This
can be reached by CITS-organized coach tour or, more adventurous-
ly, by train to **Yiliang** and from there by bus. The Stone Forest is a
strange place, with limestone pinnacles and rocks standing like
petrified trees. The outcrops are not a fossil forest but the result of
water erosion — just like the mountains of Guilin, except on a
smaller scale. The area is the home of the Sani people, who delight
in offering their handicrafts to visitors and often give song and dance
performances in the local hotel. (For information on more extended
trips from Kumming, see pages 195–202).

Expeditions

Inner Mongolia

The grasslands of China's Inner Mongolia Autonomous Region are relatively little visited by tourist groups. This is a shame, since the region offers some of the most tranquil, undeveloped landscapes in the whole country. With a northerly wind blowing off the Siberian steppes, winters are harsh in the region but summers are warm and glorious. From May to September, herds of cattle, sheep, goats and camels roam the grasslands, and Mongolian herders follow their animals, using as a home the decorated felt tents which we know as *yurts*, but which the Mongolians themselves call *ger*.

The Mongolian people are the descendants of the armies of Genghis Khan, who conquered the entire land mass of Central Asia, from the Caspian Sea to the present borders of North China, in the early 13th century, and who — under Kublai Khan — went on to conquer the whole of China and to found the Yuan Dynasty. Today, the Mongolian people are divided by an international boundary which puts Outer Mongolia under the Soviet sphere of control, with Inner Mongolia under that of the Chinese. The Mongolians have been forced to live with this division.

Mongolian family at home

Latent Mongolian nationalism has made the Chinese government acutely sensitive about their northern border, shared with the Soviet Union. In the 1960s, during the Cultural Revolution, the use of the Mongolian language, dress and customs was prohibited. Today, the teaching of Mongolian in schools and universities has been reintroduced, but the Mongolians of China believe their culture is doomed because Chinese is now the language of education — and thus of privilege. They fear the destiny of the Manchus, whose language ultimately became a relic of their nomadic past.

Most foreign travellers come to Inner Mongolia to experience the nomadic lifestyle. However, the model *yurts* laid on for foreign guests are usually situated in pastoral communes which provide permanent winter dwellings for the herders and their families. These are a welcome innovation for the Mongolian nomads, but they do not give a true picture of the hardships of a traditional nomadic life-style.

There are three such communes open to tourists outside Hohhot, the capital of Inner Mongolia. **Xilamulunsumu** can be reached as part of a day trip from Hohhot. The more distant communes of **Huitengxile** and **Baiyinhushao** require an overnight stop. All offer traditional Mongolian hospitality of a *yurt* 'At Home': butter, tea and mutton ribs. With luck, you will also be offered fermented mare's milk and even a Mongolian-style singalong. The Mongolians are enthusiastic singers and, when there are no Chinese around, they enjoy singing of those 13th-century battles when they conquered the Chinese.

A visit to a *yurt* 'motel' offers you the chance to dress up in Mongolian costumes and pose for photographs alongside tasselled camels. Some prefer, however, to travel out across the grasslands on horseback or by jeep. The rolling hills and limitless expanse of undulating meadows may seem monotonous at first glance, but if you travel quietly, you will be pleasantly surprised. You can catch glimpses of wildfowl bathing in the shallow pools which lie in small hollows. Wild irises grow amidst the grass, and skylarks rise from the pastures, singing into the clear blue heavens. Lone herdsmen watch their flocks grazing, occasionally moving them on with a flick of their lasso whip. Sometimes, by the verge of a track, you will see a white arrow pointing seemingly to nowhere. These are used by aircraft pilots to help them find their bearings.

Hohhot

The present capital of Inner Mongolia was founded in the 16th century by a group of nomads known as the Tumet. The city grew and prospered under the Qing Dynasty, and with the founding of the People's Republic of China in 1949, it was renamed Hohhot — meaning 'Green City' in Mongolian.

The city is not green, but it does have a liveliness imparted by the outgoing nature of its Mongolian inhabitants. City-dwelling Mongolians are hard to distinguish from the Chinese because they wear the same clothes. But the Mongolian is more gregarious and spirited in his outlook on life than his Chinese cousin.

The history of the region is well-documented in the **Museum of Inner Mongolia**. The museum cannot be missed, since a white statue of a prancing horse rises from its roof. During the Cultural Revolution, Chinese officials turned the statue so that it faced Beijing. Now the statue once again faces north towards the grasslands.

Popular on tour itineraries is a visit to the **Tomb of Wang Zhaojun**. Wang Zhaojun was a Han-Dynasty princess who, in the first century, was married off to a barbarian chieftain to seal an alliance. Most Chinese consider her marriage an act of self-sacrifice — a potent reminder of how the Chinese have traditionally viewed their nomadic neighbours.

The Mongolians adopted the Tibetan Buddhist faith in the Yuan Dynasty, and Inner Mongolia had many fine lamaseries before the Cultural Revolution. Some of those damaged lamaseries are now being restored. Of particular interest in the city is the **Dazhao Lamasery**, founded in the 16th century. The nearby **Xilitu Monastery** is the home of a Living Buddha. The young man who was designated as the present incarnation of the Living Buddha is sometimes introduced to foreign journalists.

For many, the most attractive sight of Hohhot is the **Five Pagoda Temple** (Wutasi). In fact, it is not really a temple but just a stupa with five small stupas on its roof, which was once part of a long-destroyed monastery. The main stupa contains the Buddhist treasure of the Diamond Sutra, written in Mongolian, Tibetan and Sanskrit. The exterior of the five roof stupas is covered by a wealth of finely worked carvings, some of them of Buddhist themes, and others depicting galloping horses.

Inner Mongolia has a large community of Hui people, Chinese Muslims. The **Great Mosque** (Qingzhensi) of Hohhot is open to visitors. It was built in the 17th century and, like all late mosques

built in China, it has no minaret. The imperial court ordered minarets to be replaced by pavilions, in which were placed inscriptions reminding the Muslims of their loyalty to the emperor.

In the eastern suburbs of Hohhot stands a rare piece of architectural history. The **Wanbuhuayan Pagoda** dates from the tenth century and has survived with little change, despite a series of renovations over the centuries. The pagoda is a beautiful brick-and-wood structure in seven storeys.

Baotou

Baotou is Inner Mongolia's only major industrial centre and is very much the creation of the town planners of the 1950s. The city offers very little for the sightseer, but beyond the city are several interesting destinations.

A two-hour bus ride into the Daqing Mountains takes you to the **Wudang Monastery**. The monastery was once one of the most important lamaseries of the region, and today it is still an important spiritual centre for Mongolian Buddhists. The Wudang Monastery is a Yellow Hat Sect, Tibetan-style lamasery, and it is said to have been modelled on the Potala Palace in Lhasa. It continues a tradition of Buddhist festivals and ceremonies, sending monks out to pray for rain when the grasslands are dry.

South of Baotou is the **Tomb of Genghis Khan**. Since he is father of the Mongolian people, his tomb has become a focal point for Mongolian festivities. In spring every year, a *suduling*, very similar to the Highland Games in Scotland, is held near the tomb. Young Mongolian men gather to test their prowess in the skills of wrestling, spear-throwing and riding.

From Baotou, visits to the **Ordos Desert** can be arranged. The tours take visitors to a place known as **Noisy Sands Bay** (Xiangshawan), where the sands have such a high metallic content that they literally rumble when you slide across them.

The Silk Road

Beyond the known world of China stretch the gravel and sand deserts and barren mountain ranges of Central Asia. In the second century, this vast expanse of barely inhabitable land was home to nomadic tribes and small pockets of settlers, who farmed the land wherever oasis springs watered the earth. These tribes of nomads were seen as a potential military threat to the western regions of the Han empire, and large expeditionary forces were sent to subdue them, and subsequently to woo them into alliances of friendship with the Chinese emperor. The power of the Han Dynasty brought an era of stability to these Central Asian lands — and from this balance of forces arose the opportunity for establishing that great trade route known as the Silk Road.

In fact, the route from the settled lands of China to the **Karakoram Mountains**, which separate the modern borders of China's Xinjiang Province, Kashmir and Pakistan, was well known to a few intrepid traders of even earlier times. The Chinese love of jade, much of which comes from the Karakoram range, made the hard journey across the deserts and mountains worth the effort for the high premiums paid in the palaces of China. By the time of the Han Dynasty, it was Chinese silk, prized in the noble homes of the Near East and the Roman Empire, which gave the major impetus to the development of the routes which came to be known as the Silk Road. The Road was in fact a chain of caravan trails, reaching north across the Gobi Desert, then as far south as present-day India and Iran, before leading to Antioch on the eastern shores of the Mediterranean. A strong empire in China could control and keep open the trade routes to the west, while drawing in great wealth.

Along with trade came travellers — and with them, ideas. The Silk Road may have seen the exchange of small but precious gems, porcelain, furs and silk, but in the long term the greater exchange was of science, religion and art. In the Han Dynasty, the Silk Road brought Buddhism to China, and by the Tang Dynasty, Islam, Nestorian Christianity and Zoroastrianism were to find roots in Chinese soil. The two latter faiths never flourished beyond the Tang Dynasty, but Islam was to grow to be a major force in Chinese culture, particularly in the areas traversed by the Silk Road.

The modern traveller, journeying through regions which were once part of the Silk Road, will find it easy to conjure up images of those early wandering imams and monks, bringing their faith to Central Asia's oasis towns. Large communities of Muslims continue to flourish, and vast Buddhist carved caves mark the river corridor out from China to the beginning of the Taklamakan Desert. But it should not be forgotten that along this route — carried by unknown hands — came the Chinese inventions of the compass, gunpowder and paper moving westwards, inventions which ultimately were to unleash the forces which would bring about the demise of the Silk Road. Advances in navigation first made by the Arabs, and later by the Hiberian nations of Spain and Portugal, were to lead to a flourishing maritime trade with China. And it was this opening of the sea routes that in turn brought ruin to the oasis kingdoms and cities built on the wealth of the caravanserai.

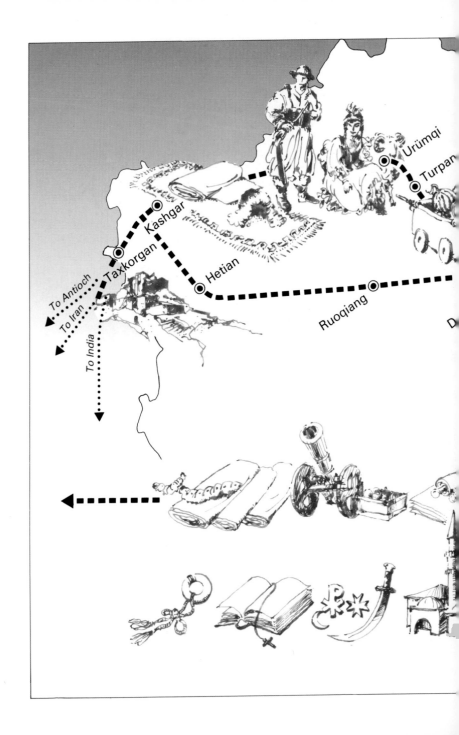

Urümqi

Turpan

Kashgar

Taxkorgan

Hetian

To Antioch

To Iran

To India

Ruoqiang

The Silk Road

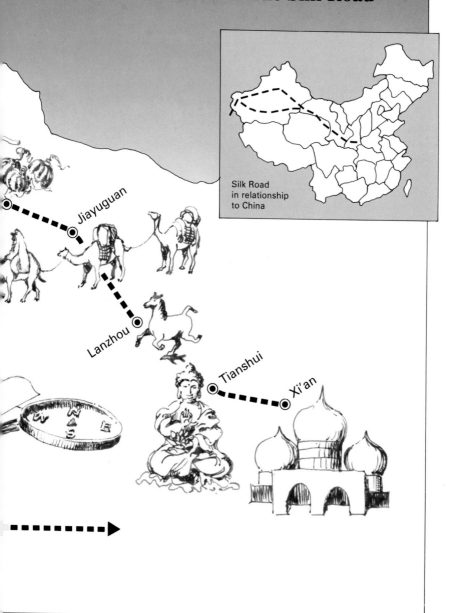

Silk Road
in relationship
to China

Jiayuguan

Lanzhou

Tianshui

Xi'an

Today, camel caravans and nomadic herders still follow parts of the ancient routes, but international boundaries and a revolution in transport have left the Silk Road a mere memory of a legend. Yet that memory still excites the imagination of present-day travellers, who are rewarded after long, hot and dusty journeys with glimpses of lost cities, strange landscapes of wind-carved rocks, scenes from bazaars little changed from medieval times, remote mountain ranges and lakes of great beauty. The Silk Road is once more profit-making as the Chinese tourism authorities cash in on the romance of Central Asia.

From Xi'an to Lanzhou

Xi'an, known by its former name of Chang'an, marked the traditional starting point of the Silk Road in the journey to the west. Modern Xi'an is much smaller than it was in the Tang Dynasty, but it still holds reminders of its former glory. The **Shaanxi Provincial Museum** has many treasures of Silk Road days — Tang figurines depicting hook-nosed merchants from Western Asia, steles with Nestorian Christian inscriptions, and coins from as far afield as Greece.

In tracing the Silk Road, many modern travellers choose to fly from Xi'an to Lanzhou, the capital of Gansu Province. However, for the visitor with time to spare, a series of train and bus trips between the two cities is recommended because of the wealth of archaeological sites which can be visited en route. The journey yields as many sidetrips as the traveller can afford — to the small towns along the route to Lanzhou, and to the southern grasslands of Gansu where Tibetan and Mongolian communities of herders live interspersed with the Hui (Chinese Muslim) people.

Xianyang is the site of the capital of the Qin Dynasty which unified China in 221 BC. The Afang palace of the first emperor has been excavated, but little now remains since the wooden structure was burnt down on the defeat of the Qin by the Han. Descriptions of the grandeur of the palace have been preserved in the history compiled in the Han Dynasty, the *shi ji*. It is said that the megalomaniac Qin emperor had replicas of the palaces of his defeated rivals built within his own palace, and brought artefacts from the conquered states to be used in his own household. Indeed, in the excavations at Xianyang, coins from the distant southern state of Chu were uncovered.

West of Xi'an lies **Baoji County**, a region which was at the centre of early Zhou Dynasty culture. For those interested in the extraordinary bronzes of this era, the Zhou Yuan Cultural Relics Administration should be visited. Shaanxi Province is famous for its lively tradition of folk arts and customs. Small villages in this area still set up a high swing at New Year, where the women of the village can enjoy a custom said to have originated in Central Asia. In the small town of **Fengxiang**, once a major trading centre on the Silk Road, the tradition of making decorative clay and cloth tigers has made it well known amongst collectors of folk art.

A once-important city for Silk Road traders was **Baoji City**, now a major rail junction. The city, set on the banks of the River Wei, has a quiet and prosperous air. The Ming-Dynasty **Jintai Monastery**, built high on a hill overlooking the city and the surrounding mountains, is the most striking city sight. In the monastery is a stele carved in the calligraphy of the famous Three Kingdoms scholar-general Cao Cao. This general was the ruler of the state of the Northern Wei from 220 to 265, and is famous for his poetry as well as his calligraphy. The inscription in the Jintai Monastery is in the 'melon-skin' style (being barely legible even to the Chinese). The area around Baoji includes excavated Neolithic settlements and the Painted Pottery of the Yangshao culture (see page 34). At **Baishouling** there is an exhibition of Neolithic pottery, some of which is very ingenious in design.

Tianshui is the first town you reach after crossing the border between Shaanxi and Gansu Provinces. Famous for its carved lacquerware, the town has been little touched by modern development schemes. It is here that the traditional one-storey houses and memorial arches so common in 19th-century cities can still be seen. Tianshui was the birthplace of Li Guang, the famous 'Flying General' of the Western Han Dynasty. He was sent by his emperor to fight the Huns of Central Asia, and helped bring peace and prosperity to the region. His tomb, where only his possessions could be buried after his death in battle, can still be visited.

Just beyond the city of Tianshui is the major Buddhist cave complex of **Maijishan**. The name, which means 'Wheat Rick Mountain', is fitting since the small mountain rises in a blunt-ended cone of soft yellow stone. Maijishan is one of the five most important Buddhist cave centres, the others being Yungang in Datong, Longmen at Luoyang, the great Dunhuang caves also in Gansu, and Dazu in Sichuan (see also pages 67, 167, 190). Many of the caves are almost inaccessible, but the outer face of the mountain is carved with magnificent Buddha images. The interior of the caves is decorated with frescoes and clay statues.

A few miles to the north of Maijishan rises **Xianren Cliff** (Immortal Cliff). Many of the carvings date back to the fifth century. Within the caves there is an eclectic mix of statues: Buddhist and Daoist figures as well as Confucian sages stand side by side.

Northwest of Tianshui, on the northern bank of the River Wei, stands a whole complex of caves and temples. The caves, situated in Wushan County, are little visited and floods sometimes cut off access. On one cliff-face, known as **Lashao Temple**, are carved the three figures of the Sakyamuni Buddha and his two disciples. The Buddha is sitting serenely in the lotus position and his two disciples stand on either side, holding lotus blossoms. The carvings were originally painted and some of the colours still remain. Beneath the Buddha's feet is a series of bas-reliefs featuring strange animals, some of which bear a close resemblance to the carved lions seen in Persian sculpture.

The capital of Gansu Province is **Lanzhou**, which sprawls along the banks of the Yellow River. It is an industrial centre for the northwest. The city's main attractions are the treasures in the **Gansu Provincial Museum**. It is in this museum that the visitor can find the famous cast-bronze flying horse which was sent on a cultural tour of major world capitals in the 1970s. The horse dates from the Eastern Han Dynasty of the second century AD, and celebrates the new breed of horses which was brought along the Silk Road from Ferghana to the imperial court of China. These horses had greater speed and stamina than the native breeds, qualities which made them extremely valuable. The bronze horse vividly portrays the speed of the Ferghana, with its flared nostrils, windswept mane and tail, and one of its hooves poised on the back of a flying swallow. Fine examples of Neolithic pottery, known as Yangshao ware (see page 34), are also in the museum, along with Zhou ritual bronzes and a reconstruction of a Han tomb.

Expeditions from Lanzhou

Bilingsi is an important cave complex dating from the fifth century. You can get to it by taking a two-hour boat ride along the Yellow River. The hundreds of caves with their statues and frescoes depict the life and works of Buddha and his disciples.

The **Labrang Lamasery** is one of the most important Tibetan Yellow Hat Sect religious centres in China. Situated southwest of Lanzhou, close to the small town of **Xiahe**, it is the focal point of the local Tibetan community. Labrang was founded in 1709 under the patronage of the Qing Emperor Kangxi. It became an important centre of Buddhist scholarship and worship due to the continued benefaction of the Qing emperors, who were much attracted to the Buddhist faith. Labrang is also the home of a Living Buddha — believed to be a reincarnation of a Bodhisattva returned to earth to teach. Labrang now houses 1,000 lamas, but previously it had more than 4,000. Originally, too, it owned most of the surrounding farmland, but the Communist regime confiscated the land and destroyed part of the monastery. Since the lamasery is an important spiritual centre, it maintains the traditional calendar of Buddhist festivals. It is likely that visitors will see part of the religious life of the lamasery and, if lucky, may even see one of the great debates held publicly by the lamas. At New Year, the lamas perform demon-mask dances to usher in good fortune for the coming year. A few miles away, there is an attractive Tibetan-style guesthouse.

On the road to the Labrang Lamasery lies the small town of **Linxia**, the capital of the Hui Autonomous Prefecture. The Hui people are Chinese Muslims, whose ancestors adopted the faith during the Tang Dynasty when Arab and Central Asian merchants travelled to, or even settled in, China. As a reminder of the region's Arab connections, the tomb of an Arab missionary stands on the summit of a local hill. In Chinese, the imam was known as Han Zeling, but his Arab name is believed to have been *Hamuzeli*. The Dongxiang minority people also live in this area. They too are Muslims, like the Hui, but their bright blue eyes and aquiline noses betray more Western antecedents.

From Lanzhou to Urümqi

After leaving Lanzhou, the inhospitable nature of the old Silk Road and surrounding landscape becomes increasingly evident. The barren slopes of the Qilian range lie to the south, and to the north, the Gobi Desert stretches beyond the western limits of the Great Wall. The winds in this region are fierce. Crops are grown in the crevices of flat stones laid out across the fields to keep the earth from blowing away. The land is bone dry, except where streams and springs give life to patches of vegetation. The modern traveller is only too well aware of how difficult the journey must have been in the days when Silk Road merchants travelled by foot with a camel caravan. Today, the best way to gain an impression of the Silk Road terrain is by train and bus.

Jiayuguan is the pass which marks the western limit of the Great Wall. Many people break their train journey here to see the Ming fortress, built to guard the strategic pass between the Qilian

Mountains to the south and the Black Mountains to the north. It is also here that some of the earliest segments of the Great Wall can be seen. Much of the wall, which has crumbled to an undulating earth mound, dates back to the Han Dynasty and bears little resemblance to the Ming section which can be seen at Badaling, north of Beijing.

From Jiayuguan, the journey to **Dunhuang** is by bus or train. However, Dunhuang does have an airstrip, and some visitors on a tighter schedule fly in.

The Buddhist caves of Dunhuang are one of the Silk Road's most impressive landmarks. The caves are located at three separate sites, the most important being the **Mogao** complex. However, for those with time to spare, the two other sites should be explored. The caves were first worked in the fourth century, but no carvings from that era have survived. The earliest caves that can be seen date from the fifth century. Monks and craftsmen lived and worked in Dunhuang for over four centuries, and the many caves reflect the changes of style during that period.

The early frescoes, dating from the Northern Wei Dynasty, take their theme from the Jataka stories of Buddha's life. The execution is dynamic, with swirling clouds and *apsaras* (Buddhist angels) trailing floating ribbons. The later paintings of the Sui Dynasty show a greater stillness of composition, and there are fewer illustrations from the Jataka tales and more serene iconographic Buddha and Bodhisattva figures.

Close to the caves is a small, sickle-shaped lake, set amidst sand dunes. A walk to the **Crescent Moon Pool** makes a refreshing break after the dark interiors of the cave.

The oasis town of **Turpan**, on the railway line to Ürümqi, is an extraordinary contrast to the barren gravel desert on all sides. In its fields are grown sweet grapes and the famous Hami melon. Where the line of fields and trees ends, the desert begins with a brutal abruptness. The water for Turpan comes from underground channels, which bring the snowmelt from the nearby Tianshan range. The Turpan oasis was an important way-station on the northern section of the Silk Road, and in the early centuries it was a centre of Buddhism. Later migrations by the Muslim Uighur people led to the region coming under the influence of Islam. One of the city's most famous sights is the **Suleiman Mosque**, founded in the late 18th century. Its minaret, built in the Afghan style of unglazed mud-bricks arranged in bold geometric patterns, is much photographed.

Close to the city lies the Turpan Depression, which at 150 metres (505 feet) below sea level, is the second lowest place on earth. Beyond the city rises the Flaming or Fire Mountains, whose deep-red rocks absorb the sun's heat and create furnace-like temperatures. Travellers walking in the mountains have had the soles of their shoes melted. Set amidst these mountains is the Buddhist cave centre of **Bezeklik**. The complex is also known, like many others on the Silk Road, as Thousand Buddha Caves. Carved between the fifth and 14th centuries, they have been very badly damaged, but many fine Tang frescoes have survived.

Turpan is close to the ruins of two ancient cities which were abandoned when trade along the Silk Road fell into decline: a period towards the end of the Yuan Dynasty and the beginning of the Ming. **Gaochang** (Karakhoja) was a first-century walled city of which very little now remains save for massive crumbling walls and foundations. The cemetery of Gaochang, known as **Astana**, has had some of its tombs excavated, one of which — from the Tang Dynasty — contains fine murals. The smaller abandoned city of **Jiaohe** (Yarkhoto) has an incredible setting; on the top of a cliff, on an island between two rivers.

Urümqi, the capital of the Xinjiang Uighur Autonomous Region, has no historical connection with the Silk Road. However, it is an important connection point for modern travellers. Xinjiang has 11 airports, the highest number for any region in China, and so adventurous travellers can choose to travel to more remote destinations by air. Road journeys can be dusty, hot and tiring. Most travellers make an air connection to **Kashgar** (also known as Kashi), which is the most westerly city within China's borders. Kashgar is the starting point for the trip along the Karakoram Highway to Pakistan.

The city of Urümqi is modern and, by and large, wholly lacking in attractive architecture — except for a few sections where traditional Russian design has survived. The city's standard government offices and cinemas were built in the 1950s by the People's Liberation Army Construction Corps. Urümqi may have a uniformity common to most major Chinese cities, but its inhabitants are widely dissimilar. The majority of the people in Xinjiang are Uighurs and Khazakhs. Uighurs are Muslims, but they are also well known for being heavy drinkers, and street brawls in Urümqi are quite common. The Uighur men dress like most of the Han Chinese, but Uighur women cut a more colourful figure, with braided hair, veils and bloomers peeping out below their dresses. There is little to see within the city, but the **Xinjiang Provincial Museum** contains an interesting exhibition of the region's early history and much material on the minorities of Xinjiang. From Urümqi, most visitors take one or two trips to the surrounding mountain ranges.

Expeditions from Urümqi

The most popular, and perhaps the most overrated of these, is to the **Tianshan** (Celestial) **Mountains** and the **Celestial Lake**. The journey up into the cool alpine meadows of the Tianshan is a welcome relief after the heat of the desert, but the trip is crowded on weekends and holidays, so be warned.

The day-trip to the **Nanshan** (Southern) **Mountains** is a more attractive alternative, since fewer people make the journey. The Khazakh people live amidst the mountain pastures, enjoying equestrian sports; they are often quite happy to put on a display of local polo. Tour group visitors are usually invited into the local *yurt* for a meal of home-baked bread, cheese and mutton kebabs.

Two longer trips to **Karamay** and **Altay**, north of Urümqi, can be made by air. Beyond the city of Karamay, which is an important support base for regional oil exploration, lies the strange, wind-eroded landscape known as **Devil's City**. The land holds little life, but thousands of years ago — when the climate was damper and cooler — many animals lived in the region. The fossils around Devil's City are easily accessible and are now being excavated. Small wind-polished, semi-precious stones can be found scattered among the rocks.

Further north, in the Altay Mountains, close to the border with Mongolia and the Soviet Union, are strange rock pictures carved by early nomads. The rocks overlook good pastureland and, not surprisingly, the scenes depicted are of grazing animals and hunting parties. In one of the pictures stands the unmistakable form of an elephant. It is recorded in the histories of the Han Dynasty that elephants and tigers roamed this region as late as the second century BC.

Aksu lies southwest of Urümqi and is usually a refuelling stopover for flights to Kashgar. Close to the neighbouring city of Kucha are the **Kezi'er Thousand Buddha Caves**. The caves are worth the detour because of their well-preserved frescoes, believed to date from the fourth century. Of the 236 caves, only 75 have remained intact. The statuary has all but disappeared, but the strange murals depicting man-beasts, double-headed birds and Buddhist immortals could almost be characters from the unbelievable tales of Marco Polo about his own journey along the Silk Road. Aksu is modern, but it does have a candlelit night-market. Kucha too has an excellent market, held every Friday. The small town of **Wensu** has retained its Central Asian architecture and is worth visiting for that alone.

Kashgar (Kashi) retains all the romance of the Silk Road era, having been little touched by Chinese attempts at modernisation. It is smaller than Urümqi and easy to explore on foot or bicycle, a city which could have jumped out from the pages of the *Arabian Nights*. Because of Kashgar's trade with Pakistan, its bazaars are full of goods from China as well as the Indian subcontinent. There is a choice of hats of every description: fur-trimmed, embroidered and plain. Silks from China are on sale, as are semi-precious stones and the beautiful hand-woven rugs of the region.

The city has a long history, stretching back over 2,000 years. In the Han and Tang Dynasties it was under Chinese control, but the indigenous people of the region are believed to be Indo-European in origin. Blue-eyed and hook-nosed features are common in Kashgar. The city is Islamic in character, but in pre-Tang times it was an important meeting point for Buddhist monks and craftsmen. On a cliff-face north of the city at the **Sanxian Caves**, remnants of Buddhist murals can be seen.

In the last century, Kashgar with its foreign consulates was the listening post in the 'Great Game' between Britain and Russia in their bid to secure control over the region. In May 1986, when the Karakoram Highway was opened, Kashgar once more became an important city for foreign travellers moving between China and South Asia.

The Road to Pakistan

The route from Kashgar to the Pakistani border over the **Khunjerab Pass** may be one of the most spectacular and exhausting road trips in the world.

As the road heads south, travellers pass through the small town of **Gez**, which has a large community of Kirgiz people. The Kirgiz are nomadic herders, whose women have a liking for elaborately embroidered head cloths, heavy silver jewellery, and waistcoats decorated with buttons. From Gez, the road sweeps past the two great peaks of Mount Kongur and Mount Muzagata. Around **Taxkorgan**, in the foothills of the Pamir Mountains, live the Tajik people. The Tajiks are pastoralists descended from Persian stock. The Tajik women are also colourful, using buttons, tassels and silver discs to decorate their plaits. The nomadic Tajiks live in houses built of earth and grass, and many of their tombs are built in the shape of a saddle — reputedly because of their love of being on horseback. The town of Taxkorgan is dominated by the still-impressive but crumbling ruin of a Han-Dynasty fort.

From Taxkorgan, it is approximately a two-and-a-half hour journey by road to the border crossing to Pakistan. In earlier days, the route was extremely hazardous and entire camel caravans could be frozen to death on the passes when a snow storm swept in. Luckily, the modern traveller on the Silk Road is better insulated against such dangers for the route is only open in the summer and autumn months, from 1 May to 30 November.

Tibet

There are many mountains in the world, but few have contained such a uniquely spiritual civilization as the Himalayas of Tibet. Since Tibetan history began to be recorded in the seventh century (when Buddhism took root in the country), the people of these mountains created a society in which monasteries acted as the centres of learning, of medicine, and ultimately of economic and political power. Buddhism blended with the ancient Tibetan animistic beliefs of Bon and became the core of Tibetan culture, thereby transforming a group of warrior tribes into a theocratic state.

Yet the peaceful doctrines of Buddhism did not always prevent the Tibetans from warring with each other, or with their neighbours. Due to the high altitude and scarce soils, farming was limited to a few river valleys, where only barley could be grown successfully. Tibet therefore could not develop a social system of settled farming communities in the manner of its Chinese neighbours to the east. The young men of Tibet could only herd, trade or join a monastery. Up until the middle of this century, the term 'monk' covered the widest possible range of character and activity. Some monks were cooks, others were the craftsmen of the brotherhood, and a chosen few were educated to become lamas — those who, in turn, transmitted Buddhist teachings and the traditions of Tibet's culture and medical knowledge to others.

The great unifier of Tibet, King Songsten Gampo, patronized the establishment of Buddhism in the seventh century, along with the development of a Tibetan script in which the scriptures themselves could be written. He also made tactical marriages to two Buddhist princesses, one Nepalese and one Chinese. The king's descendants ruled Tibet until the middle of the ninth century, when the monarchy came into conflict with the monasteries. After the last king was assassinated by a monk, rival monasteries created power bases, and the country was divided into regional spheres of influence. Tibet's earliest monasteries were controlled by rival sects, the most powerful of which were the Red Hats. In the 14th century, a scholar named

Tsong Khapa founded the Yellow Hat Sect, which subsequently eclipsed the older Red Hat Sect and proved to be a force for reunification.

From the Yellow Hat Sect evolved a line of master monks known as Dalai Lamas, a title meaning 'Ocean of Wisdom'. In the 17th century, when the fifth Dalai Lama came to power, his ascendancy over all other lamas was established, and he was proclaimed to be the reincarnation of Chenrezi, the Bodhisattva of Mercy. The fifth Dalai Lama ruled from Lhasa but brought Shigatse, the second city of Tibet, under his control by enhancing the power of that city's Yellow Hat monastery, Tashilhunpo. Tashilhunpo's abbot had been the Dalai Lama's tutor and, in honour of his wisdom, the Dalai Lama had him named the Panchen Lama, meaning 'Great Scholar'. The Panchen Lama was then proclaimed to be a reincarnation of the Amitabha Buddha, thus making his status in Shigatse unchallengeable.

The theocratic government of Tibet ruled for the following two centuries with no interference from China, though it exercised a little of its own influence at the Qing court. The Qing rulers, who were Buddhists, often invited high-ranking Tibetan lamas to Beijing in order to teach and advise their court. However, by the mid-19th century, the British in India and the Russians were alert to the possibility of using Tibet as a pawn in their power game for control of Central Asia. This scheming in turn reminded the Qing rulers of the importance of Tibet in Chinese political concerns. In 1904, adopting their usual 'gunboat diplomacy', the British sent the Younghusband Expedition into Tibet to force a treaty of trade and friendship on the Tibetans. In 1910, it was China's turn to invade Tibet, seeking political concessions. The 13th Dalai Lama fled to Darjeeling and requested British aid to oust the Chinese. But it was the newly unified Chinese Communist government which finally gained control of the country, sending in its own army to 'liberate' Tibet in 1950.

The impact of a Chinese Marxist regime on the theocratic government of Tibet was catastrophic. Where the Chinese saw only backwardness, poverty and religious superstition, the Tibetans saw a world where man lived in harmony with his environment and the world of the spirit. The meeting of opposites was less than fortunate. In 1959, after an abortive uprising, the 14th Dalai Lama fled with 80,000 of his followers over the Himalayas and into India.

This self-imposed exile by the current Dalai Lama has created an unsolved problem for the Chinese, who have ruled Tibet with what can only be called cruel condescension, even if it has been slightly

tempered in the last few years. The Dalai Lama has remained in exile, despite behind-the-scenes negotiations between representatives of his exiled government and Beijing. The Chinese will not let him return to Lhasa to live and rule as spiritual leader because they see him as the potential focus for political discontent. The Dalai Lama declines to return if he is to be forced to settle in Beijing.

The only clarity in the situation is that the Chinese set a high value on the strategic importance of Tibet. They have also redrawn Tibet's borders so as to reduce the actual territory traceable on the map as Tibet. Whole Tibetan regions have been absorbed into the surrounding provinces of Sichuan and Qinghai. Yet despite Chinese rule, anti-Buddhist propaganda, persecution and the policy of forcibly importing Han Chinese and Hui Muslims into their communities, the Tibetans have retained their sense of cultural identity and their love of the Dalai Lama.

It is hardly surprising that in the bleak but majestic landscapes of Tibet's highlands, the world of the spirit seems more real than the world of men. The silent landscapes of snow and ice, mountains, lakes and meadows have an unearthly beauty, often being regarded as holy places by the Tibetans who pass through them in their mortal lives.

Lhasa

Because of Lhasa's altitude, 3,500 metres (12,000 feet) above sea level, most visitors need to take it easy the first few days in order to become acclimatized to the thin air. The best way to do this is to start your itinerary with a few short outings, with rests in between. Strolls around the city and out along the banks of the **Lhasa River** are an excellent and not too taxing introduction to life in Tibet.

Chinese political control is apparent in the sharp contrast between the old Tibetan part of Lhasa and the newer section of the city constructed by the Chinese. The old district, which clusters round the Jokhang Temple, contains a web of narrow lanes and houses of rough-hewn stone, brightened with whitewashed walls and painted woodwork. The new section of the city is drabber, but it has wide boulevards with housing and office blocks set well back from the road behind high compound walls.

The Tibetans still dress in their traditional costumes — mainly because the clothes are so well adapted to the rigours of the climate. The men and women wear *chubas*, thick belted garments made from sheepskin. In winter the men wear felt or fur hats. The women wear

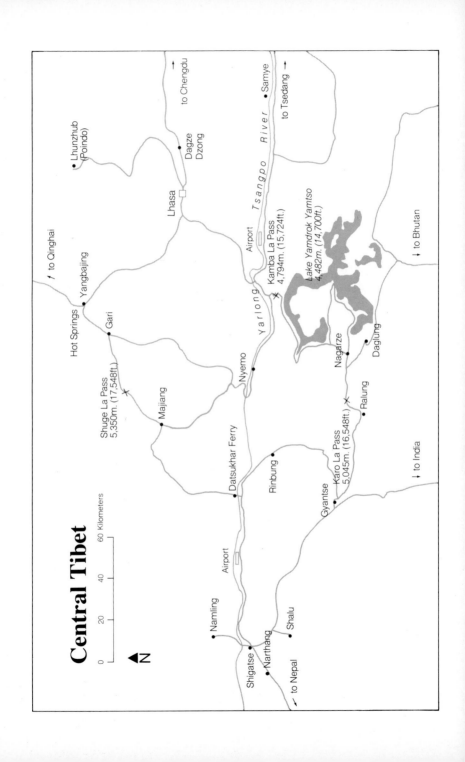

Central Tibet

N

0   20   40   60 Kilometers

to Qinghai

to Chengdu

Lhunzhub
(Poindo)

Dagze
Dzong

Lhasa

Hot Springs

Yangbajing

Gari

Shuge La Pass
5,350m. (17,548ft.)

Majiang

Nyemo

Airport

Samye

to Tsedang

Tsangpo River

Kamba La Pass
4,794m. (15,724ft.)

Lake Yamdrok Yamtso
4,482m. (14,700ft.)

to Bhutan

Nagartze

Daglung

Yarlong

Datsukhar Ferry

Rinbung

Ralung

Karo La Pass
5,045m. (16,548ft.)

to India

Gyantse

Namling

Airport

Shalu

Shigatse

Narthang

to Nepal

their hair in braids or tucked under coloured scarves, and — on special occasions — elaborate headdresses. Their long dresses are usually black, brown or blue in colour, but the working pinafores of woven stripes (only worn by the married women of Central Tibet) are brightly coloured.

A walk around the old section of Lhasa is full of discoveries: small temples being restored and lovingly decorated, street stalls selling anything from snacks to daggers, prayer flags fluttering above walls, and glimpses into courtyards of Tibetan homes. Tibetans are generally friendly and welcoming and, in their love of open-air picnics, can show zealous hospitality. Foreign travellers have been known to reel back to their hotels in a stupor after generous (and unrefusable) refills of local liquor.

Travellers exploring the city should make time for an outing to **Gumolingka Island** in the Lhasa River — a favourite summer picnic place for Tibetans. The **Moslem Quarter** of Lhasa has its mosque and *halal* restaurants. The Moslem district lies to the southeast of the **Barkhor Pilgrim Path**. The Barkhor circles the Jokhang Temple, and you must walk around it in a clockwise direction (this is true of all Buddhist sites in Tibet) in order not to offend, or collide with, Tibetan pilgrims. On the Barkhor, devout pilgrims often make the circuit in a series of full-length body prostrations.

The **Tibetan Hospital of Traditional Medicine** makes a fascinating visit for those interested in herbal remedies and their history. Traditional medicine was once taught in the monasteries, the most famous of which was the old medical college on the summit of Chokpori Hill in Lhasa. It was reduced to rubble by the Chinese army in 1959, and a steel antenna was erected on the site. Religious pilgrims still walk the slopes of the hill.

Tibetan carpets, with their Buddhist motifs, are extremely attractive, and one can watch them being made at the **Lhasa Carpet Factory**. Tibetan performing arts are being revived, and the **School of Tibetan Performing Arts**, founded in 1980 as a gesture of Chinese tolerance, allows foreign visitors to attend music and opera rehearsals.

After years of closure, small city temples are being restored for worship. The **Ramoche Temple** in the north of the city, and the cave temple of **Palalubu** at the foot of Chokpori, are open to foreign visitors. Less well visited are the monasteries of **Chomoling**, **Muru Ningba**, **Tengyeling** and the convent of **Ani Gompa**.

You can also visit the old summer palace of the Dalai Lama, the **Norbulingka**. The palace and its park are about a 15-minute walk southwest from the **Lhasa Hotel**, in the west of the city. It was built

by the seventh Dalai Lama as a summer retreat, and today it houses a small zoo which has rare Himalayan bears and snow lynxes.

Built on a hill overlooking the city, the **Potala Palace** is Tibet's best-known landmark. Once the spiritual and temporal palace of the Dalai Lama, it is now a museum with shrines and chapels maintained by monks. The Potala has two sections, known as the White and Red Palaces. The White Palace, built in 1653, rises in terraces to the central Red Palace, built in 1693, which is crowned with an ornate gilded copper roof. Inside the Potala, most of which is off-limits to visitors, there are open chapels and galleries which have fascinating wall paintings. The apartments of the 13th and 14th Dalai Lamas are open to visitors, as is the tomb of the 13th Dalai Lama. For security reasons, the tomb must be visited with a guide or a monk, because the interior has treasures of gold and precious gems. You can climb up to the roof for a fine view over the city and the river valley.

The **Jokhang Temple** is Tibet's holiest religious foundation and the home of the most precious Buddha image the country possesses — the Sakyamuni Buddha, brought from China by the Tang-Dynasty princess Wen Cheng, who was wedded in a marriage alliance to the great King Songsten Gampo. The Jokhang is the most important site of pilgrimage in Tibet, so visitors should be particularly respectful of worshippers. In the main hall of the temple is a lovely mural showing the arrival of Princess Wen Cheng in Tibet. The roof of the Jokhang can also be visited.

Set against the bare hillside of Mount Gyengbuwudze, on the western outskirts of Lhasa, the **Drepung Monastery** was once the largest and the wealthiest in Tibet. A Yellow Hat foundation, the monastery had senior monks who were instrumental in the training of Dalai Lamas, and who specialized in esoteric psychic practices. The monastery was also the home of the State Oracle who, in trance, advised the Dalai Lama on important decisions. The Drepung was divided into four Tantric Colleges, each of which had its own special field of learning. In the chanting hall of the **Nuosenle College**, there is a model doll of the State Oracle in the regalia worn for prophecy.

On the northern outskirts of Lhasa lies **Sera Monastery**, a Yellow Hat Sect monastery which was once rival to Drepung. Set against Tatipu Hill, Sera had three Tantric Colleges which were famous for their Bon tradition of occult teaching. Monks have returned to Sera and can be seen at prayer in their deep red robes and distinctive yellow hats which sweep upwards like a curved shell over their forehead. Worth looking for is the image of the horse-headed god in the **Gyetazang College** chanting hall. The treasury of the monastery is the gilded Chenrezi image, the Bodhisattva of Mercy, of whom all Dalai Lamas are said to be incarnations. The Chenrezi image is in the **Tsug-gyeng College** chanting hall.

Twenty-seven kilometres (17 miles) south of Lhasa is the **Droma Lhakang Temple**. Less visited than most, it is dedicated to the Indian Tantric master, Atisha, who came to Tibet in the 11th century. Atisha settled in Tibet to teach, and he was instrumental in the revival of Buddhism after two centuries of fighting and destruction which followed the overthrow of the royal family in the ninth century. The temple has many images of the Tibetan goddess Tara, who was the guardian deity of Atisha. Tara is said to have been a princess who, when challenged by monks saying that a woman could never achieve enlightenment, set out to prove them wrong. When Tara did achieve enlightenment, she was deified. It is easy to identify her image, since it is usually depicted in white or green.

Seventy kilometres (45 miles) east of Lhasa is the Yellow Hat Sect monastery, **Ganden**. It was once Tibet's third largest religious community, after Drepung and Sera, but was badly damaged by the Chinese army. It is now being rebuilt. The impressive ruins and the two rebuilt chanting halls can be seen.

Gyantse

The traveller in Tibet often visits Gyantse on the way to Shigatse. The impression today is of a small and inconsequential city, but that was not always so. Gyantse commanded the meeting-point of two major caravan routes, one to India and the other to Nepal, making it a place of strategic and military importance as well as a fortified city of great wealth. Until the early part of this century, Gyantse was Tibet's third city and a major gathering-point for nomads, who would come to sell their wool for export.

The wealth of the city was manifested in the foundation of **Palkhor Monastery**, built in the 14th century. The monastery has been badly damaged, but on no account should it be passed by. The monastery's Nepalese-style stupa with painted eyes is of great interest. Known as the **Kumbum**, meaning 'Place of a Thousand Images', the stupa has a gilded tower topped by a parasol wrought in filigreed metal. The monastery itself has a vast wall, on which large *thankas* — Buddhist paintings on silk — are hung in the open air during the summer months.

Gyantse's fortress, the **Dzong**, was damaged by British artillery in 1904, during the Younghusband Expedition. The fortress was further damaged by Chinese troops in the 1960s. For those with time for a detour, a visit to the town of **Yadong**, just over 160 kilometres (100 miles) south of Gyantse, is recommended. Yadong has a wonderful prospect over the forests and peaks of the Himalayas. Close to the town is an old wooden monastery, built in Sikkimese style.

Shigatse

Shigatse is set in the valley of the country's major river, the **Yarlong Tsangpo**. This river is better known by its Indian name, the Brahmaputra, for it flows from the western mountains of Tibet, down through India to the Bay of Bengal. Near Shigatse, the Yarlong Tsangpo is a fast-flowing river of snowmelt which waters the farm fields around the city.

Shigatse once rivalled Lhasa for the political and spiritual control of Tibet. It was a centre of monastic learning, and had its own noble families, who used their wealth to found monasteries and thus create power bases. The city was dominated by the Red Hat Sect until the time of the fifth Dalai Lama who, with the backing of a Mongolian warlord, managed to subdue rival sects and unite the country under the leadership of the Yellow Hat Sect (see page 174). The Panchen Lama, the abbot of the **Tashilhunpo Monastery**, reinforced the rule of the Dalai Lama from Lhasa.

The journey to Shigatse from Lhasa is usually made by the southern route, past **Yamdrok Yamtso Lake** and via Gyantse. However, there is a longer but equally interesting northern route, which gives a contrasting picture of the Tibetan landscape. Many travellers visit Shigatse by one route and return to Lhasa by the other. Furthermore, some travellers go from Shigatse to Nepal, since the route is now open to foreign visitors and is highly recommended for adventure travel. (Many tours take this route to Nepal. Independent travellers are therefore advised to organize the trip well in advance *from* Lhasa, since transport is not easy to find and a visa must be obtained first from the Wepalex Commission in Lhasa. Those who have experienced it say the route should be taken from Lhasa, rather than from Nepal, since the rapid change in altitude on the ascent can cause great fatigue and dizziness. Those already acclimatized to Lhasa's altitude will find the descent more comfortable.)

Perhaps because the present Panchen Lama has become the 'guest' of the Chinese in Beijing, Tashilhunpo was spared the worst of the excesses of the Cultural Revolution, and it has now emerged once more as an active centre of worship and teaching. A Yellow Hat order, Tashilhunpo was founded in the 15th century, but it came to pre-eminence in the 17th century with the naming of its abbot as the first Panchen Lama. The current Panchen Lama is the 10th (the sixth is considered to be the greatest).

Tashilhunpo is a beautiful monastery, for it rises in stately terraces to a central gilded roof with decorated eaves and finials. Its distinctive rose-coloured walls are inset with dark wooden windows, brightened with whitewashed borders. The monastery still practises the art of making *mandalas* (abstract meditation pictures) of coloured sands. The courtyard of Tashilhunpo has a high *thanka* wall, on which the huge coloured pictures are unfurled in the sun during festivals.

Visitors can view the **Panchen Lama's Palace**, which remains uninhabited while the Panchen Lama is in Beijing. In the palace is a temple containing the tomb of the fourth Panchen Lama; it has a stupa wrought in gold and precious stones. On the upper level of the temple hang embroidered *thankas* made for the monastery in Hangzhou in the 1920s. Of special interest are the Panchen Lama's throne displayed in the main chanting hall, the sutra hall where the Buddhist canon (scriptures) is kept, the 20th-century statues of the Maitreya Buddha made in gold, copper and brass, and the roof with its chapels.

Travellers can join worshippers on a walk back to Shigatse from the monastery on a pilgrim path (again, the walk has to be done in this direction, since the route is clockwise. No Buddhists walk in pilgrimage in a counter-clockwise direction). Also close to the Tashilhunpo is the Panchen Lama's **Summer Palace**. It is not open to the public.

Twenty-two kilometres (14 miles) south of the city is the **Shalu Monastery**, a Red Hat Sect monastery founded in the 11th century. The original buildings were demolished by an earthquake, and the present structure dates from the 14th century, when it was rebuilt in Mongolian style. Its most famous abbot was Buston, who was a clever administrator and an accomplished historian of Buddhism. The monastery was famous for its occult training. The influence of Bon, the ancient animistic religion of Tibet, was maintained in its teachings. You may notice the counter-clockwise swastikas (Buddhist swastikas are clockwise), which are Bon symbols. Like Tashilhunpo, the monastery has a collection of 20th-century embroidered *thankas* from Hangzhou, and a tradition of making coloured-sand *mandalas*.

From Shigatse to Nepal

Despite the lack of comfort on the journey, this route is popular because of the breathtaking contrasts of scenery visible from the road. The traveller passes through upland river meadows, dun-coloured deserts, through passes offering spectacular vistas of the Himalayan peaks, and down into the warmer forest glades of Tibet's border with Nepal. The trip also offers a chance to see more off-the-beaten-track monasteries and villages.

West of Shigatse stand the almost unearthly walls of the **Sakya Monastery**. Its name means 'tawny soil', and its massive windowless walls rise from the earth like an enormous abstract painting of grey and maroon, with a single white-and-yellow stripe breaking the colour change. It was once the leading Red Hat Sect monastery of the region and enjoyed Mongolian patronage during the Yuan Dynasty, when one of its abbots went to the court of Kublai Khan to convert the emperor. Kublai Khan made the monastery the centre of power in Tibet during his reign. The monastery has suffered damage, but sections of the 13th-century building can still be seen.

On the road to Nepal, the peak of Mount Everest, the highest mountain in the world, towers above the horizon in its lofty splendour. A detour can take the traveller to the base camp of the mountain at **Rongbuk**. This journey, if walked, should only be taken after careful preparation, with enough food for ten days and adequate sleeping and cooking equipment.

North of **Nyalam**, on the road to Nepal, is a cave where the eccentric Buddhist saint and poet, Milarepa, spent much of his life. He is famous for his severe asceticism, acts of compassion and wild songs of poetry. The cave is close to a monastery dedicated to Milarepa. It was destroyed in the Cultural Revolution, but repair work is now underway; craftsmen and artists having been brought in from Nepal to help.

The last Tibetan town before crossing the border is **Zhangmu**. A sleepy town which appears to tumble steeply down a hillside, it has a beautiful setting of pine forests, deep river gorges and cascading waterfalls.

When to Visit Tibet

Travellers should think seriously before travelling in the colder months. The summer is the most popular tourist season, and summer visitors often have a chance to observe Tibetan festivals and celebrations — of either a religious or sporting kind. Keep an ear to the ground for news of Tibetan horse races, wrestling matches and drinking sessions, which take place throughout the warmer months. The Tibetan Lunar New Year (which falls in January or February) is cold, but it does provide a wonderful opportunity to enjoy a week of archery contests, religious dances and other ceremonies. The last day of the old year sees a dance by lamas in masks, known to foreigners as the 'Devils' Dance'. This is when evil influences are driven out to usher in an auspicious New Year.

Sichuan

The vast inland province of Sichuan in southwest China is shaped like a deep dish of lowland river plain, wedged within a serrated rim of towering mountains. To the west the foothills of the Himalayas jut skywards in snowy chains, and to the north the deep-brown folds of the Longmen range separate Sichuan from the neighbouring province of Shaanxi. To the east, the turbulent Yangzi and its tributaries flow between the deep cuts of mountain ranges which sweep from north to south.

Sichuan's name means 'four rivers' — the four tributaries of the Yangzi: the Jialing, Minjiang, Tuojiang and Wujiang. The rivers run in deep gorges through sparsely inhabited upland regions, before they reach the rich soils of the alluvial plains at the centre of the province. The most famous of these gorges are the Sanxia, or Three Gorges, of the Yangzi.

The fertile river plains of Sichuan are the granary of China, producing enough rice and wheat to export surpluses to other parts of the country. With 11 frost-free months, deep soils and an abundance of rainfall, double cropping and three rice harvests a year are possible. The villages of the lowland regions of Sichuan are prosperous and attractive, tucked into bamboo thickets amidst glittering fields of wet paddies and neat terraces of vegetable fields and orchards. The agrarian reforms now being undertaken throughout China were pioneered here by Premier Zhao Ziyang in the early 1980s. At that time he was head of the provincial party committee in Sichuan. He was so successful in restoring Sichuan's agricultural economy that the Sichuanese coined a rhyme: *Yao chi fan, Zhao Ziyang*. Translated, it means, 'If you want to eat, find Ziyang' (*zhao* meaning 'find', as well as being a surname).

The most remote mountainous regions of Sichuan are often populated by minority peoples. Perhaps these are the most attractive regions for the foreign visitor to explore. Indeed, increased trade and tourism are giving the hope of greater wealth to even the least prosperous of them. Of Sichuan's major cities, the traveller is most

likely to visit Chengdu, the capital, and Chongqing, the major industrial centre, before leaving the province to steam down the Yangzi. However, the recent opening to foreigners of the highways to Tibet and Shaanxi, the Buddhist caves of Dazu and the minority regions of the west, has meant that Sichuan now offers as wide a choice of adventure destinations as neighbouring Yunnan Province. Nowadays, it is even possible to visit Tibetan communities without flying direct to Lhasa.

For details of the Yangzi port cities, including Chongqing, see pages 204–7. For the Buddhist mountain of Emeishan in western Sichuan see pages 228–32.

Chengdu

Chengdu may be a large, modern city, but its ways are more those of the countryside than the town. Life is taken at an easy pace, teahouses are always full, and market stalls overflow with an abundance of farm foods brought in from the surrounding villages. The city centre is softened by trees shading the pavements and wide boulevards. The old city hugs the Jin River in a tangled pattern of lanes overhung by two-storey frame houses painted a dusky red. Chengdu rose to prominence in the Three Kingdoms period (220–265) as the capital of the state of Shu (even today, Sichuan is referred to by the name of Shu). Chengdu is the provincial capital, although Chongqing in the east of the province is the foremost industrial centre. The city was once among the most splendid in China, with its own grand city walls — pulled down in 1949 — and Vice-regal Palace, destroyed in the 1960s. Where the palace once stood now rises a monumental granite statue of Mao Zedong, granite-faced and stone coat flapping.

In the rural western suburbs of Chengdu stands **Du Fu's Thatched Cottage**. Du Fu was a Tang poet, who lived in Chengdu in the eighth century. During the later Song Dynasty, a thatched cottage shrine was built in memory of the original cottage, which he described in the poem 'My thatched cottage is wrecked by the autumn wind'. The present buildings date from 1500 and 1811, when major restorations were undertaken. In the front hall are two wooden screens, one of which has a biography of the poet carved out in Chinese characters. In the shrine itself stand clay figurines of Du Fu, which date from the Ming and Qing Dynasties. The garden walks around the shrine are lovely, and many different types of bamboo have been planted to shade the paths.

Set in the southern suburbs of the city are a series of halls called the **Zhuge Liang Memorial Halls**. They commemorate the great military strategist Zhuge Liang, who was adviser to the King of Shu in the Warring States period (475−221 BC). The halls were first built in the fourth century, but the present buildings date from 1672. On display are three bronze drums, believed to have been used by the armies of Shu under Zhuge Liang.

Finally, the **Precious Light Monastery** is worth a visit. It was founded in the Han Dynasty and houses a fine collection of Buddhist treasures as well as modern paintings. A craft market held outside the monastery walls is popular with both local and foreign visitors.

Outings from Chengdu

The hydraulic system, shown in an exhibition hall at **Du River Dyke**, was created in the third century BC by Li Bing, a minister in the ancient state of Shu. Its scale and sophistication are a tribute to the scientific genius of ancient China. The network of dykes and canals not only controlled flood levels on the Min River, but also created an irrigation system vital to the agricultural development of the region. Close to the dyke are several old temples, one of which — the **Two Princes Temple** — is dedicated to Li Bing and his son.

The great statue of the Maitreya Buddha carved on a river cliff at **Leshan** is one of the most splendid sights Sichuan has to offer. The statue stands at the confluence of the Min, Qingyi and Dadu Rivers to the south of Chengdu. Carved in the eighth century, the Buddha is 71 metres (220 feet) high, and is the largest Buddha image carved in China. It has an extraordinarily gentle and serene face, which is now overhung with trees growing in the gardens at the cliff-top. The best way to see the statue is to take a boat along the river. On either side of the statue stand warriors who, though they are imposing, are dwarfed by the size of the Buddha.

Opened to tourists only in 1982, the **Buddhist Caves of Dazu**, to the southeast of Chengdu, are reason enough to visit Sichuan. The caves are scattered over 40 different locations and contain more than 50,000 carvings dating from the Tang and Song Dynasties. The carvings are in isolated areas and thus have escaped much of the destruction suffered by Buddhist centres elsewhere. The two most visited cave centres are **Beishan** and **Baodingshan**. However, adventurous visitors can easily reach the more remote cave centres with the help of local guides.

The sculptures of Beishan date from the late Tang Dynasty and are scattered over the following sites: Fowan, Yingpan Hill, Guanyin Hill, Beita Temple and Fo'er Cliff. The most outstanding are the carvings of grottoes number 136 (known as the 'Wheel of the

Universe') and number 245, with its small-scale carved illustrations of the Buddhist scriptures. The sculptures of Baoding Shan date from the Southern Song Dynasty and are found at 13 different locations. The monk Zhao Zhifeng made the master plan for these Buddhist carvings, and a miniature of that master plan survives to this day. They are made special by the number of works detailing everyday scenes of rural life — look carefully and you will see a maiden kneeling to feed her chickens, farmers out herding their cattle, and scenes with children. There is a beautiful carving of a reclining Buddha, which shows him entering *nirvana* (the Buddhist paradise). Buddhist deities flank his chest at top and bottom, in attitudes of reverence and worship.

The road from Chengdu to the border with Shaanxi Province is open to foreign travellers. The journey can be made by hiring a jeep as a group, or by local bus. This Northern Highway is famous in Chinese history, since it was the only link between the remote region of Sichuan and the northern provinces of China. In times of war, the route — with its high mountain passes — was of great strategic importance. Many of the stories encountered along the way relate to the stories of the Three Kingdoms period, when the state of Shu was at war with its northern rival, the Wei. On the way north there are five famous passes — Seven Bends (Qipan), Skyward (Chaotian), Flying Immortals (Feixian), Heavenly Might (Tianxiong) and Sword Door (Jianmen).

The small town of **Jiange** is remarkable for its ancient wooden buildings, which have survived from the Ming Dynasty. North of Jiange is the famous **Green Cloud Corridor**, a section of the road shaded by 7,900 ancient cypresses planted on the orders of a Ming-Dynasty governor, Li Bi. On either side of the northern section of this route, the women of the mountain villages still wear their traditional headdress of blue turbans and silver hair ornaments.

The Road to Tibet

The overland route to Tibet is fraught with dangers. Landslides frequently block roads and heavy rains cause mudslips, washing away the road and stranding vehicles for days. The route also crosses several high-altitude passes. Thus, it should be travelled only by those who are fit, well prepared and have a clear set of transportation arrangements.

The road heads southwest from Chengdu to the town of **Ya'an**, which is famous for its tea processing. Bricks of tea shaped like large saucers are part of the staple diet of the Tibetans. From Ya'an, the

road passes Mount Erlang and crosses the Dadu River. At **Luding** you can see the famous iron-chain suspension bridge, which the Red Army crossed in 1935 during the Long March. In the town is an exhibition hall giving details of the episode. Luding marked the traditional entry point into Tibet before the borders were adjusted in the 1950s. This region was once known as Xikang, but it has since been made part of Sichuan.

Kangding is the next town west of Luding. It is the capital of the Garze Tibetan Autonomous Prefecture. These small mountain towns are wholly Tibetan in character, despite recent influxes of Chinese settlers brought in to 'stabilize' the region. Kangding is famous for its horse racing, the big races being held every year on Buddha's Bathing Day (the eighth day of the fourth lunar month: early summer).

At **Xinduqiao**, the highway divides into two sections. The northern part goes through Garze, Maniganggo and the Chola Mountains, to Dege and Qamdo. The southern section goes via Bamda, Rawu and Bomi. Both roads run through spectacular scenery, offering views from the high passes over the folded mountain mass of the Qinghai-Tibetan plateau. Dege, on the northern run, is well worth a visit, since it has a traditional Buddhist printing press, where sutras are printed by hand from wood blocks. Also on the northern route is Qamdo, the largest town in eastern Tibet. The men of Qamdo have a reputation for being fierce warriors and hunters, who in earlier times made their living from banditry.

Minorities

Fourteen different minority groups live in Sichuan: the Tibetans, Yi, Miao, Qiang, Hui, Tujia, Bouyei, Naxi, Bai, Zhuang, Dai, Mongolian, Manchu and Lisu. Their communities are predominantly in the remote mountainous regions of the north, west and southwest of the province. Many of their districts are being opened up by local authorities in order to attract foreign travellers and bring greater prosperity to the minorities. Many of these minorities can be found in other Chinese provinces. Of special interest are the Qiang people, who live in **Maowen County**, north of Chengdu. The Qiang are known for their small castle dwellings, which were built on hilltops. The castles are no longer inhabited, but they were made with such fine craftsmanship that they are still standing after 700 years. The Qiang people are thought to have been the first people to domesticate animals. To this day, they retain their distinctive dress of brilliant-coloured robes and cloth turbans decorated with tassels.

Yunnan

Yunnan Province is in the far southwest of China. It is of special interest to many travellers because of its large and diverse population of minority peoples. The 24 minorities of the province have lifestyles, religious customs and costumes more in common with their Tibetan and Southeast Asian neighbours than with the Han Chinese. However, it is less known that Yunnan is the original home of many of the plants and trees which we in the West associate with China. Camellias, rhododendrons and tea, to name but three, all trace their origins to the high-altitude plains of Yunnan.

Yunnan is mainly a high plateau, rising steeply towards the northwest and the Himalayan mountain chains. The average elevation of the Yunnan plateau is about 2,000 metres (5,000 feet), the lower-lying regions being in the south, on the borders of Burma, Laos and Vietnam. The high altitude of the plateau and the tropical location of the province give it a mild and warm climate throughout the year — ideal for travellers, even in the winter months. Three great rivers flow south through Yunnan from the northern border with Tibet: the Salween, Mekong and Yangzi. The Salween and Mekong continue on into Burma and Laos, but the Yangzi turns in an enormous loop to flow north into neighbouring Sichuan Province.

There are three great adventure destinations in Yunnan, whose paths — though well-trodden — are still unspoilt: Dali, Lijiang and Xishuangbanna. All three regions are renowned for their natural beauty of setting, historic sites and, of course, their minority peoples. Dali and Lijiang lie to the northwest of Kunming, the provincial capital, in the high plateau region of Yunnan. Xishuangbanna is in the south of the province, where the tropical jungles and riverside villages make the region a natural geographical and cultural extension of Southeast Asia.

The predominance of these three destinations should neither deter the independent traveller from including them on an itinerary, nor detract from the exploration of other, less well-documented regions. Yunnan, perhaps more than any other region except Tibet, appeals to the traveller for whom the journey itself is the adventure.

Dali

West of Kunming, 400 kilometres (250 miles) along the old Burma Road, stand the **Azure Mountains**, whose slopes rise in soft furrows above the lakeside plain of Dali. The richness of the plain's black soils, the marble deposits buried in the mountains, the waters of

Erhai Lake teeming with fish, and the ribbons of small streams which water the fields, all help to make Dali a prosperous region.

Dali is the name of the region and of the region's most important town. It was once the capital of the Nanzhao Kingdom, when Yunnan was ruled by its own tribal people and had little interference from the Chinese empire. At its height of power in the eighth and ninth centuries, the Nanzhao Kingdom sent armies to conquer parts of present-day Burma and Laos. In the tenth century, the kingdom was renamed Dali, but it was only brought under Chinese rule in the Yuan Dynasty.

The predominant ethnic group in Dali is the Bai, whose young women adorn themselves in bright red tunics, multicoloured aprons and intricate hats with tassels, braided ribbons and woven fabric. The older women also wear the red tunics, but their hats and pinafores are less colourful.

The perfect way to enjoy the local sights is by boat on Erhai Lake. CITS arranges boat trips or, with a little bargaining, you can hire boats on the waterfront. The western shore of the lake is flat, with cultivated fields, and the rocky eastern shore is interesting for its small, dry-stone-walled villages, with their moored fleets of boats. The lake's islands are worth exploring: **Golden Shuttle Island** for its Buddhist temple and pavilion (now being restored), and **Xiaoputuo Island** for its picturesque temple dedicated to the Bodhisattva of Mercy, Guan Yin.

The town of **Xiaguan** has a lakeside park with a botanical garden famous for its camellias, azaleas and magnolia. Also in Xiaguan is a **Tea Factory**, where Yunnanese tea is processed into 'bricks' for export to Tibet.

The more attractive stone-built town of Dali itself, with its whitewashed walls and grey tiled roofs, invites exploration. In the north of the city stand the **Three Pagodas**, the largest of which is striking in its unadorned simplicity of form. Close to the Three Pagodas is the **Marble Factory**, where the stone is cut and polished to reveal natural patterns resembling clouds and mountains. For those who love legends and a good walk, a visit to **Butterfly Spring** is recommended.

Outings from Dali

To the northeast of Dali rises **Chicken Foot Mountain** (Jizushan), so named because of its striated ridges which resemble a chicken's foot. Sadly, this Buddhist holy mountain was very badly damaged during the Cultural Revolution, and little remains of its former glories.

However, a seventh-century pagoda has survived, as have small sections of the old walnut forests which once supplied timber to the people of the plain. For those with time to spare, a visit from Dali to the renowned Buddhist caves of **Stone Bell Mountain** is highly recommended. The caves are in a remote area north of Dali, but they reward the traveller with carvings dating back to the Nanzhao Kingdom. Of special interest is a cave full of carvings which depict female genitalia. With special permission from CITS, visitors may plan a trip to the early iron suspension bridge called **Rainbow Bridge** (Jihongqiao). The Chinese people were the first in the world to build iron suspension bridges. The present structure of this one dates from 1475, but a similar bridge is known to have existed at this site for a thousand years or so.

Lijiang

Part of the delight in going to Lijiang lies in the journey itself. From Dali you have no choice but to go by road. As it climbs upwards into the mountainous region of northwest Yunnan, the road passes through forest glades of rhododendrons and azaleas, while ahead rise the stark, snow-tipped peaks of the **Jade Dragon Snow Range**.

Lijiang is the home of the Naxi people, who speak a language of the Tibeto-Burman group, and dress in black or deep blue. It is even said that their preference for black extends to keeping black goats! Other smaller minority groups live around Lijiang, including the Lisu, Pumi and Nuosu Yi. The Pumi are more brightly clad than the Naxi people, and the Lisu can only be seen by visiting the more remote districts close to the Nujiang (the Chinese name for the Salween River).

The Naxi were traditionally a matriarchal tribe, whose property was passed through the youngest female child; the men were in charge of music-making and child-rearing. In the present more liberal climate in China, the traditional Naxi orchestras are being revived. The Naxi are also notable for their shamanist traditions. Shamans (spirit mediums) were common in ancient China, and they still survive amongst the remote Siberian tribes, in Korea, and in Tibetan communities. The shamans, or *dongbas*, of the Naxi were responsible for transmitting the learning of the tribe into their own pictographic script — now being translated into Chinese in a major attempt to preserve the Naxi heritage.

Lijiang itself falls into clear parts: old and new. The old part is infinitely more interesting, with its pebbled paths, potted mountain plants and small restaurants serving *baba* — deep-fried wheat cake, offered with a variety of fillings. **Black Dragon Pool** is the principal attraction of the town, with its **Moon Embracing Pavilion** (a modern reconstruction, since the Ming pavilion was burnt down in 1950 by a drunken cadre and his mistress in a fit of suicidal romanticism — or vandalism). One of the adjacent buildings is used to house the **Dongba Cultural Research Institute**, and another, the **Dragon God Temple**, is a setting for flower and art shows. The **Five Phoenix Hall**, a piece of whimsical architectural bravura, was once part of the Fuguo Monastery which no longer exists.

The latter formed part of the Five Temples of Lijiang, which were reduced thus to four when two of the Fuguo buildings were transported to Black Dragon Pool. These temples were founded under the patronage of Mu Tian Wang, the 17th-century Naxi king. He was a religious man, instrumental in the growth of the Red Hat Sect of Buddhism in his domain. The **Jade Summit Temple** is famous for its setting in a pine forest, and for a camellia tree which in late February or early March blossoms in such profusion that locals claim it has 20,000 blossoms. A trip to the **Temple of Universal Benefaction** includes a pleasant walk up a mountain trail. In the temple, Tibetan *thankas* have survived destruction, as have a few Buddha images. A few miles south of the town, the **Peak of Culture Temple** was famous in its time as a meditation centre. Above the temple is a hole in the earth, near a sacred spring where monks would stay for over three years to engage in intense meditation. The fourth temple to survive, the **Zhiyunsi**, in the nearby town of Lashiba, has been converted into a school.

Outings from Lijiang

The mighty Yangzi River sweeps through the northern part of Yunnan, and can be seen at the dramatic **Tiger Leaping Gorge** as it roars through sheer walls, 4,000 metres (10,000 feet) below. At the point where the Yangzi makes its great turn northwards lies **Stone Drum Village (Shigu)**, so named because of a memorial stone drum commemorating a victory by Chinese and Naxi troops over a Tibetan force in 1548. **Shigu** is known in modern Chinese history as a crossing-place of the Red Army on its Long March. In 1936, the survivors of the Communist army reached Shigu, where the local citizens helped ferry them across the river to escape the Nationalist troops in pursuit.

The village of **Nguluko** is interesting for two reasons: it is typical of the smaller Naxi villages in its setting, and in the 1920s it was the home of the Austro-American explorer and botanist, Joseph Rock,

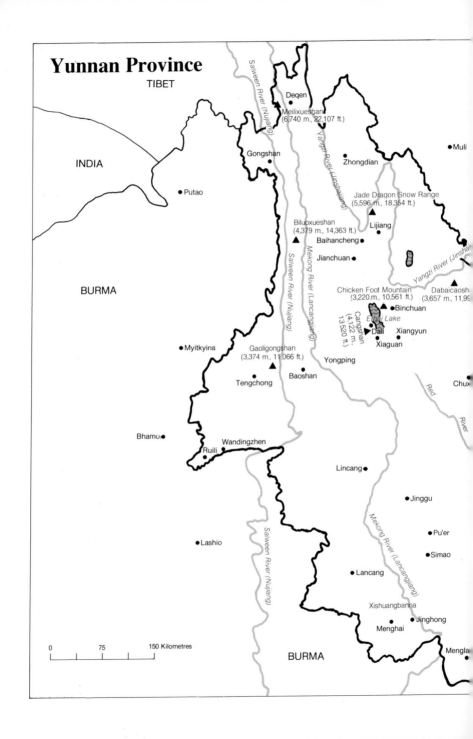

Yunnan Province

TIBET

INDIA

BURMA

Deqen

Meilixueshan
(6,740 m., 22,107 ft.)

Gongshan

Putao

Muli

Zhongdian

Jade Dragon Snow Range
(5,596 m., 18,354 ft.)

Biluoxueshan
(4,379 m., 14,363 ft.)

Lijiang

Baihancheng

Jianchuan

Chicken Foot Mountain
(3,220.m., 10,561 ft.)

Dabaicaosh
(3,657 m., 11,99

Binchuan

Cangshan
(4,122 m.,
13,520 ft.)

Erhai Lake

Dali

Xiangyun

Xiaguan

Myitkyina

Gaoligongshan
(3,374 m., 11,066 ft.)

Yongping

Chux

Baoshan

Tengchong

Bhamo

Wandingzhen

Ruili

Lincang

Jinggu

Pu'er

Simao

Lashio

Lancang

Xishuangbanna

Jinghong

Menghai

Mengla

BURMA

Salween River (Nujiang)

Yangzi River (Jinshajiang)

Salween River (Nujiang)

Mekong River (Lancangjiang)

Yangzi River (Jinsha

Salween River (Nujiang)

Red River

Mekong River (Lancangjiang)

0   75   150 Kilometres

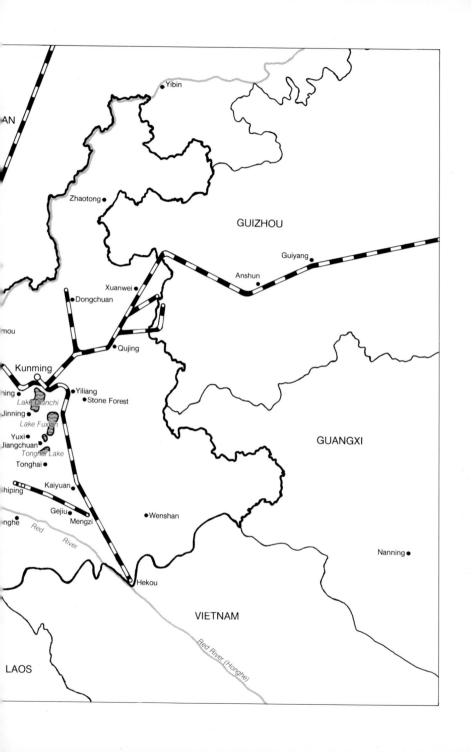

who pioneered research on Yunnan's flora and Naxi ethnology. His house can still be visited, and is now the home of one of his former muleteers. The ancient town of **Baoshan**, to the north of Lijiang, is a rare sight because it is one of China's few remaining walled towns.

Xishuangbanna

The region of Xishuangbanna lies in the south of Yunnan Province, on the very borders of Laos and Burma. It is especially worth a visit in April to see the famous Water Splashing Festival, when the Dai people celebrate a legendary triumph over a destructive demon by splashing each other — and any passer-by — with water. If you wish to visit the town during the festival, be sure to plan well ahead. It is difficult to find lodging.

The Dai people of Xishuangbanna share their Buddhist practices and festivals with their Burmese and Laotian neighbours. The Dai girls wear sarongs wrapped from the waist, and the temple and stupas closely resemble such architecture found in Southeast Asia. Chinese influence in this area is political rather than cultural. The tropical climate and diseases have always made it an unattractive place for Chinese settlers, and in fact it is only in recent times that malaria and cholera have been brought under control.

The capital is **Jinghong**, an unassuming city which comes to life only on market days. The **Tropical Crops Research Institute** in the western district of the city is often visited. Beyond Jinghong and close to the Mekong River are many interesting Dai villages built on stilts. Stilt houses are common throughout Southeast Asia as an answer to the problem of the river floods. The roofs of the Dai houses are similar to the double-eaved Malay and Thai houses, designed for maximum ventilation and to protect against the heavy tropical rains.

At the town of **Menghai**, west of Jinghong, tea growing and processing is the main industry. The tea grown is the famous Pu Er variety. At nearby **Mengzhe**, also an area of tea plantations, is the **Manlei Great Buddha Pagoda**.

Visitors can take a river journey on the Mekong from Jinghong. The boat pushes southward on the yellow back of the river and stops at the farm known as **Olive Plain**, where travellers can rest and take walks in the surrounding villages.

Another fine expedition is follow the road from Jinghong to the Burmese border. At Damenglong, there is the **Manguanglong Monastery**, the spires of its various pagodas resembling tapering tips and with lotiform decoration in the Burmese style.

The Yangzi River

The Yangzi River offers adventure-travellers many kinds of expeditions. The river can be travelled by ship or luxury cruiseliner for the 2,500 kilometres (1,500 miles) between Chongqing and Shanghai. There are also sidetrips to small riverside towns and a boat ride up the Daning River. But for those keen to see the remote upper reaches of the Yangzi — impossible to navigate due to its turbulent course through mountain meadows and narrow gorges — overland expeditions to northern Yunnan, Tibet, and even as far as the river's source in Qinghai, are possible.

The Yangzi, like the Great Wall or the Yellow River, often serves as a symbol of the suffering of the Chinese people. Over the centuries, floods have brought harvests of despair to the farmers who lived alongside the lower reaches of the river. Raised embankments and flood walls are testimony to their struggle to control the river. However, the present government has made a major effort to keep the Yangzi safe for navigation, and has undertaken major hydraulic schemes to keep the waters in check. In addition, massive hydro-electric power projects will harness the Yangzi's energy to generate electricity for a power-hungry economy. This is all changing the face of the river. The rapids of the Three Gorges are still an unpredictable force, but they are no longer so threatening since Chinese troops dynamited most of the major obstacles in the 1950s. The Gezhouba Dam at Yichang has broken the river's flow, and the projected Three Gorges Dam, which is still on the drawing-board (and looks set to stay there), could flood thousands of hectares of farmland, causing whole villages and towns to disappear.

Yet the 'taming' of the Yangzi has not taken away the sense of adventure. In the last few years, the Chinese government has lifted more and more restrictions on travel to small towns along the river's course. A voyage up or down the Yangzi now offers a glimpse of river communities previously unknown to the foreign traveller.

However, for all its sidetrips and diversions, the river itself is the heart of the Yangzi expedition. Few travellers can fail to be impressed by the dawn voyage through the towering walls of the Three Gorges, or the excitement of turning out of the mouth of the river into the hectic waterway of Shanghai's Huangpu Creek. But the river has its quieter moments: the evening flight homeward of geese across the bows of the ship, a glimpse of a riverside pagoda, the passing of small craft with their lamps lit at night, or the thick flow of the river as it pushes past the shoreside fields of young rice.

With a little imagination, the history of the river can be brought to life, too — the epic battles of the Three Kingdoms, Kublai Khan crossing the river with his navy on his way to conquer the Song empire of the south, and more recently, the tea clippers of the 19th century which raced from Hankou to London with the first of the season's tea.

The River Journey

Yangzi travellers can choose the longer journey upstream, embarking at Shanghai or Wuhan, or the downstream trip embarking at Chongqing. Most tour groups are taken along the Yangzi in cruiseliners, making the most of sidetrips to riverside towns. However, independent travellers usually take the regular East is Red steamers, with a change of boat at Wuhan. The steamers do not allow the visitor to stop off at many of the smaller places along the way, so an organized tour is — at the moment — the best way to see the river.

Chongqing is the embarkation point for the journey downstream. The city is one of southwest China's major industrial centres, and it served as the capital of China during the Japanese occupation in the Second World War. The city's famous foggy weather saved it from being destroyed by Japanese bombers. Chongqing's history stretches

back to the fourth century BC, when it was known as Yuzhou. At the confluence of the Yangzi and Jialing River, it was a settlement of strategic importance, serving as the capital of the ancient state of Ba during the Zhou Dynasty. The men of Ba were renowned as great warriors and were buried in boat-shaped coffins, perched on river cliff ledges. Some of these strange coffins can be seen in the **Chongqing Museum**.

The modern name of Chongqing, which means 'Double Celebration', dates from the Song Dynasty, when a Song prince who had resided in Yuzhou became emperor. To celebrate his enthronement, he renamed his city Chongqing.

Set on a promontory on the north bank of the Yangzi, the city has outgrown its original site and spilled over to the adjacent banks of the Yangzi and Jialing. Cable cars and bridges connect the newer districts of Chongqing with the older cliff-side city centre. Most visitors are taken to **Pipa Hill** at dusk to view the city. It is an attractive sight of steep lamplit streets sweeping down to the dark waters of the river below. Tour itineraries include visits to the **Red Rock Villa** and the **Cassia Garden**, which were Communist head-quarters during the 1930s and 1940s. However, escape the city if you can and travel out to the **Southern** or **Northern Hot Springs** to bathe, visit temples, and wander through gardens with lotus and fish ponds.

Nearby **Fengdu** was traditionally known by its nickname of 'Ghost City' and it has a temple dedicated to the King of the Underworld. This strange association dates back to the Han Dynasty, when two scholar recluses who lived in the town were believed to have achieved immortality. The combination of their names results in the title 'King of the Underworld'!

Fuling was the site of the royal tombs of the fourth-century state of Ba (it was from here that many of the boat-shaped coffins, now in the Chongqing Museum, were excavated). The most important archaeological treasure in Fuling is a set of carvings along the rocky shore of the Yangzi, which are only exposed when the river drops to a very low level. There are stone inscriptions surrounded by carved fish, giving information on ancient hydrology and cosmology.

The name of **Shibaozhai** means 'Precious Stone Fortress'; the precious stone in question is a 30-metre-high (100-foot) rock which juts into the air. This rock is said to resemble a stone seal. (Seals in traditional China were carved at the base and used as a form of official signature.) In the Qing Dynasty, a temple was built on top of the rock. Originally, you could only visit the temple by climbing up an iron chain, but in the late 19th century a nine-storey wooden pagoda was built next to the rock so that the ascent could be made by staircase. An extra three storeys were added this century, and now the 12-storey red pagoda rises alongside the rock to the base of the temple. The legend of the precious stone tells of a hole in the rock, through which flowed a ceaseless supply of rice which was used to feed the monks of the temple. A greedy monk thought that he could make his fortune by enlarging the hole to get more rice, but he was punished when the miracle of the rice flow ceased the moment the hole was made bigger.

Shibaozhai is one of the most attractive small towns along the Yangzi because much of its traditional architecture still remains and the views over the wooded slopes of the river cliffs have not been spoilt by industrial development.

Wanxian is the overnight stop for the East is Red steamers before they negotiate the Three Gorges by morning light. The city is an ancient river port and once had a thriving junk-building industry. River passengers enjoy the stopover here because of the city's night market, which sells delicious, locally grown citrus fruits and a wide selection of bamboo and rattan handicrafts. On the outskirts of the town is **Taibai Rock**, where the Tang Dynasty poet, Li Bai (Li Po) is said to have stayed. The rock face around the memorial pavilion to the poet is covered with stone inscriptions, some of which date back to the Tang Dynasty.

Facing south over the river, the town of **Yunyang** is famous in stories from the Three Kingdoms period (220−265). This period in Chinese history has much of the romance which the English associate with the tales of King Arthur, except that there is a firmer historical background for the Chinese tales. In Yunyang it is said that General Zhang Fei of the Kingdom of Shu (the kingdom which covered most of present-day Sichuan) was assassinated. In his honour, the **Zhangwang Temple** was built, which still stands today. Stone carvings from the fifth and sixth centuries have been housed in the temple, which has a tranquil setting amidst gardens and rock pools.

Fengjie guards the western entrance of the Three Gorges, and because of its splendid scenery it became the temporary home of many great Chinese poets. The city is much celebrated in verse. It was here that Liu Bei, the King of Shu, died in despair after his armies were routed by the forces of Wu. The famous general of the state of Shu, Zhuge Liang, trained his troops in military strategy in the fields around Fengjie. The city has an attractive setting, and parts of its Ming-Dynasty ramparts as well as one city gate are still intact. It has open-air markets, where the varied produce of the local countryside is sold. Local teahouses also prosper in this market town.

Baidicheng — or White Emperor City — is reached by ferry from Fengjie. It offers splendid views into the mouth of the Qutang Gorge, and has a temple which was originally dedicated to the mythical White Emperor. In the Ming Dynasty, the temple was re-dedicated to General Zhuge Liang. The Forest of Steles Hall in this temple has several rare stone carvings. The Bamboo Leaf Poem Tablet is one of only three in China. The carving dates from the Qing Dynasty, and the characters of the poem are engraved in the form of three bamboo branches.

The Three Gorges

The Three Gorges of the Yangzi extend for 200 kilometres (125 miles) of the river's course, and span the provincial boundary of Sichuan and Hubei. The first gorge on the downstream voyage is the Qutang. It is the shortest gorge, but visually the most dramatic. The second, the Wu (Sorceress) Gorge, has enchanting scenery of forest-clad slopes rising into strangely formed mountain peaks. The final gorge, the Xiling, is the longest of the three, enclosing banks of shoals and rapids which turn the muddy river to a coffee-like froth.

The gorges push the river into a funnel of furious water, which in places has a velocity of 80,000 cubic metres (105,000 cubic yards) a second. The river is squeezed to a width of less than 100 metres (330 feet) at some points, and the water flow can reach 25 kilometres (15 miles) an hour. In the small valleys which extend like fingers from the gorges, farmers plant rice, maize, sweet potatoes and oranges, and collect lacquer sap and medicinal herbs from the hillsides.

The most spectacular of the gorges, the **Qutang Gorge**, was known to foreigners in the last century as 'The Windbox'. The name seems inappropriate on a fine day with a light mist hanging between towering cliffs, which themselves soar in deep shadow to over 1,200 metres (4,000 feet) either side of the river. Yet in a storm, with a high water level, the gorge was impossible to navigate, and many lost their lives while travelling through the Qutang. Look out for the Meng Liang stairway, a strange rock-face which stops half-way up the river cliff. High on the slopes of the rock-face were found some of the 2,000-year-old coffins from the state of Ba, now on exhibit in the Chongqing Museum.

Passengers on the cruiseliners can disembark at **Wushan** and transfer to small motorboats for a river journey through the Three Lesser Gorges of the Daning River. The Daning is a tributary of the Yangzi which rises in Shaanxi Province, flowing south into the Yangzi. The Three Gorges of the Daning are known as the Dragon

Gate, the Misty Gorge and the Vivid Green Gorge. The boats motor upstream for 50 kilometres (30 miles) through the tranquil scenery of verdant river cliffs and terraced fields, before turning back to course downstream with the current. In the quieter reaches of the gorges, golden-haired monkeys still roam in chattering bands. The region is famous for rare medicinal herbs.

The twelve peaks of **Wu Gorge** all have poetic names. They include Fir Tree Cone Peak, the Gathered Immortals Peak, and the Assembled Cranes Peak. The Chinese have a great love of weaving legends around strange natural phenomena, and these gorges and mountains are therefore among their best-loved landscapes. The most renowned peak in this sense is **Goddess Peak**, which is said to resemble the figure of a maiden kneeling in front of a pillar. Legend has it that the young goddess was the daughter of the Queen Mother of the West, who fell in love with this lonely spot and made her home here. Yet the most historic site in the Wu Gorge lies at the foot of the Gathered Immortals Peak. It is known as the **Kong Ming Tablet**, and has carved inscriptions in the calligraphy of General Zhuge Liang. They are large enough to be seen from the boat as it moves on to the small town of **Peishi**, which marks the border between the provinces of Sichuan and Hubei.

Xiling Gorge, the next on the river, runs for 75 kilometres (45 miles) through slopes planted with orange groves. The gorge is divided into seven smaller gorges, the most famous of which are the Gorge of the Sword and the Book on the Art of War, the Gorge of the Ox's Liver and Horse's Lung, the Gorge of the Yellow Ox, and the Gorge of Shadow Play. The shoals and rapids within Xiling were the most treacherous of all obstacles in the Three Gorges. Until the 1950s, boats were hauled over them by trackers, whose back-breaking job would guarantee them an exceedingly short lifespan. A folk song about the Blue Shoal has the following words: 'May the gods protect us as we sail through the Blue Shoal. If the Dragon King gets angry, then both men and boats are finished.' The Blue Shoal, like all other river obstacles, was dynamited in the 1950s to make it safe for navigation.

Just beyond the Three Gorges, the flow of the river is broken by the 70-metre-high (230-foot) barrier of the Gezhouba Dam. The dam harnesses the energy of the Yangzi's current, and the projected annual output of the dam is 138 billion Kwh. Boats have to pass through one of the three shiplocks on either side of the dam.

Yichang marks the end of the upper reaches of the Yangzi and the beginning of the broader, middle reaches of the river. The city was an important river port, where goods were unloaded from the

The Yangzi River

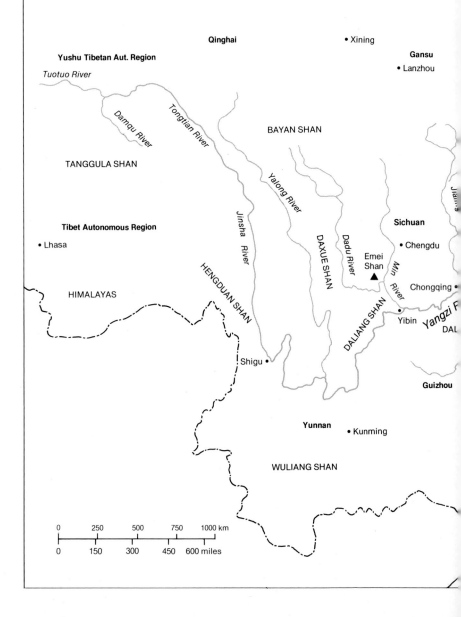

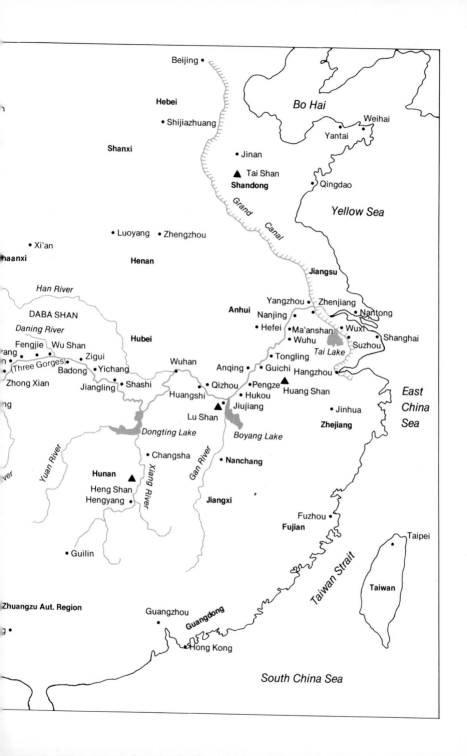

larger ships used further downstream, or from the smaller ships which travelled upstream through the gorges. West of the city there is a small cave, which is famous for its Tang and Song inscriptions of poetry. It is known as the **Three Travellers Cave**, after three Tang-Dynasty poets who first met there. The hill above the cave is an excellent place to go to enjoy a view of the eastern entrance of the Xiling Gorge. Yichang also marks the site of the legendary Yiling Battle between the Three Kingdom States of Shu and Wu. The Wu army was smaller and weaker, but it used fire to destroy the camps of the Shu army. The King of Shu, Liu Bei, was bitterly disappointed after this battle and died soon afterwards in Fengjie. The nearby town of **Shashi** is known for its riverside **Pagoda of Longevity**, built in the reign of the Qing Emperor Qianlong.

South of the Yangzi lies **Dongting Lake**, once China's largest freshwater lake. However, silting and land reclamation have reduced its size, and now it ranks second. Legends about Dongting abound. One Tang-Dynasty story has the lake as the home of the King of the Dragons. **Junshan Island**, within the lake, is worth visiting to see the Silver Needle Tea; the tea was once sent to the emperor as part of the yearly tribute.

The Lower River

The triple city of **Wuhan**, which spans the confluence of the rivers Han and Yangzi, is for many travellers the end or the beginning of their river cruise. The city has always been the Yangzi's major inland river port, since it marked the furthest point to which the seagoing vessels could sail. In the last century, the city became a treaty port and grew rich on the tea trade which ran out of **Hankou** (one of the three connected cities).

Hankou was the city with the foreign concessions, and to this day has remained the commercial centre of Wuhan. It looks less like a Chinese city than the two other cities of **Hanyang** and **Wuchang.** In Hanyang there are two famous sights — the **Lute Pavilion** and the Buddhist **Guiyuan Monastery**. The Lute Pavilion comprises a series of terraces and pavilions set amidst attractive gardens. It lives up to its musical name, since it is now a popular place with elderly music lovers who gather here for open-air performances. The Guiyuan Monastery was founded in the Qing Dynasty and became an important centre for Chan (Zen) Buddhist scholarship. The monastery has a collection of 500 carved and gilded *luohans* (Buddhist disciples), which are considered works of great craftsmanship. Attached to the monastery is a vegetarian restaurant.

Chinese Painting

Chinese painting has a long and eminent history, being considered the ultimate accomplishment of the Chinese scholar. However, there are two traditions of Chinese painting — the scholar and the professional/artisan. Both these traditions have overlapped and influenced each other, but in general the scholar tradition has retained the greatest prestige.

The development of the scholar tradition becomes clear with the advent of the Tang Dynasty, even though few of the surviving Tang paintings are original. They are mainly copies made in later centuries. Indeed, copying was considered an important part of the practical study of painting, and there is a long tradition in Chinese painting — as in the other arts — of learning from past masters.

By the Song Dynasty — considered by many to be the apogee of Chinese landscape painting — there was an established tradition of painting styles and repertoires as well as a rich vocabulary of symbols and emblems used as an inner language in the paintings. The main categories of subject matter evolved into four classes — landscape, people and objects, birds and flowers, grass and insects. Of the four, the most esteemed was that of landscape. In the Northern Song Dynasty, masters such as Li Cheng, Fan Kuan, Guo Xi and Xu Daoning created magical, monumental landscapes and mists in which, if humans had a place at all, it was a minor one.

It is in these classic landscapes that the fundamental difference between Western and Chinese painting can be located: perspective. After Giotto's work in 13th-century Italy, Western painting developed with a single fixed perspective. However, Chinese painters, although they were aware of perspective, rejected the device of a single disappearing point, creating instead landscapes in which the viewer *becomes* the traveller within the painting. The problems which such a technique creates are solved by the inventive use of space and, giving the picture shifting layers of perspective. Expanses of mist and water convey subtle shifts of vision. As you view a hanging scroll, your eye moves upwards to the summit of the mountains in a series of scene-changes. With a horizontal scroll — traditionally viewed an arm's length at a time — the same effect is achieved from right to left.

The second major difference between Western and Chinese art lies in the medium itself. Most Western masterpieces are worked in oil. Chinese paintings are worked in black ink on silk or absorbent paper, sometimes using mineral colours — and those sparingly. The two traditional colours of Chinese painting are blue and green. Since the artist chose to capture the spirit or essence of his subject, rather than recreate it in loving detail, the use of black ink in a variety of tones and strokes has always been much more evocative than definitive in intention. Using brush and ink leaves no room for error. Once the brush is on the paper, it must be moved with strength and fluency if the painting is not to be rendered lifeless. Unlike the artist in oils, the Chinese painter has no chance to change or paint over his initial strokes. The importance of the brushstroke meant, in turn, that the development of the Chinese artist was intimately linked to that of the calligrapher. The scholar painter aimed to achieve an easy, inspired fluency of style which was unerring. To some extent, this explains why the noted poet and calligrapher of the Song Dynasty, Su Dongpo, saw the arts of poetry, painting and calligraphy as indivisible. In Chinese art, part of the beauty of the painting lies in the poem which the artist selects to write at the side of his work, as well as the style in which he decides to write it. Manuals on brushwork were compiled so that young artists could admire and copy the past masters, learning for example how they painted trees in winter or spring and precisely which brushstrokes they used.

Nature was the major preoccupation of the Chinese scholar artist. He made choices of subject in harmony with his own mood and the season of the year. Indeed, he believed that nothing could be painted without an understanding of the essential character of nature. Thus, landscape painting for him was less a celebration of the individuality of a particular place than an evocation of the spirit of *all* landscapes, captured in one particular scene at one particular season.

In his treatment of birds, animals and flowers, the Chinese painter also had little in common with his Western counterparts. The *nature morte* (still-life) of European painting would have been distasteful to him. The Chinese tradition is to show animals and flowers alive in their natural setting. Much attention is paid to detail here, and the artist is expected to depict how the plant or tree changes with the seasons, how an animal or bird moves and stands. This does not mean that Chinese renderings of flora and fauna are realistic. Rather, they are 'true' to the nature of the subject.

This also applies to the inner vocabulary of the Chinese painting. These emblems and symbols are an important part of the artist's intent. The four favourite subjects of the scholar painter are bamboo, plum, chrysanthemum and orchid, all of which reflect the qualities which the scholar strives to achieve in his own conduct. The bamboo bends but is not broken. The plum blossoms in winter, rising above adverse conditions, as does the chrysanthemum, while the orchid represents fragrance and elegance of form. The scholars of the Ming and Qing Dynasties turned these four subjects into a veritable fashion.

Wuchang, on the south bank of the Yangzi, is important in
Chinese revolutionary history. It was here that the military uprising
started, which was ultimately to topple the Qing Dynasty and bring
about the founding of the Chinese Republic. Visitors can see the
Headquarters of the 1911 Revolution, which is known locally as the
Red House. A statue of Dr Sun Yat-sen stands outside the building.
Another place of special interest in Wuchang is the **Hubei Provincial
Museum**, which houses artefacts excavated from the Warring States
period tomb of the Marquis of Zeng. An impressive collection of 65
bronze chime bells forms part of the tomb's treasures.

After the Yangzi crosses the provincial boundary to flow through
Jiangxi, the boat reaches **Jiujiang**. Once an important river port for
the tea trade, Jiujiang now thrives on its cotton industry. The city
lies just west of **Boyang Lake**. The lake is one of China's best-known
nature reserves, a wintering ground for rare white- and red-crested
cranes, as well as storks and wildfowl. Jiujiang is the stopping-off
point for visits to the mountain resort of **Lushan**. Lushan is attractive
in spring, when the azaleas are in flower, but it receives a heavy
swell of visitors in the summer months, when the mountains offer a
cool retreat from the baking temperatures of the Yangzi plain.

Close to Jiujiang is **Stone Bell Hill**, where Boyang Lake empties
into the Yangzi River and waters of different colours flow together,
mixing like ceramic slip. The hill has been a tourist attraction since
the Han Dynasty, mainly because of its unsolved mystery — there is
a bell-like sound within the hill, which some people believe is caused
by flowing water. In the Song Dynasty, the poet Su Dongpo was so
intrigued by the hill that he came here three times.

Xiaogushan is a small riverine island which, through silting, has
now become part of the north bank of the river. Legend tells of a
maiden, Xiaogu Niang Niang, who when fleeing with her lover on a
flying umbrella, dropped her slipper into the river. The slipper
miraculously turned into an island. The girl and her lover fell from
the sky and became mountains divided by the river. There is a
temple on the island dedicated to Xiaogu Niang Niang, which is
visited by infertile women who come in the hope of bearing a child.
Nearby, again on the north bank, in Anhui Province, is the famous
Ming **Zhenfeng Pagoda** of Anqing.

For river travellers, **Wuhu** is the stopping-off point for the
mountains of Huangshan and Jiuhuashan (see pages 227 and 233).
Within the town itself is Zhe Hill, which gives an excellent view over
the Yangzi from the **Zheshan Pagoda**, built in the Song Dynasty.
Three of Wuhu's famous temples were destroyed in the Second
World War, but the surviving **Guangji Temple**, at the foot of Zhe

Hill, has recently been renovated and has a well-known collection of Buddhist paintings depicting the horrors of hell. The monastery was once the retreat of the Tang Emperor Dezong, who became a Buddhist recluse. The **Zhongjiang Pagoda**, which means 'mid-river' pagoda, was built at the confluence of the Qingyi and Yangzi Rivers. The pagoda served as a lighthouse until this century. The traditional crafts of Wuhu are wrought-iron pictures and old-fashioned, large-handled scissors.

For **Nanjing**, see pages 71−9.

Zhenjiang was a city of great strategic importance in the Three Kingdoms period and it served as the capital of the state of Wu. It is here that the Grand Canal intersects the Yangzi, thus making Zhenjiang an important trading centre. The hills around the city were the source of inspiration for many painters of the Southern Song school. In the middle of the river at Zhenjiang rises **Jiao Hill**, where the Song-Dynasty painter Mi Fei, and the poet Lu You, had stone inscriptions carved in their own calligraphy. The nearby **Jin Hill** was once a riverine island, but silting has joined it to the southern bank of the river. The monastery of Jin Hill is still an important place of Buddhist pilgrimage. To the northeast of the city lies **Beigu Hill**, considered to be the most beautiful of Zhenjiang's hills. It appears in many of the stories in the *Romance of the Three Kingdoms* (see Recommended Reading at end of book).

To the north of the Yangzi, on the Grand Canal itself, lies the city of **Yangzhou**, once one of the wealthiest of Chinese cities. Its merchants thrived on the salt trade, which was an imperial monopoly, and the city's prosperity led to it becoming a centre for the arts. Indeed, Yangzhou has retained its traditional charms. One of the most delightful ways to pass your time here is to stroll through the lanes which thread between the city's canals. The buildings around the **Slim West Lake** are some of the finest, with their simple whitewashed walls and contrasting dark-grey tiled roofs, which sweep up into flying eaves. A large community of Arab traders resided in the city in the Yuan Dynasty, and the city mosque, the **Xianhe Si**, dates from the 13th century. Puhaddin, who was the 16th-generation descendant of Mohammed, came to China in the mid-13th century and was buried in Yangzhou. In the **Museum** there is a good collection of the works of the Eight Eccentric Painters of Yangzhou, who lived in the 18th century. Unlike most scholar-painters of the time, who regarded painting as a purely academic pursuit, these painters were so eccentric that they actually made their living from the sale of their works to the wealthy merchants of Yangzhou.

For **Shanghai**, see pages 112−9.

Fujian

The coastal province of Fujian in southeast China is one of the areas least explored by foreign visitors. Yet the province offers some of the best sightseeing, historic sites and local cuisine found anywhere in China, with the bonus of a warm, sub-tropical climate which makes winter visits an attractive option. The four main cities of Fujian are the capital Fuzhou, Xiamen (Amoy), Quanzhou and Zhangzhou. In the northern mountains of the province is the scenic area known as the Wuyi Mountains.

Fujian has a long indented coastline backed by steep and rugged mountains where much of the soil is too poor for farming. The Fujianese have traditionally earned their living from the sea, and by growing fruit and vegetables. In the 19th and early 20th centuries, the land tenure system forced many poorer peasants to emigrate. The overseas Fujianese community is second only to that of the Cantonese. Most overseas Chinese from Fujian settled in Southeast Asia, with a large proportion in the Philippines. Many Taiwanese are originally from Fujian, and the dialects spoken either side of the Taiwan Straits (Taiwan lies only 160 kilometres — 100 miles — away from Fujian) are mutually intelligible. There is growing trade between Fujian and Taiwan, which is encouraged on the mainland side but illegal in Taiwan. Rare medicinal herbs and fungi collected in the mountains of Fujian have a ready market in Taiwan, while the People's Republic has a voracious appetite for Made in Taiwan consumer goods (which can be anything from fashion clothes to telescopic umbrellas). The rewards seem to outweigh the risks in this semi-clandestine trade.

Fujian has a long history of trade with the outside world, and the city of Quanzhou had a large foreign population during the Tang and Yuan Dynasties. Most of the foreign traders who came to the shores of Fujian were Arabs. Their descendants, and their converts' descendants, still live in distinct Muslim communities throughout the province. Many of the mountain people of Fujian are not Han Chinese. One of the largest minority communities is the She people. Young people from the She villages can often be seen working in the cities in order to save enough money to get married. The girls wear headdresses of bright scarves over a frame shaped like a coathanger without the hook. They are very shy and never seem to mix with the local Chinese or wish to be photographed.

There are some wonderful off-the-beaten-track places to visit in Fujian, if you are willing to take local buses and wander at will. If you are visiting in the warmer months, the coast has some lovely golden sand beaches. (A Welsh development agency wants to turn one of them into a holiday resort as a joint-venture.) Local cooking is good. There are fresh vegetables throughout the year and lots of delicious seafood. The smaller hotels and guesthouses are reasonably clean and efficient. This is probably because the province sees many overseas Chinese tourists, who come back to visit their ancestral villages. However, if you choose to explore alone, watch out for the bus-drivers of Fujian. On one minibus ride I took, the driver seemed to be intent on running over as many chickens in as short a space of time as possible. If in doubt, travel with an organized tour coach — it may save on tranquillizers.

Fuzhou

The provincial capital of Fuzhou has a glorious setting on the banks of the Min River, against a backdrop of mountains. The city has grown up around three hills — Yushan, Gushan and Wushan — which are areas of scenic interest, with numerous pavilions, temples and museums. The city is famous for its lacquerware and puppet troupe, but other reasons to visit the city are its excellent seafood restaurants, various craft factories, and excursions to the numerous old temples around the city.

Yushan lies in a striking location at the mouth of the Min River and, although small (the hill is only 60 metres — 200 feet — high), it has three temples, several pavilions and the famous **White and Black Pagodas**, which are the landmarks of the city. You will also find the **Fuzhou Antique Shop** on Yushan.

On the eastern outskirts of Fuzhou, you will also find **Drum Mountain** (Gushan), one of the scenic resorts of the city. Its best known temple is the **Bubbling Spring Temple**, which is reached by walking up a stone stairway lined with flowering shrubs. The temple is a major religious centre, with a community of several hundred monks.

West of Yushan lies the small hill of **Wushan**. The hill was originally a place of Daoist retreat. It has many small pavilions sited to offer views over the countryside and river estuary. There are several stone carvings on the hillside, the most remarkable of which is an image of Buddha on the southeast slope.

The city also has two famous temples which have lovely settings. The **Gold Mountain Temple**, outside the city on an island in the middle of the Wulong River, is reached by raft. The **Xichan Temple** (close to Fuzhou University) is a lively city temple, which has been restored by donations from overseas Chinese. A visit to the **Snow Peak Temple** in the hills beyond Fuzhou offers a chance to enjoy a drive through the countryside and walks in the hills.

Quanzhou

South of Fuzhou, on the banks of the Jin River, lies the ancient port city of Quanzhou. Its quiet, prosperous air belies its distinguished history as China's first port in the Song and Yuan Dynasties. Its harbour silted up in the Ming Dynasty, and it is now of minor importance, but nonetheless it remains the commercial centre for the surrounding farmlands.

As a reminder of Quanzhou's history as a great international port, the large Muslim community flourishes. From the Tang to the Yuan Dynasties, Arab merchants traded and settled in Quanzhou, leaving behind a thriving community of Muslims. The **Grand Mosque** is a short walk from the Overseas Chinese Hotel. The mosque was built in the first years of the 11th century and continues to be an active centre of worship. Just to the east of the city is **Lingshan** (Ling Hill), which is the burial site of two Muslim missionaries who came to the city in the Tang Dynasty. In the old quarter, to the northwest of the city, the **Kaiyuan Temple** is one of the most famous in the region. It was founded in the Tang Dynasty and has some fine examples of Buddhist architecture and statuary dating from the Song Dynasty. To the east is the **Ancient Boat Exhibition**, the remains of a Song-Dynasty seagoing ship excavated downstream of the city and now housed in this hall. To the north, there is a fine stone bridge over the Luoyang River, called — unsurprisingly — **Luoyang Bridge**. It dates from the Song Dynasty and is now only open to pedestrians.

Zhangzhou

Like Quanzhou, Zhangzhou was also a major port city, until it was eclipsed by the nearby port of Xiamen when its tidal creek silted up. Zhangzhou now serves as a market for the farmers of the rich, fertile plain of the Jiulong River. The area is famous for its tropical fruits, such as pineapples, bananas, lychees and *longyans* (Dragon's Eyes), as well as for the popular Chinese New Year flower, the narcissus, which is grown for special effect in water. The city is also renowned for its art galleries, craft factories and local opera troupes, which often give open-air performances.

In the south of the city lies **Nanshan Temple**, an important Buddhist monastery which runs a vegetarian restaurant open to the public. One of the monastery's treasures is a milk-white jade Buddha, which was brought to China from Burma.

Seven kilometres (four miles) south of the city is the **Hundred Flower Village**, a botanical garden which was started in the Ming

Dynasty. It is a wonderful place to come and enjoy flowers and a display of *pen jing* (miniature trees, usually known by the Japanese name of *bonsai*). In the summer, the lychee season can be enjoyed with a visit to the lychee orchards, which are a few kilometres east of the garden.

Xiamen

On the southern coast of Fujian, the thriving commercial city and port of Xiamen is one of the success stories of China's current economic reform programme. Because of its beautiful setting, on an island linked to the mainland by a narrow causeway, no heavy industry has been allowed in the city, and it has a pleasant pollution-free atmosphere. Its rocky shores face several offshore islands on the eastern side, one of which — **Gulangyu** — is the city's own resort, with old villas and car-free lanes. Another close-lying island, **Quemoy**, is held by Nationalist troops of the government of Taiwan.

The inevitably sensitive coastal defences meant that Xiamen was off-limits to foreign tourists until the early 1980s. The city is now open as a Special Economic Zone, and it has a growing electronics industry as well as a port with good facilities for seagoing vessels. An extended runway has even been constructed at Xiamen Airport to allow Jumbo jets to land.

The lovely island of Gulangyu has golden sand beaches for swimming in warmer months, narrow lanes full of hawker stalls, and the Lotus Flower Monastery, known locally as the **Sunlight Monastery**. It stands on the high point of the island called **Sunlight Rock**, which, climbed at dawn, gives an excellent view of the sunrise over the sea. The island has four churches, and every Christmas Eve a carol service is held on the island.

East of Xiamen's city centre, the Buddhist **Nanputuo Monastery** rises in terraces and courtyards against the slopes of Wulao Mountain. The monastery has one of China's few Buddhism schools, and runs an excellent vegetarian restaurant in a side courtyard of the temple.

Wuyi Mountains

Finally, in the northwest of the province, is the marvellous resort area of the Wuyi Mountains. The Chinese have been keen mountain visitors for centuries, and this area has been popular since the second century BC. A trip to these mountains takes you through scenery as evocative as the landscapes of Guilin. Most visitors enjoy a trip on

the **Nine Twist Stream**. The trip is a gentle punting expedition past sheer cliffs, strange rock formations and flowery river banks. Because of the region's great beauty, it has received many famous visitors over the centuries, and the various stone inscriptions by the side of the river have been carved in the calligraphy of famous painters, poets and scholars. Of special interest is the exhibition of 3,000-year-old boat-shaped coffins which were found on ledges high up on the river cliffs.

Mountains

Mountain-climbing was a traditional pastime in ancient China. Emperors went to mountains to make sacrifices to heaven and the deities. Scholars went to draw inspiration for poetry and painting. Mystics went to become Buddhist monks or Daoist hermits. Ordinary people went to pray and worship. Thus mountain-climbing in China was more than a sport. It was a popular religious and cultural activity. This partly explains why Chinese mountains are so well laid-out with walking trails, stone markers, hermitages, monasteries, guesthouses and tea pavilions.

The Chinese have divided their mountains between Daoist and Buddhist peaks. Daoists were philosophers with an interest in alchemy, herbal medicine and the general world of nature. They regarded the pursuit of immortality and oneness with the cosmos as a way of life. The common people, however, also established and worshipped a pantheon of Daoist deities. The Buddhists believed that the path to enlightenment lay in good works, a knowledge of the Buddhist scriptures, and in meditation far from the everyday world. Both Daoists and Buddhists therefore saw mountains as a natural refuge. In early times, the religious affiliation of a mountain was not so clearly defined — various religious communities often shared the same mountain. Today, however, the divisions are clear. The four Buddhist mountains are Emeishan in Sichuan, Wutaishan in Shanxi, Putuoshan off the coast of Zhejiang, and Jiuhuashan in Anhui Province. The five Daoist mountains are Taishan in Shandong Province, Huashan in Shaanxi, Northern Hengshan in Shanxi, Southern Hengshan in Hunan and Songshan in Henan. Huangshan in Anhui Province belongs to neither category, and is not a holy mountain.

The Southern and Northern Heng mountains and Mount Song have not been included here, since they are not as yet easily accessible to foreign travellers. All of the mountains described here are open to foreign visitors, but some may still require special permits, so travellers should check in advance with their travel agent or with the nearest branch of CITS. Few travellers would plan to scale all the peaks of China's mountains, but try to include a trip to at least one or two of them as part of a regional tour. Some more enterprising international travel companies now include mountain trips as part of their itinerary.

Taishan

Taishan (Mount Tai) rises above the folded landscape of the Shandong Peninsula in northeast China. As early as the time of Confucius, in the fourth century BC, it was famous as a centre for pilgrimage. As Confucius said, 'From the summit of Mount Tai the earth seems small.' Qin Shi Huangdi, the first emperor of China, climbed Mount Tai to make a sacrifice in the second century BC, but history records that he was buffeted by storms because he lacked the necessary righteousness!

Throughout the ages, emperors regularly visited Mount Tai, leaving behind records of their visits — examples of their own calligraphy, for example, set in stone at favoured scenic points. The present-day traveller can join the less grand pilgrims and sightseers who throng the mountain through the spring, summer and autumn months, and enjoy the climb of 7,000 steps and an overnight stay at the guesthouse on the summit. (Even though the tourist influx has resulted in the installation of a cable car, walking is still the best means of experiencing the mountain.)

Mount Tai is just over 1,500 metres (5,000 feet) in height, and a fit person can usually climb to the summit in four to five hours. In order to arrive before sunset, the less fit should start the ascent early in the morning, since the steps on the last part of the climb are extremely steep and need to be negotiated in good light. The best time of year to climb the mountain is in spring, but friends have climbed it in the dead of winter, when it was cloaked in snow, and have found the experience delightful — if a little chilly.

Most visitors hope for a clear morning on which to enjoy the sunrise over the sea of clouds that lies above the plain. This is best described by Mary Augusta Mullikin and Anna M. Hotchkis in their book, *The Nine Sacred Mountains of China*, written in the mid-1930s: 'On a clear day the view from the top is one continuous line of interlacing mountains lying to the north and east, whereas to the south the plain spreads out in a glory of light, as though the tawny soil had become a golden yellow carpet.'

Chinese city dwellers come to the mountain for sightseeing holidays, and they enjoy the **Dai Temple** at the foot of the mountain as well as the various shrines and temples en route. But many country folk, particularly the women, still visit the mountain as part of a pilgrimage. Taishan is dedicated to the Daoist deity, the Jade Emperor, but the most popular shrine and temple is dedicated to the Jade Emperor's daughter. It is called the **Princess of the Coloured Clouds Temple**. The peasant women of Shandong visit her temple to pray for sons and grandsons, a prayer of greater urgency in these days of one-child families, when all parents and grandparents wish for a male heir to carry their name. They throw sweets, small coins and scarves as offerings to the princess.

Huangshan

Huangshan (Yellow Mountain) in Anhui Province was never classified as a sacred mountain, but in recent years it has become one of the most popular destinations in eastern China, largely due to its proximity to Shanghai. That should serve as a warning. The mountain is a favourite with Chinese holidaymakers, and therefore the summer months should be avoided — unless, of course, you like crowds.

Unlike the smooth-topped Taishan, Huangshan rises in a series of craggy peaks which inspired a whole school of painting in the late Ming period. The peaks themselves have literary names which reflect the traditional reverence Chinese scholars feel for mountains — Lotus Flower Peak, Bright Summit and Heavenly Capital Peak being the most popular. Between Purple Cloud Peak and Peach Blossom Peak are hot spring pools which are a pleasure to bathe in after a stiff walk.

Huangshan, at just over 1,800 metres (6,000 feet), does not offer easy hiking, and a good pair of canvas, rubber-soled shoes should be worn, since the granite trails are tough on the feet. Overnight guesthouses on the summits offer simple accommodation, but hikers should remember to bring warm and waterproof clothing (those swirling seas of clouds look wonderful from a distance, but walking through them can be damp and demoralizing without thick clothing), and some supplies of high-energy food such as chocolate and dried fruit.

Huashan

Huashan, with its fearsome five peaks, rises over 2,400 metres (8,000 feet) above the plains of Shaanxi Province, to the east of Xi'an. The mountain used to be off-limits to foreigners, but it is now open to travellers, only the fittest and most well-prepared of whom should accept the invitation. The mountain paths are carved out of bare rock in many places, and some of the trails lead past dizzying precipices.

Like Taishan to the east, Huashan is a Daoist mountain and a site of imperial sacrifices. History records that the founders of the Shang and Zhou Dynasties made sacrifices on this mountain, which dominated a strategic pass at a great bend of the Yellow River. Its peaks are dotted with small Daoist shrines and large temples, some of which are used as guesthouses. The most spectacular view can be had from the **West Peak Monastery**, which sits astride a narrow ridge of bald granite, topped with wind-sculpted pine trees.

Wutaishan

To the northeast of the city of Taiyuan, in Shanxi Province, soars the five-peaked mass of Wutaishan. The mountain is sacred to Buddhists. It represents Manjushri, the Bodhisattva of Transcendent Wisdom, known in Chinese as Wen Shu. The mountain lies close to the grasslands of Inner Mongolia, and it was an important site of pilgrimage for Mongolians who had adopted the Tibetan version of the faith.

Sadly, all but two of the numerous Buddhist monasteries, which once covered the slopes of Mount Wutai, have now gone. Those surviving are **Nanshan Monastery** and **Foguang Monastery**, the latter being a rare example of original Tang temple architecture. The buildings from 850 still stand. In descriptions of Wutaishan in the 1930s, the mountain was a bustling centre of activity: Mongolian pilgrims arrived at the temples on their short ponies, and Tibetan lamas mixed with Chinese Buddhist monks in friendly confusion. With the recent reopening of the mountain to pilgrims and tourists, the temples are once again becoming centres of worship.

The mountain is cold, even in midsummer, so hikers should bring adequate layers of clothing as well as basic supplies such as torches, high-energy foods, fold-away rainwear and comfortable shoes.

Emeishan

Emeishan lies to the southwest of the city of Chengdu in Sichuan Province. It is a Buddhist mountain and represents Pu Xian, the Bodhisattva of Universal Kindness. As it is higher than most of China's other sacred mountains, rising to a lofty 3,000 metres (10,000 feet), Emeishan cannot be visited in less than three days — which include two overnight stops at monastic guesthouses scattered over the mountain slopes.

Wildlife in China *Martin Williams*

Wildlife enthusiasts hoping to see good numbers of unusual birds and mammals while on a sightseeing tour of China are likely to be disappointed. Damage to the environment, excessive trapping and hunting, along with pressure imposed on ecosystems by the huge number of people, have caused a lack of wildlife in much of the country. Visitors with only a casual interest in wildlife notice that few birds are to be seen, whether around tourist sites or on journeys through the countryside.

Yet there are areas which are rich in wildlife species that are unique to China or at least rare in other countries. The panda reserves in north Sichuan, whose forests also host rare pheasants; Boyang Lake, the winter home of over 90 per cent of the world's Siberian Cranes; the tropical forests in Xishuangbanna, which harbour over 400 species of birds and over half of China's mammal species — these are among the sites which even the most well-travelled naturalists would find rewarding. Giant Pandas, Manchurian Tigers, River Dolphins, Golden Monkeys and Crested Ibises are among the endangered species which have recently received protection due to the introduction of conservation measures by the Chinese government.

Reaching the prime wildlife areas may require some effort, and some are inaccessible to foreigners or restricted to visitors on organized tours. Hence — particularly for those with money but little time — joining a specialized tour may be the best means of seeing wildlife in China.

Some localities which may be visited by independent means are given below. The emphasis is on birds, since birdwatchers predominate among the naturalists who have explored China in recent years. Note that the environs of some tourist sites have proved convenient for birdwatching. The Great Wall at Badaling and the Summer Palace near Beijing are examples. Buddhist temples can also be good, since they are often surrounded by woodland in areas which are otherwise deforested.

Changbaishan, Jilin Province. The slopes of this mountain have superb forests, and good numbers of birds breed here. Manchurian Tigers are occasionally reported.

Zhalong Nature Reserve, Heilongjiang (about 250 kilometres — 155 miles — south of Qiqihar) is a huge wetland. Red-crowned and White-naped Cranes breed here, and four other crane species breed nearby or pass in migration. Around 500 Siberian Cranes spend April and early May in the area.

Beidaihe, Hebei Province, is a seaside resort and one of Asia's best places for observing bird migration. Around 280 species of birds migrate each year. Over 700 cranes of four species pass in early spring (20 March to 4 April is usually the best period). Early April to late May is the main spring migration period for most other birds (late April to mid-May being the best). Early September is excellent for shorebirds and Pied Harries, and the autumn migration continues until the middle of November, with cranes, geese, Oriental White Storks and Great Bustards passing in numbers around the beginning of the month. By this time, most smaller birds have headed south.

Yen Chinao Nature Reserve, Jiangsu Province, is a coastal wetland where Sanders Gulls breed, and in winter over 200 Red-crowned Cranes and several thousand ducks and shorebirds are seen on the marshes. Though the reserve is large, one birdwatcher recently saw 50 Red-crowned Cranes during a half-day's walk from the village of Yan Cheng.

Qinghai Lake, Qinghai Province. It seems that the rather sparsely populated Qinghai-Tibetan plateau is relatively rich in birds, and visits to the environs of Koko Nor (beside Qinghai Lake) have yielded some very interesting species, including several which are unique to China.

Jiuzhaigou, in Sichuan Province, offers the chance to see where Giant Pandas live (wild pandas are very rarely seen). Visits to the area have produced sightings of some very rarely seen species, and pheasants may also be found.

Emeishan, in Sichuan Province, has forests which have proved very good for bird watching. One species — the Emeishan Liocichla — is unique to the mountain.

Xishuangbanna, in Yunnan Province, still boasts tigers and elephants in its tropical forests, and the birds include Rufous-necked Hornbills, Green Peafowls and Silver Pheasants. There are seven protected areas of forest, and access to all is restricted. Some reasonable birdwatching may be done on the road to the north of Menyang, which passes through one of these protected areas. CITS in Jinghong can help with hiring a jeep with driver.

Boyang Lake, in Jiangxi Province, boasts 1,600 Siberian Cranes, 2,000 White-naped Cranes, 40,000 Swan Geese and over a quarter of a million ducks, among others, in its 'greatest bird spectacle in Asia' each winter (late November to February). CITS in Nanchang may be able to arrange visits.

Hong Kong. Birdwatchers travelling to and from China via Hong Kong should visit the World Wildlife Fund reserve at Mai Po Marshes, which is excellent for birdwatching from late autumn to early May. WWF of Hong Kong organizes tours of the reserves. It is also possible to obtain a permit from the Agriculture and Fisheries Department. The Tai Po Kau Foresters Reserve is also good for birdwatching.

There is a wide choice of walking trails to be followed, but the ascent to the summit requires some steep climbing — so be prepared. Once you are up there, the view is breathtaking (assuming you are lucky enough to be there on a fine day). If all the circumstances are correct, you will not only see the sun from the summit but also the strange light-effect known as 'Buddha's Halo', which appears between the clouds.

The walks on Emeishan are truly beautiful. Unlike the trails on the northern mountains, which cut through rock and pines, those on Emeishan twist through cool bamboo thickets where countless butterflies dance in the summer sunlight. Farmers in the area have not yet discovered insecticides, which means that butterflies as well as many insects flourish amidst the mountain glades. Fast-flowing streams rush past small farmsteads, where poor farmers dispense meagre but kind hospitality to strangers. At the overnight stop of the **Pavilion of the Clear Singing Waters**, two Streams — the Black and the White — meet each other in a frothing torrent (hence the name of the pavilion). Monks run the guesthouses, and their food is simple and vegetarian. Washing facilities are minimal, but on a warm afternoon you can have a bucket-bath out in the sun.

There are said to be pandas living on the western slopes of the mountain, where there are no walking trails. However, it is unlikely that you will catch a glimpse of these shy creatures. A walk to the summit will more probably bring you face-to-face with a horde of chattering monkeys. Beware of their friendship — they are unrepentant beggars, and dislike being refused anything.

Emeishan has become a popular tourist destination in the summer months, so it is advisable to book your stay in advance through CITS. The guesthouses on the mountain accept bookings through vouchers bought at the office in **Baoguo Monastery** at the foot of the mountain. Tour buses take travellers up a back road to a half-way point on the mountain, if time is limited. Otherwise, start walking from the monastery and use the walking trail maps available from the monastery's office. There are several routes to choose for the summit, but take into account the weather and your physical fitness. If you do decide on the summit, be sure to travel light — the walk is strenuous — and don't forget to pack snacks, waterproof clothing, a thick jersey and a complete change of clothing in case of bad weather.

Putuoshan

The easterly Buddhist peaks of Putuoshan are dedicated to Guan Yin, the Bodhisattva of Mercy. Putuoshan rises out of the sea as a rocky island off the coast of Zhejiang Province. The island, seven kilometres (four miles) long by five kilometres (three miles) wide, is a remarkable sanctuary of peace and beauty, which has been a Buddhist site of pilgrimage since the Tang Dynasty.

The island was closed to foreign tourists until very recently, and is reached by boat from either Shanghai or Ningbo. The island's monasteries were closed during the Cultural Revolution, and the thousands of monks and nuns who lived there were forced to return to their towns and villages. Some of the original Buddhist inhabitants have now returned, and in the last few years Putuoshan has again become an active centre of Buddhist worship.

The most famous of Putuoshan's monasteries are the **Pujisi**, **Huijisi** and **Fayusi**. The Pujisi buildings date from the Qing Dynasty, but the tiles of the roof of the monastery's Great Hall come from the Ming palaces of Nanjing, destroyed by the Manchu troops when they conquered China in 1644. The Huijisi on Buddha's Peak was founded in the Ming. The Fayusi is smaller than Pujisi but has a more attractive setting, rising in terraces amidst tree-clad slopes.

Jiuhuashan

The Buddhist peaks of Jiuhuashan lie south of the Yangzi River in Anhui Province. Jiuhuashan is dedicated to the Bodhisattva, Di Zang. It rises with over 90 peaks to 900 metres (3,000 feet) against the backdrop of a wooded plain. The trails make comfortable walking, except for those to the summit, and just under 100 monasteries have survived to this day. The most famous of these, the **Dizangsi**, is dedicated to the Di Zang Bodhisattva. This Bodhisattva is believed to be able to open the gates of hell to release the suffering souls, so the monastery was by tradition a point of pilgrimage for bereaved relatives. Some of the mountain temples were founded as early as the fourth century, but most of the buildings that have survived to this day date from the Qing period.

Hong Kong

With its crowded street markets, plethora of restaurants, elegant shopping plazas and cityscape of towering highrises set between mountains and sea, Hong Kong is an exciting and vivid place. Here, traditional Chinese values and customs co-exist with an outward-looking commercial sophistication and a good mix of Western institutions and ideas. The people of Hong Kong are extraordinarily hard-working and investment-conscious (widely believed to be due to the preponderance of first- or second-generation refugees amongst its population). There is also a tradition of wealthy, and even not so wealthy, families sending their children overseas to study. A Hong Kong banker may take his vacations in California and enjoy a round of golf on Sundays, but he will also remember to sweep his family graves at the Qing Ming festival and decorate his home with branches of blossom at the Chinese New Year. This fascinating blend of Orient and Occident is one of the main reasons why Hong Kong is understood to be a 'Gateway to China' — and a primary reason why it is included in this book.

The main centres of population in Hong Kong are Hong Kong Island itself and Kowloon. The Island and the tip of Kowloon peninsula were ceded to Britain 'in perpetuity' by the so-called 'Unequal Treaties' which concluded the two Opium Wars between Britain and China in the 19th century. Thereafter, Hong Kong flourished as the base for British opium trading. In 1898, Britain leased more of Kowloon and the New Territories from China. The lease was for 99 years and is thus due to expire in 1997. This explains why Britain has had to reach an agreement with China on the future of the territory. The Sino-British Joint Declaration of 1984 returns Hong Kong to Chinese sovereignty in 1997, but it gives Hong Kong the status of a Special Administrative Region, able to keep its capitalist lifestyle for another 50 years.

The lease of 1898 gave Hong Kong a large number of offshore islands as well as the New Territories. It is these islands, and the remoter areas of the New Territories, which offer a glimpse into the older rural world of Hong Kong. The farmers of the New Territories and the outlying islands are mainly Hakka people; they are easy to identify, since the women wear a traditional headdress of a woven rattan hat with a black cloth fringe. In the New Territories, you can still see the traditional walled villages of the Hakka (fortified against their Cantonese neighbours, with whom they rarely intermarried in the past). One of these villages, in Shatin, is now preserved as a museum in the middle of a highrise estate.

Hong Kong's rural life is slowly dying as farmers get older and their better-educated offspring take up work in the city. After all, Hong Kong is the fourth largest financial centre and one of the biggest ports in the world. Business dominates Hong Kong. If you walk down a busy street in Central, the financial district on Hong Kong Island, you will see people clustering around video displays in bank windows. They are watching the stock market's movements. The Hong Kong Exchange may only have the total value of one day's dealing on Wall Street, but it is important because of its regional position and its slot in the international time zones.

Business has made Hong Kong prosperous — and it shows. The biggest Paris and Italian fashion houses have several branches in Hong Kong, and the new buildings rising in Central are being designed by world-famous architects. The new Bank of China headquarters, due for completion in August 1988, has been designed by I.M. Pei, the famous Chinese-American architect who recently designed a new building for the Louvre in Paris. Gone are the days when the label 'Made in Hong Kong' meant something cheap and shoddy. 'Made in Hong Kong' now has prestige and style, as the face of the city readily reflects. Shops and restaurants are full, and secretaries dress for work as if for some kind of cocktail party. The residential districts of the territory, which are mainly highrise (the incredible density of population putting a tremendous premium on land), are at their smartest on the Peak and the south side of Hong Kong Island, as well as in the quieter coastal regions of the eastern New Territories. Here you can see the villas of the territory's many film stars and multi-billionaires. The upper echelons of Hong Kong society are, without a doubt, mega-rich.

City Sights

The visitor to Hong Kong has a dazzling variety of choice over ways to spend time profitably in the territory. Many people enjoy the shopping, of course, and the wonderful restaurants and nightlife. But there are are other ways to spend your days — which could mean anything from a ferry ride to one of the outlying islands, a day out at the famous marine centre of Ocean Park, or a visit to one of the old temples or markets of Kowloon. Here I have merely listed a small selection of possible sights and pleasures. The rest is up to the individual visitor.

The Peak, also known as Victoria Peak, is the mountain-top residential district of the rich and powerful. It is also a marvellous place to look out over the city, the harbour and the islands. If you are fit, and the weather is not too hot, you can walk to the top.

There are two shady, quiet paths — one starts from Magazine Gap Road, the other from Conduit Road. The most popular and comfortable way to the top is the eight-minute journey by the **Peak Tram**. The terminus is in Garden Road. Once at the top, you can walk up to the summit or take the circular trail which starts just to the right of the exit of the Peak Tram terminus. The ultra-modern **Peak Tower Restaurant** (which looks like a cross between a lost spaceship and an antique Chinese vessel) offers good food with stunning window views. The old-fashioned **Peak Café**, over the road from the terminus, has open-air seating, a reasonable menu and a relaxed atmosphere.

The **Botanical Gardens**, just up the hill from Central, are usually overlooked by foreign visitors but are much loved by local residents. In the morning, old people gather to swap gossip and do their calisthenic exercises. The gardens are pleasant, but the small zoo is the main attraction with its leopards, orangutans and wonderful landscaped aviaries full of rockpools, waterfalls and exotic foliage. The zoo is famous for its pioneer work in captive breeding of such endangered species as the Philippines Palawan Peacock and the Chinese Crane.

For ordinary Hong Kong people, a ride on the **Star Ferry** is the cheapest way of crossing the harbour. For visitors, the Star Ferry is also the best way to enjoy a view of the whole harbour from the water. The fleet of ten green-and-white Star Ferries all have 'star' in their names — Celestial Star, Morning Star, Solar Star, for example.

Between Central district and Western district there are two parallel roads, Queen's Road and Des Voeux Road, bisected by a series of small lanes. It is fun to explore the Lanes, since each of them has a speciality. Cloth Lane is most popular with visitors for its fabric stalls. But there are also lanes selling fashion clothes, and bargain watches (which usually stop a few days after purchase, so *caveat emptor*!). My own favourites are the lanes with goldfish, singing birds and 100-year-old eggs.

Outings from Hong Kong

Hong Kong's largest island, off the west coast of the Island itself, is **Lantau**. It is still relatively undeveloped, but that may all change, since the Hong Kong government is considering a plan to build a new container terminal and second airport on its southern shore. Nonetheless, for the moment Lantau is a haven of peace and quiet. The most well-known sights on Lantau are the **Polin Monastery** (gaudy and commercialized, but scenic) and a tea plantation, where rides on retired racehorses are offered. But the island is worth visiting for its grand landscapes of cloud-tipped mountains, pastoral valleys and cove beaches. The walking trails are well-marked and take you through some stunning scenery.

To the south of Hong Kong Island, **Lamma Island** is smaller than Lantau and has no cars. It is sadly disfigured by the two enormous chimney stacks of a coal-fired power station. It is known, however, for its excellent waterfront seafood restaurants.

To the southwest of Hong Kong Island, **Cheung Chau** is famous for its Bun Festival, held every year in May. The festival features stilt-walkers, traditional costume parades and mountains of sticky buns (which, until the practice was discontinued as too dangerous, young men used to climb for a prize pinned to the top). Cheung Chau is now badly overbuilt and is a dormitory for Hong Kong commuters. Yet there are some pleasant pubs and bars, as well as a windsurfing school on the island.

Off the east coast of the New Territories lie the two lovely islands of **Ping Chau** and **Tap Mun**. Ping Chau can only be visited at weekends by public ferry and requires an overnight stay with sleeping bag in one of the island's deserted houses. It lies close to China and is shaped like a grassy aircraft carrier. The absence of inhabited villages has made it a natural wildlife sanctuary, bright with butterflies, dragonflies and shy birds. The nearby island of Tap Mun is also small, but it has thriving villages, restaurants and a famous Tin Hau Temple popular with local seagoing fishermen (Tin Hau being a Daoist goddess of South China who is believed to protect fisherfolk). Tap Mun can be reached every day by ferry. Ferries to both islands depart from University, a stop on the Kowloon-Canton Railway.

In the eastern New Territories, the **Sai Kung** peninsula is the most beautiful and unspoilt area. This is because much of the land was designated into Country Parks in the 1970s. Visitors can explore the hills and seashore on walking trails, picking up one of the small ferries which run between the villages. The beaches are clean and uncrowded, and the walks offer glorious views over **Mirs Bay** and the China coast. Further north, the town of **Fan Ling** is a good place for a game of golf. The Royal Hong Kong Golf Club allows non-members to play on weekdays.

For those interested in farming and gardening, the Kadoorie Experimental Farm near **Tai Po** is an excellent place to visit. It has helped to introduce modern farming methods to the villages of the New Territories, improved the local pig stock, and has wonderful landscaped gardens of native flora. Visits can be made, but by appointment only (Tel: 0-981317).

Shopping and Entertainment

Much of what is produced for export in China is on sale in Hong Kong. There are large **China Products** emporiums throughout the territory, which sell Chinese-made goods at reasonable prices. The advantage of shopping in these stores is that everything, from all the different regions of China, is under one roof. The best known of these shops is **China Arts and Crafts** — one is near the Star Ferry terminus on Kowloon side, the other at the bottom of Wyndham Street in the Island's Central district.

Central has all the most expensive brand-name shops. Prices may or may not be lower than New York or London, depending of course on currency fluctuations. Better value is offered at the factory outlet shops themselves, which sell goods made for export at knock-down prices. Lists of these factory outlet shops can be found in a brochure distributed by the Hong Kong Tourist Association.

If you like shopping combined with some local colour, then try to visit some street markets by night. There are many throughout the Island and Kowloon, but the most popular with foreign visitors is **Temple Street Market** in Kowloon, near the Jordan MTR (underground/subway) station. Here you can buy hand-painted T-shirts as well as taste a casserole of garlic snails. My favourite market is around **Sai Yeung Choi Street**, near the Mongkok MTR station.

As far as eating is concerned, the choice is so great that it is best to consult the Hong Kong Tourist Association handbook for a comprehensive listing. If you have just come out of China and are longing for Western food, then Hong Kong has some of the best Western restaurants in the world. Particularly recommended are those of the Peninsula and Mandarin Hotels, along with the French restaurant Au Trou Normand in Tsimshatsui, Kowloon.

Some of the most interesting local restaurants are the traditional teahouses, where the old-fashioned flavour of Chinese breakfast and lunch *dim sum* (small steamed and fried snacks) can be savoured. The best-known traditional teahouses are the Luk Yu in Stanley Street, on the Island, and the bird teahouse — where old men go with their pet caged birds — called Wan Loy, on Shanghai Street in Mongkok, Kowloon.

Finally, Hong Kong is famous for its late, late nightlife. In Causeway Bay, the shops don't close until nearly 11 pm every night, and the discos can go on until 4 am. All the hotels have good bars and nightclubs, some with live music. The local hostess bars range from the cheap and cheerful to the very, very expensive. These should be visited with some caution and a prior look at prices.

Hotels: A Select List

The following list is by no means comprehensive. The choice is a personal one, based mainly on the more exhaustive information provided in the individual guides in the China Guides Series. However, the descriptions and the prices quoted are the most up-to-date available at the time of going to press. For the latest details, you are advised to check with your local travel agent or branch of CITS.

Xi'an

Golden Flower Hotel (Jinhua Fandian)
Changle Xi Lu
tel. 32981
tlx. 70145, fax 32327

金花饭店
长乐西路

205 rooms, US$105 (single), US$135 (double), US$250 (suite). From December to March attractive rates are available for two- and three-night packages inclusive of room, breakfast, airport shuttle and excursions. (Amex, Diners, Visa, MasterCard, JCB, Federal)

Opened in April 1985, this joint-venture hotel is operated by SARA Hotels of Sweden to a high international standard. It is undoubtedly the best hotel in Xi'an. The hotel offers Western and Chinese restaurants, a bar lounge and adjoining small disco (open 8 pm—midnight and later at weekends), one of Xi'an's few nightspots. The attractive rooms are amongst the largest of any of China's new hotels. There is also a Western-style business centre (open 7am—8pm). Currently the hotel is adding 300 rooms, an indoor/outdoor pool, health club, various restaurants and conference facilities.

Bell Tower Hotel (Zhonglou Fandian)
southwest of the Bell Tower
tel. 22033, 24730
tlx. 70124, cable 8988

钟楼饭店
钟楼西南角

321 rooms, US$70—90 (single), US$80—95 (double), US$100—40 (suite)

This ideally located hotel, which first opened under local management in 1983, reopened under Holiday Inn management at the end of 1987, with revamped facilities (plus a new health club) and much-improved service. Western food is served in its Tower Café, and there is also a good Chinese restaurant.

**Xi'an Garden
(Tanghua)**
Xiaozhai Dong Lu

唐华饭店
小寨东路

301 rooms

Next to the Big Goose Pagoda, and set in expansive grounds, this Japanese-owned international-standard hotel was set to open in April 1988. The garden complex, which covers 100,000 square metres, will also contain a Tang Culture and Arts Museum and the Tang Theatre Restaurant.

Jianguo Hotel
Huzhu Lu

建国饭店
互助路

700 rooms, US$45 (single), US$60 (double), US$70 (super double)

This new highrise joint-venture hotel which has five restaurants, a pool, health centre, and large Friendship Store, was scheduled to open in August 1988. It is located just south of the Golden Flower, off Jianhua Bei Lu, close to the zoo.

**People's Mansion
(Renmin Dasha)**
Dongxin Jie
tel. 715111

人民大厦
东新街

472 rooms, Rmb85–260 (double)

Recently renovated, this Chinese-run hotel with its imposing Soviet-style facade now boasts 472 air-conditioned, heated rooms (most with telephones).

There are four dining rooms, a coffee shop and two bars (open 8 am–12pm). Other facilities include souvenir shops and a games room. CITS and CTS are both located in the back building.

Bicycles can be rented at the hotel gate for Rmb5 a day.

Beijing

Great Wall Sheraton
Donghuan Bei Lu,
Chaoyang
tel. 5005566
tlx. 20045
fax 5001938, 5003398

长城饭店
朝阳东环北路

1,007 rooms, US$100–850, executive floor, business centre, nightclub, Clark Hatch health centre, indoor/outdoor swimming pool, tennis, billiards, theatre (max 900), ballroom (max 1,800), conference and banquet (max 1,000). (Amex, Diners, Visa, Mastercharge, Federal, Great Wall Card)

With a vast, reflecting glass facade, impressive pyramid-shaped atrium lobby, scenic elevator, and plush interiors, this is one of Beijing's smartest hotels. Its many facilities include restaurants offering French, Sichuan, Cantonese and international cuisine, together with a 24-hour coffee shop.

Shangri-la
29 Zizhuyuan Lu
tel. 8021122,
tlx. 222231, fax 8021471

香格里拉饭店
紫竹院路29号

786 rooms, US$80–380, business centre, health club and indoor swimming pool, music room, ballroom and function rooms (max 750). (Amex, Visa, Mastercharge)

This hotel is managed by the Shangri-la International Group. The attractively designed rooms in the main building are very spacious and amongst the best in Beijing. The smaller, west building has 76 guestrooms and 44 fully-equipped office suites, which may be rented by the day or on long lease. The hotel is in the northwest part of the city, 10–15 minutes by car to Tiananmen. Restaurants include a brasserie, coffee shop, and the Shang Palace, offering high-quality Chinese food (a hallmark of Shangri-la hotels).

Jianguo
Jianguomenwai Dajie
tel. 5002233, tlx. 22439

建国饭店
建国门外大街

457 rooms, US$85–185, ballroom (max 200), indoor swimming pool, delicatessen. (Visa, Diners, Amex)

The Jianguo was the first foreign-managed hotel in Beijing and is a favourite with business visitors and the few independent travellers who are lucky enough to get a room. Competition to secure a booking is fierce year-round. The hotel has a reputation for high-quality food in the Cantonese, Japanese and European restaurants and in the coffee shop. Its bar — Charlie's — is one of the best in town. The Jianguo is within walking distance of Beijing's two major new office blocks for foreign companies — the CITIC Building and Noble Tower.

Holiday Inn Lido Beijing
Jichang Lu, Jiangtai Lu,
tel. 5006688, tlx. 22618

丽都假日饭店
机场路将台路

1,000 rooms, US$77–175, health club, bowling centre, indoor swimming pool, billiards, TV games, supermarket, delicatesssen, disco. (Amex, Diners, Visa, Mastercharge)

This very successful operation is the largest Holiday Inn in Asia. The whole complex is a massive expatriate enclave, with offices and residential apartments, a large sports club, as well as hotel rooms. Located northeast of the city centre, the hotel is 20–30 minutes' journey into town. A hotel shuttle bus service takes guests to key stops downtown. The Lido has a reputation for good food with a smart European restaurant, a coffee shop, a noodles and congee restaurant, and a quality Cantonese restaurant.

Beijing Hotel
Dongchang'an Dajie
tel. 507766,
tlx. 22426, cable 6531

北京饭店
东长安大街

910 rooms, Rmb100—300. Business centre,
conference and banqueting hall (max 1,000)

First opened in 1917, this is undoubtedly the
capital's grand old hotel. It is ideally located at
the corner of Beijing's main shopping street,
Wangfujing. Rooms are almost impossible to
secure without a contact in the city — the hotel
rarely confirms bookings from individuals outside
China.

The giant complex has three wings, with a
fourth under construction. Recent renovations
have smartened up the gloomy public areas,
while the service (reputed to be surly at best) has
noticeably improved, even extending to room
service after midnight. The restaurants offer a
whole range of Chinese regional dishes, as well
as Japanese and European food.

Diaoyutai State
Guesthouse
(Anglers' State
Guesthouse)
Sanlihe Lu
tel. 668541

钓鱼台国宾馆
三里河路

Rooms from US$100. Extensive gardens, lake
(fishing and boating)

A few select tour groups and business
delegations stay in this secluded guesthouse
complex, until recently reserved for high-ranking
Chinese officials and visiting guests of the
Chinese government. The buildings are set in
attractive wooded parkland, which date back to
the 11th century. Many of the public rooms and
suites contain exceptionally fine Chinese antiques
— furniture, paintings, bronzes and porcelain.
Food is restricted to Chinese cuisine and service
is, of course, excellent.

Club Mediterranée
Nanhu Island,
Summer Palace,
Yiheyuan
tel. 281931, 281936

南湖宾馆
颐和园

US$100 (double), 23 rooms and suites, restaurant
and conference hall (max 30)

Club Med has achieved the apparently
impossible, by taking on management of two
small villas right in the Summer Palace grounds.
Both villas — which are completely self-
contained — have been restored without losing
the Chinese flavour of the original. The villas,
which together accommodate 36 guests, are open
to any business visitor or tourist.

**Fragrant Hills
(Xiangshan) Hotel**
Xiangshan
tel. 819242,
tlx. 285491, cable 7391

香山饭店
香山

*288 rooms, Rmb130−240, health club, outdoor
pool, tennis, gardens*

I.M. Pei's masterly blend of Chinese and
Western architecture is set in the former hunting
park at the Fragrant Hills, some 20 kilometres
(12 miles) northwest of Beijing. This is a long
way out for anyone who wants to travel to the
city centre everyday (usually at least an hour by
taxi), but the magnificent setting has its
compensations.

Friendship Hotel
Basishiqiao Lu
tel. 890621, cable 2222

友谊宾馆
白石桥路

*1,500 rooms. Rmb66−145, outdoor swimming
pool, gymnasium, theatre, tennis*

This massive Russian-style complex in extensive
grounds accommodates tourists, business visitors
and some resident foreigners. This is a relaxed,
pleasant place to stay, specially in summer, with
a good range of facilities. Its distance from the
city centre is the main drawback, although the
hotel's shuttle bus service has partially eased
transport difficulties.

Beiwei
Beiwei Lu
tel. 338631

北纬饭店
北纬路

226 rooms, Rmb93−210

This hotel is well located in the southern part of
the city centre, near Liulichang and the Temple
of Heaven. It has Chinese and Western food,
and recent renovation work has improved its
uninviting rooms to make it one of the better
budget hotels in the city.

Nanhua
11 Nanhua Xi Lu,
Hufang Lu, Xuanwu
tel, 337916, 332619,
cable 7916

南华饭店
宣武区虎坊路
南华西路11号

50 rooms, Rmb 120−180

Located in a small *hutong* near the Beiwei Hotel,
this small, new hotel has friendly staff who
welcome foreign guests.

Nanjing

Jinling Hotel
2 Hanzhong Lu
Xinjiekou
tel. 44141, 41121
tlx. 34110 cable 6855
fax. (025) 43396

金陵饭店
汉中路2号

768 rooms and suites, US$60−700. Business centre (World Trade Center Club Hong Kong); convention and exhibition facilities; indoor swimming pool and health club; adjacent shopping arcade. Most international credit cards accepted

This centrally-located luxury hotel, a mere 20 minutes' drive from the airport, is the first choice of most foreign businessmen and tourists. It boasts several restaurants and a revolving lounge on the hotel's 36th floor where one can dance in the evening.

An annexe to the hotel is a shopping complex with a good bookstore, souvenir shops and a sub-branch of CITS.

Dingshan Guesthouse
90 Chaha'er Lu
tel. 85931
tlx. 34103
cable 6333

丁山宾馆
察哈尔路90号

Main building: 126 rooms and suites. Rmb148 (double), Rmb250 (suites). Business centre, gift shop, banquet rooms. (Visa, MasterCard, Amex) Annexe: 220 rooms, Rmb85 (double); dormitory Rmb10 (per bed)

A large complex encompassing several buildings, this hotel offers a range of room prices and good facilities. Its main Chinese restaurant is highly popular.

Guangzhou

Garden Hotel
(Huayuan Jiudian)
368 Huanshi Dong Lu
tel. 73388
tlx. 44788
cable 4735

花园饭店
环市东路368号

1,147 rooms and suites, standard double Rmb100

The Garden is managed by the Peninsula Group who runs the Jianguo Hotel in Beijing. The Group's reputation for excellent hotel restaurants is confirmed in the 15 bars and restaurants here.

Business facilities include a conference hall and business centre. There are two pools (one for children), a gym, health club, tennis, squash and badminton courts, sauna, and shopping arcade. Reservations can be made through the Peninsula Group Reservations Centre in Hong Kong, Swissair, Cathay Pacific Airways, and travel agents worldwide.

China Hotel (Zhongguo Dajiudian)
Liuhua Lu
tel. 66888
tlx. 44888
cable 6888

中国饭店
流花路

1,017 rooms, standard double 107 Rmb

This is a massive complex and offers a 19-storey guest room complex, a 15-storey office tower, a shopping arcade and some 250 deluxe apartments for businessmen and their families working in Guangzhou. Since the hotel sits between the Trade Fair Exhibition Hall and the Dongfang Hotel, it is fast becoming an informal business centre for the city. Business and communication facilities, including convention facilities, are among the best in the country.

An astonishing 18 food and beverage outlets aim to satisfy all tastes from gourmet European cuisine to Cantonese home cooking. For relaxation there is an outdoor pool, tennis court, gym and sauna, and nine-lane bowling alley. Confirmed reservations are through New World Hotels International (HK), telex 51878 NWHIL HX, tel. 3-694111.

White Swan (Baitiane Binguan)
Shamian
tel. 86968
tlx. 44149
cable 8888

白天鹅宾馆
沙面

Double rooms Rmb333, 407 (with view); suites from Rmb518; all major credit cards accepted.

The White Swan offers a tranquil environment and a superb location on the old foreign enclave of Shamian Island. Best views over the Pearl River are to be had from the eighth floor upwards. A member of 'Leading Hotels of the World', the White Swan is run by arguably the most successful local Chinese management team in China. Recent additions include an attractive riverside garden, a second swimming pool, a competitively-priced health club offering all the facilities one would expect from an international hotel. A new business centre is under construction, as is a flyover to the Trade Fair Exhibition Centre area.

Liuhua (Liuhua Binguan)
Renmin Bei Lu
tel. 68800, 64304

流花宾馆
人民北路

660 rooms, double Rmb57

This is conveniently situated near the railway station. It has mainly Overseas Chinese guests, but is now open to foreigners. It has a coffee shop and eight restaurants, mostly serving Cantonese food, but also with food from Chaozhou and Dongjiang. Rooms may be booked through CTS (Hong Kong), tel. 5-252284.

**Foreign Affairs Hostel
(Waishibu Zhaodaisuo)**
2 Si Jie, Shamian
tel. 84298, 89251

外事部招待所
沙面四街2号

Single bed Rmb6

This dormitory-style hostel is popular with young travellers. There are three beds to each room and they are assigned on a first-come, first-serve basis. There are no private bathrooms.

Shanghai

**The Huating Sheraton
Hotel**
1200 Caoxi Bei Lu
tel. 386000, tlx. 33589

华亭宾馆
漕西北路1200号

Double room (standard) US$110, (deluxe) $125, executive suite $250, presidential suite $1,000

The first hotel in Shanghai to be managed by an international chain, the Huating is housed in an enormous S-shaped 28-storey building with over a thousand guest rooms, including 40 suites. It offers all the services that one expects of an international-style hotel — business centre, conference facilities (including simultaneous interpretation, courier and fascimile) and recreational facilities such as indoor swimming pool, gymnasium, sauna, billiards room, ten-pin bowling alley and tennis court.

Jinjiang Hotel
59 Maoming Nan Lu
tel. 582582, tlx. 33380

锦江饭店
茂名南路59号

Double room Rmb170−200, suites Rmb300−360

In the heart of the old French quarter, the Jinjiang was originally a private hotel for French residents in Shanghai. Now, with three new buildings added, it has about 800 rooms. It is a first-class hotel.

The Jinjiang complex encompasses a row of shops, a hairdresser's, a mini-supermarket, and a café.

**Western Suburbs
Guesthouse (Xijiao
Binguan)**
1921 Hongqiao Lu
tel. 379643, tlx. 33004

西郊宾馆
虹桥路1921号

Double room Rmb310, suite Rmb600

Set in 32 hectares (80 acres) of beautifully kept grounds, this is a secluded, luxurious, and expensive guesthouse, used mainly by official delegations, foreign companies, and some upmarket tour groups. The guesthouse complex consists of seven buildings; Building Number Four, originally the private house of a rich businessman, has a swimming pool, a disco, and a magnificent garden room, now used as a lounge.

**Shanghai Hilton
International**
250 Huashan Lu
tel. 563343, tlx. 33612

上海希尔顿酒店

华山路250号

This 800-room hotel has all the facilities usually associated with hotels of this kind — swimming pool, poolside lounge, roof-top bar, executive business centre and secretarial services, as well as a health club with gym and saunas, an outdoor tennis court, two squash courts and underground parking for more than 100 cars. Four rooms are specially adapted for the handicapped.

Peace Hotel
20 Nanjing Dong Lu
tel. 211244

和平饭店

南京东路20号

Wide range of tariffs, with a double room (standard) priced at around Rmb170

Built in the late 1920s and formerly known as the Cathay, this famous landmark, with its distinctive green-roofed tower, stands at the corner of Nanjing Lu and the waterfront. The former Palace Hotel, dating from 1906 and standing opposite on the south side of Nanjing Lu, has now been incorporated to form a smaller south wing of the Peace Hotel.

Reminders of the hotel's past remain in the softly-lit lobby, with its revolving doors, art deco windows and lamp stands, and in the ornate, heavily decorated dining room on the eighth floor, which overlooks the waterfront and the river. It has all the usual services, plus a desk in the lobby which helps book day-trips to nearby places of interest.

Ruijin Guesthouse
118 Ruijin Lu
tel. 37253, tlx. 336030

瑞金宾馆

瑞金路118号

Double room Rmb150–250, suite Rmb385

Set in well-kept grounds, the Ruijin is a first-class hotel which numbers many State dignitaries among its guests. There are four villas, the first of which used to house a secret Kuomintang organization.

Park Hotel
170 Nanjing Xi Lu
tel. 225225

国际饭店

南京西路170号

Double room (standard) Rmb100

Built in 1934, with an excellent location overlooking the old racecourse (now Renmin Park), the Park Hotel was well known for its chefs and its fashionable daily tea dance. There are few reminders today of the hotel's past, but of its kind the Park remains one of Shanghai's best hotels. Service on some floors, each with its own service desk and staff, is excellent.

Shanghai Mansions
20 Suzhou Bei Lu
tel. 244186, tlx. 33007

上海大厦
苏州北路20号

Double room Rmb150

This typical 1930s-style skyscraper commands a
magnificent view from the north bank of the
Suzhou Creek, looking down along the
waterfront and across the city of Shanghai. Built
in 1934, it was a smart residential hotel, which at
one time housed the US Military Advisory
Group on the lower floors, with apartments for
the foreign press above.

Pujiang Hotel
17 Huangpu Lu
tel. 246388

浦江饭店
黄浦路17号

*Dormitory Rmb14 (including breakfast), double
room Rmb73–100*

Formerly the elegant Astor House, this
run-down hotel overlooks the Huangpu River
and the Waibaidu Bridge. It offers dormitory
accommodation. Each room has its own
bathroom, but each room may sleep up to 17
people.

**Seagull Hotel (Hai'ou
Fandian)**
60 Huangpu Lu
tel. 251043, tlx. 33603

海鸥饭店
黄浦路60号

Double room Rmb88

Built as an appendage to the International
Seaman's Club in 1985, this 14-storey hotel is
associated with Shanghai's Workers'
International Exchange Centre. Catering
particularly to technical exchange groups and
workers' delegations, the Seagull organizes visits
to factories, schools and hospitals for its guests.
Its facilities include rooms for ping-pong, chess
and mahjong.

Hangzhou

Hangzhou Hotel
78 Beishan Lu
tel. 22921
tlx. 35005/6
fax. 22921-2514

杭州饭店
北山路78号

Over 350 guest rooms are spread among the
West and East Buildings and three villas of this
1950s hotel, which has been completely
refurbished by Shangri-La International to bring
the Hangzhou to world-class standards. The
hotel stands on the northern shore of the West
Lake, and its facilities, including several
restaurants, business centre and shopping arcade,
are excellent.

Dragon Hotel
Hangda Lu and
Shuguang Lu
tel. 71614

黄龙饭店
杭大路曙光路

552 rooms, 9 suites

This New World hotel opened in March 1987.
Among the features of this international-class
hotel are a pool and pool-side lounge, Cantonese
and Pekinese restaurants, a banquet hall and
function room, a lobby lounge, a disco, and a
coffee shop.

Overseas Chinese Hotel
92 Hubin Lu
tel. 23401

华桥宾馆
湖宾路92号

375 rooms

This large hotel is located in town on the eastern
edge of the lake. It has a post office, *bureau de
change*, hairdresser, souvenir shop, book counter
and a surgery. It does not usually take non-
Chinese guests. However, budget travellers can
usually find a bed here except in the peak tourist
seasons of spring and early autumn, when the
hotel is booked up in advance.

Guilin

**Ramada Renaissance
(Huayuan Jiudian)**
Yanjiang Lu
tel. 3611
tlx. 48446

花园饭店
沿江路

Double rooms US$88, 98; suites US$240

The hotel has 332 rooms, some of which
overlook the large atrium coffee shop, while
others give on to the Li River towards Fubo Hill.
Facilities include tennis courts, a small outdoor
pool, Western and Chinese restaurants, health
centre, disco and car rental.

Holiday Inn Guilin
14 Ronghu Nan Lu
tel. 3950
tlx. 48456

假日桂林宾馆
榕湖路14号

Double rooms US$80, 90

Located by the Ronghu (Banyan) Lake, this
comfortable hotel is in a quiet part of town. A
health centre, Chinese and Western restaurants
and a bar are among the facilities. Holiday Inn's
service puts the hotel into the top bracket of
Guilin's hotels.

Guishan Hotel
Chuanshan Lu
tel. 4059
tlx. 48443

桂山大饭店
穿山路

Double rooms US$70−80, suites US$140−400

Run by New World Hotels of Hong Kong, this
hotel, opened in 1988, is situated on a spacious,
secluded site on the east bank of the Li River. Its
600 rooms are spread out in three lowrise
Chinese-style blocks, divided by gardens. There
are good recreational facilities, including a
bowling alley, swimming pool, health centre, and
billiard room.

Kunming

Green Lake Hotel
(Guihu Binguan)
Guihu Nan Lu
tel. 22192 ext.200
tlx. 64027

翠湖宾馆
翠湖南路6号

Deluxe suite Rmb250, special suite Rmb80, standard double Rmb72, dormitory Rmb8—10

This is Kunming's closest approximation to a first-class hotel. It was modernized in the early 1980s. Its 172 rooms all have carpeting, air-conditioning and television. There are four deluxe suites and 20 special suites; these need to be reserved well in advance of arrival. There is also an excellent restaurant. A bar and coffee shop, popular with young Chinese and foreign residents of Kunming, is on the third floor. On the top floor, a lounge/bar has a terrace overlooking Green Lake Park. Plans for the future include a sauna, a conference centre and a ball room.

Kunming Hotel
(Kunming Fandian)
145 Dongfeng Dong Lu
tel. 23918, 22063
ext. 2111, tlx. 64027

昆明饭店
东风东路145号

Suite Rmb80, standard double Rmb70, dormitory Rmb8—10

The Kunming Hotel is large, with 342 rooms. Most rooms are standard doubles with private, Western-style bathrooms. In addition, there are second-class doubles where four persons share one bathroom. The capacious dormitory on the 14th floor is famous among young travellers as a gathering place and information-swapping centre. The hotel has an abundance of restaurants. A ticket booking office is located in the main hall.

West Garden Hotel
(Xi Yuan Fandian)
Kunming Xi Jiao
tel. 29969

西园饭店
昆明西郊

This villa-style hotel is located in spacious grounds at the foot of the majestic Western Hill. It was formerly the country retreat of a warlord. The buildings and gardens are in French colonial style on the edge of Dianchi Lake. In the main villa there are ten double rooms with bath. The outer buildings contain 20 dormitory rooms with communal washing facilities. Meals are served at the villa. Two launches for visitors make excursions on the lake with simple meals aboard. Transportation to downtown Kunming is by CITS taxi or public bus on the main road.

Kunhu Hotel
(Kunhu Fandian)
Beijing Lu

昆湖饭店
北京路

This simple hotel is conveniently located near Kunming's main bus and railway stations in the southern part of the city. It is better than the average Chinese inn, but below standard for fastidious foreigners. Most rooms have four beds, and everyone shares the bathroom at the end of the hall. The atmosphere is friendly and standard Chinese fare is served in the dining room.

Restaurants: A Select List

Xi'an

May the First Restaurant
(Wuyi Fandian)
Dong Dajie
tel. 718665

五一饭店
东大街

This downtown hotel restaurant is popular for banquets and provides local-style food. The staff is efficient and service is prompt but prices are high by Xi'an standards. Roast chicken with 'five-spice' is a particularly delicious dish on the menu. It is open 8 am – 10 pm.

East Asia Restaurant
(Dongya Fandian)
Luoma Shi
tel. 719492

东亚饭店
骡马市

All the chefs in this restaurant, which is near the Bell Tower, were originally from Shanghai, and officially they prepare the cuisine of Suzhou and Wuxi, cities close to Shanghai. In practice most of the food is local in style. They serve their own 'East Asia' hotpot (*Dongya huoguo*), a close relative of the Mongolian hotpot.

Baiyunzhang Beef and
Mutton Ravioli House
Intersection of Dong
Dajie and Juhuayuan
tel. 719247

白云章牛羊肉饺子馆
东大街菊花园口

Located very close to the Xi'an Restaurant, this is the place to try one of the most celebrated ordinary dishes of north China, *jiaozi*, whose nearest Western equivalent is the Italian ravioli. *Jiaozi* can be prepared and cooked in a number of different ways but essentially are made of hard-wheat pasta filled with chopped meat and vegetable.

Beijing

Donglaishun
16 Donghuamen, at the
north entrance of
Dongfeng Market
tel. 550069

This is an excellent place to try Mongolian hotpot in unpretentious surroundings with pleasant service. Highly popular with the people of Beijing, this restaurant is always busy. The lamb shashlik — chunks of lamb rolled in sesame seed and barbecued — is specially good, and for

东来顺饭店
东华门16号

the more adventurous there are other Mongolian specialities to try, such as braised camel's hump or camel tendons.

Fangshan
Beihai Park
tel. 442573

仿膳饭店
北海公园

This prestigious restaurant uses recipes from the 19th-century imperial court. Banquets are highly elaborate and expensive — a meal including delicacies such as shark's fin and bird's nest soup might cost over Rmb100 a head. But with a magnificent setting on an island in the centre of the beautiful lake in Beihai Park, this must surely rank as one of the most splendid restaurants in China.

'Sick Duck'
(Wangfujing Kaoya Dian)
13 Shuaifuyuan
tel. 553310

王府井烤鸭店
师府园13号

A Beijing duck banquet may consist of far more than just the serving of the crisp skin and meat of the tender bird. Cold duck dishes — which may include meat in aspic, shredded webs, and sliced liver — are usually served first, followed by fried duck heart, liver and gizzard, and the delicious duck soup which comes at the very end of the meal. This restaurant off Beijing's main shopping street, Wangfujing, is perhaps the friendliest in which to try a Beijing duck banquet, but there are many others which are more popular with tour groups because of their large banquet rooms.

Garden of the Horn of Plenty (Fengzeyuan)
83 Zhushikou Xi Dajie
tel. 332828

丰泽园
珠市口西大街83号

One of Beijing's most famous eating houses, the Fengzeyuan is celebrated for its Shandong food. The cuisine of this coastal province south of Beijing includes some excellent fish dishes. Particulary well known here is the sea cucumber, soup with cuttle-fish eggs, and braised fish with a rich brown sauce.

Sichuan
51 Rongxian Hutong
tel. 656348

四川饭店
绒线胡同51号

This restaurant is housed in the traditional courtyards of a grandee's home. The house itself is said to have once belonged to the warlord Yuan Shikai at the beginning of the century. This is the most famous Sichuan restaurant in China, specializing in the hot spicy cuisine of the large southwestern province which is the home of Deng Xiaoping. Any of the many specialities here is worth trying. The smoked duck, spiced beancurd, and braised eggplant have been specially recommended.

**Beijing Vegetarian
Restaurant**
74 Xuanwumennei
Dajie
tel. 334296

北京素香斋
宣武门内大街74号

The Chinese are masters at the art of vegetarian
cooking, and are capable of producing an
astonishing variety of dishes from the versatile
beancurd, which forms the basis of their
vegetarian food. The restaurant can provide a
well-balanced banquet of as many as 15 dishes
that seem like pork, duck or fish, together with
fresh vegetables, many different kinds of
mushrooms and seaweed, steamed dumplings
and noodles.

Maxim de Pékin
2 Qianmen Dong Dajie
tel. 512210
(reservations), 5121992
(bar)

北京马克西姆
前门东大街2号

Owned by Pierre Cardin, this restaurant
opened in 1983. It is well patronized by
diplomats, expatriates and business visitors. The
menu reads as a Maxim's menu should — Fois
Gras de Canard fait Maison, Crepes Fourrées
Suzette, Mousse Glacée Framboise, Iced Soufflé
Grand Marnier, Escargots Fricassée. The wine
list is good by Beijing standards. It is open for
lunch at 12 noon (when a businessmen's set lunch
is offered), and for dinner at 7 pm, closing when
the last guests leave. After 9 pm, you may go just
for drinks at the bar, where there is a small
dance-floor.

Nanjing

Qifangge
150 Gongyuan Jie
tel. 23159

奇芳阁
贡院路150号

On the ground floor of Qifangge is a 'fast-food'
dumpling and noodle snack bar. A separate
entrance leads to the upper floor where the
simplicity of white table-cloths and sky-blue chair
covers creates a pleasant ambience for enjoying
the Jiangsu specialities served here.

Guangzhou

Panxi Restaurant
151 Longjin Xi Lu
tel. 89318, 85655

泮西酒家
龙津西路151号

This is one of the city's most beautiful
restaurants, overlooking an artificial lake. There
is a lovely garden, with little bridges, peaked
tiled roofs and carp in a large fishpond. So
attractive is Panxi, though, that it takes visitors
for granted and the foreign diner who does not
come with a tour group can be disappointed. The
dim sum is still superb, with bird's nest pastry,
shrimp and meat balls, and sweets such as fried
water-chestnut pudding. Open 6.30–10.30 a.m.,
11 am–2 pm, 5–9 pm.

Beiyuan
318 Xiao Bei Lu
tel. 33365

北园酒家
小北路318号

The Beiyuan is noted for its appealing architecture of flowers and moats, little bridges, old-style ebony cabinets and large banquet rooms, each with different colour motifs. But the restaurant can actually serve up to 8,000 people in one day. It offers a good middle-brow banquet (a ten- or 15-course affair). Banqueters may sample the famous Cantonese suckling pig, served in two courses — definitely the climax of any meal. Open 5.30 am−9 am, 11 am−3 pm, 5 pm−9 pm.

Nanyuan
120 Qianjin Lu
tel. 50532

南园酒家
前进路120号

Renowned as one of the great restaurants of China, the Nanyuan has no fewer than 20 different restaurants and banquet halls, each with lovely marble furniture, scrolls along the walls, and displays of the traditional Chinese art of framed marble. The food is expensive but equally impressive — soups with chicken, bamboo and pigeon eggs: two-coloured perch balls; beancurd with crabmeat; and fried fresh milk with shrimp. Open 6−9 am, 11 am−2.30 pm, 5−8.30 pm.

Shahe Noodles
79 Shahe Dajie, Shahe
tel. 75639, 75449

沙河饭店
沙河大街79号

Visitors from throughout China come to this restaurant in Shahe, a town 15 minutes from Guangzhou, famous for its water and rice. The fortunate visitors can watch the whole noodle-making process. According to the 600-year-old recipe, the rice noodles are chopped fine, soaked for 12 hours, laid out on bamboo mats and cut a quarter of a centimetre thick. Five flavours (sour, sweet, hot, cool-and-bitter, salty), four different grades and dozens of ingredients (such as mushrooms, bamboo, beef, chicken, port) are offered. Open 10.30 am−11.30 pm.

Shanghai

Park Hotel
170 Nanjing Xi Lu
tel. 225225

国际饭店
南京西路170号

The reputation of the Park Hotel restaurants, the **Peacock** on the 11th floor and the **Fengze** on the second floor, is very high — and deservedly so. The Beijing duck served here cannot be faulted, and the escargots are excellent. One of the nicest features of eating in this hotel are the old-fashioned dining rooms and generally courteous service, especially from the older staff.

Yangzhou Fandian
808 Nanjing Dong Lu
tel. 222779

杨州饭店
南京东路308号

One of the city's most popular restaurants, the Yangzhou serves some of the best Shanghai food to be had anywhere. But since the restaurant always seems to be packed, reservations should be made well in advance.

Meilongzhen Jiujia
22 Nanjing Xi Lu, 1081
Long (Lane)
tel. 532561 and 562718

梅龙镇酒家
南京西路1081弄22号

No trip to Shanghai, they say, is complete without a visit to Meilongzhen. Dating from 1938, this is one of Shanghai's most famous restaurants. The restaurant prides itself on its Longyuan beancurd, imperial concubine's chicken (*guifeiji*) and crisp-fried duck (*xiangsu ya*).

Lubolang Canting
Yu Garden Bazaar
tel. 280602

绿波廊餐厅
豫园商场

This restaurant in the Yu Garden Bazaar overlooks the small lake and the walls of the Yu Garden. It is famous for its steamed and baked Shanghai dumplings, both sweet and savoury. Try the Moth Eyebrow dumplings which are wafer-thin crescents of light shortcrust pastry filled with diced shrimps and vegetables or with sweet fillings of red bean paste and nuts.

Suzhou

Wangsi Jiujia
23 Taijian Long, off
Guanqian Jie
tel. 27277

五四酒家
太监弄23号

The Wangsi is an established restaurant in Changshu, and this offshoot takes the prize as the best restaurant in Suzhou. The celebrated beggar's chicken, 'duck's blood' glutinous rice and cassia flower soup (a dessert), as well as dishes identified with Huaiyang cuisine, are served in a delightful upper-floor dining room.

**The Pine and Crane
Restaurant (Songhelou)**
141 Guanqian Jie
tel. 22066

松鹤楼
观前街141号

Emperor Qianlong is supposed to have dined at this old restaurant. Seven years ago it moved to its present location. The Songhelou is known for its delicate chopping, so try the finely-sliced eel with mushrooms, ham and bamboo shoot. Other specialities based on local ingredients are 'snowflake' crab claws, 'chrysanthemum' fish, watermelon chicken, wild duck, shrimps in crispy rice crust and 'squirrel' fish.

Hangzhou

**Hill Beyond Hill
(Shanwaishan)**

This restaurant is located in a beautiful setting at the Jade Spring by the Hangzhou Botanical

Jade Spring
tel. 26621

山外山
玉泉

Gardens. It serves many of the great local dishes, including one made of sweet red bean and egg named after one of the Ten Prospects of West Lake (Lingering Snow on Intersecting Bridge). This restaurant also serves the famous freshwater fish of the region, Guiyu, in a variety of ways. The fish has a light delicate flesh and is best lightly steamed with scallions.

Zhiweiguan
111 Qunying Lu
tel. 23655

知味观
群英路111号

This is one of the most enjoyable places for any meal, be it breakfast, lunch or dinner. There are no fancy trimmings, just crowds of local people having a good time and unpretentious food. Their dumplings are the best in Hangzhou (there are many kinds) and their speciality is 'cat's ear' noodles. If you have the capacity for heavy, rich, sweet food, the glutinous 'eight treasures' rice pudding is a delicious experience.

Tianxiang Lou
676 Jiefang Lu
tel. 22038

天香楼
解放路676号

A three-storey building in traditional Chinese style, Tianxiang Lou (Heavenly Fragrance Pavilion) has six dining rooms and an open-air roof garden with a view of the West Lake. It began in the 1920s as a very small eating place and became so famous that to many gourmets its name immediately suggests Hangzhou.

Kunming

Yunnan Crossing-the-Bridge Rice Noodles Restaurant (Yunnan Guoqiao Mixian Fandian)
Nantong Jie
tel. 22610

云南过桥米线饭店
南通街

This Kunming favourite has been around for more than 50 years, though it is now housed in a new building. As the name suggests, the special noodle dish reigns here. Other items are on the menu but any visit to Yunnan must include Crossing-the-Bridge Rice Noodles. This restaurant is almost always full, so plan to come before 6 pm.

Guanshengyuan Guangwei Fandian (Cantonese Restaurant)
Jobi Lu
tel. 22970, 25266

冠生园（广味饭店）
金碧路

A fixture of Kunming's eating scene for half a century, this large, two-storey Cantonese-style restaurant is a great favourite among locals for any festive occasion. Its *dim sum* is varied and good and there is a wide choice of pork prepared in different ways. Interesting chicken dishes and seafood dishes, such as abalone with oyster sauce, round out an ample menu.

Recommended Reading

Nagel's Encyclopedia-Guide to China (Geneva 1978) is the established guidebook, but it was compiled in the 1960s and first published in French in 1967. It is now out of date. It has a wealth of historical and cultural information on the major cities, very much in the style of a traditional European guidebook.

The Guidebook Company has published in its China Guides Series guides to *Beijing; Shanghai; Canton, Guilin and Guangdong; Hangzhou and Zhejiang; Nanjing, Suzhou, Wuxi and Jiangsu; Yunnan Province; The Yangzi River; Tibet, X'ian, The Silk Road; Fujian Province and Hong Kong*. These are up-to-date, accurate and well-illustrated guides complete with the best available maps, diagrams and plans of cities, scenic spots and architectural complexes.

China, A Short Cultural History by C.P. Fitzgerald (Cresset Press, London 1961) is an excellent chronological introduction to Chinese civilization. An anthology, edited by R. Dawson, entitled *The Legacy of China* (Oxford University Press 1964) covers, section by section, the philosophy, literature, arts, science and politics of China. *East Asia: Tradition and Transformation* by J.K. Fairbank, E.O. Reischauer and A.M. Craig (Allen & Unwin, London 1973) is an eminently readable historical textbook. Jonathan Spence's *Gate of Heavenly Peace* (Viking Press 1981) is a well-written survey of recent Chinese history.

The Story of the Stone by Cao Xueqin, translated by David Hawkes and John Minford in five volumes (Penguin 1973–88), is that great 18th-century novel of manners better known as *The Dream of the Red Chamber*. There are other excellent translations of Chinese literature. The *Romance of the Three Kingdoms* is available in various translations. The poems of the two Tang masters, Li Bai (Li Po) and Du Fu (Tu Fu), have been translated by Arthur Cooper in the collection *Li Po and Tu Fu* (Penguin 1973).

Chinese archaeology has attracted world attention in recent years. Two short studies explain the implications of the discoveries: *Ancient China: Art and Archaeology* by L. Sickman and A. Soper (Penguin 1968), which is an absorbing introduction to its subject. *Style in the Arts of China* by William Watson (Penguin 1974) is an interesting handbook, analysing the forms of Chinese art in terms of style. The great Swedish sinologue Osvald Siren wrote a fascinating series of books on Chinese art and architecture: *The Chinese on the Art of Painting* (New York and Hong Kong 1963), *Chinese Painting*,

Leading Masters and Principles (New York and London, seven volumes, 1956–8), *Gardens of China* (Roland Press, New York 1949), *The Imperial Palaces of Peking* (London 1924) and *The Walls and Gates of Peking* (London 1924).

Two other books on architecture can be recommended: A. Boyd's *Chinese Architecture and Town Planning* (Alec Tiranti, London 1962) and *Chinese Buddhist Monasteries: Their Plan and Function as a Setting for Buddhist Monastic Life* by J. Prip Moller (Hong Kong University Press. 2nd. edn. 1967).

Chinese Monumental Art by P.C. Swann (Thames & Hudson 1963) covers a number of topics, including the four principal Buddhist cave sites and the Great Wall. *The Nine Sacred Mountains of China* by M.A. Mullikin and A.M. Hotchkis (Hong Kong 1973) describes the five Daoist peaks and the four Buddhist mountains.

Sven Hedin, the great Swedish explorer of the early 20th century, produced some very exciting material on Xinjiang and Tibet. He wrote *The Silk Road* (Routledge & Sons, London 1938) and *Trans-Himalaya: Discoveries and Adventures in Tibet* (Macmillan 1909). *A Portrait of Lost Tibet* by R. Jones Tung is based on photographs taken in 1942–3 by Brooke Dolan and and Ilya Tolstoy, grandson of Leo Tolstoy (Holt, Rinehart and Winston 1980). A more recent pictorial study is *Tibet*, written by David Bonavia and photographed by Magnus Bartlett (Shangri-la Press, Hong Kong 1988). For those interested in both exploration and botany, *Plant Hunting in China* by E.H.M. Cox (London 1945) is recommended.

There are many books attempting to interpret the Chinese revolution. *Red Star Over China* by E. Snow (Gollancz 1938) is the classic report on the Communists at the beginning of the anti-Japanese war, illuminated by the author-journalist's long conversations with Mao Zedong. *Fanshen: A Documentary of Revolution in a Chinese Village* by W. Hinton (Vintage Books 1966) describes in detail the dynamics of revolution in a peasant society.

Simon Leys is one of the most stimulating and penetrating observers of present-day China. He has written *Chinese Shadows* (Penguin 1978) and *Broken Images* (Allison & Busby 1979). A readable and informative book on contemporary China is *The New Chinese Revolution* by Lynn Pan (Hamish Hamilton 1987). The collection of translated dissident literature *Seeds of Fire*, edited by Geremie Barmé and John Minford (Far Eastern Economic Review 1986) gives an insight into contemporary Chinese culture and socio-political controversies. For an overview of China's recent economic development, the *World Bank's Country Economic Report on China* (World Bank 1985) is highly recommended.

A Chronology of Periods in Chinese History

Palaeolithic	c.600,000–7000 BC
Neolithic	c.7000–1600 BC
Shang	c.1600–1027 BC
Western Zhou	1027–771 BC
Eastern Zhou	770–256 BC
Spring and Autumn Annals	770–476 BC
Warring States	475–221 BC
Qin	221–207 BC
Western (Former) Han	206 BC–8 AD
Xin	9–24
Eastern (Later) Han	25–220
Three Kingdoms	220–265
Western Jin	265–316
Northern and Southern Dynasties	317–589
Sixteen Kingdoms	317–439
□Former Zhao	304–329
□Former Qin	351–383
□Later Qin	384–417
Northern Wei	386–534
Western Wei	535–556
Northern Zhou	557–581
Sui	581–618
Tang	618–907
Five Dynasties	907–960
Northern Song	960–1127
Southern Song	1127–1279
Jin (Jurchen)	1115–1234
Yuan (Mongol)	1279–1368
Ming	1368–1644
Qing (Manchu)	1644–1911
Republic	1911–1949
People's Republic	1949–

Index of Places